*Always
a Sister*

Always a Sister

The Feminism of Lillian D. Wald

Doris Groshen Daniels

THE FEMINIST PRESS
at The City University of New York
New York

© 1989 by Doris Groshen Daniels
All rights reserved
Published 1989 by The Feminist Press at The City University
of New York, 311 East 94 Street, New York, New York 10128
Distributed by The Talman Company, 150 Fifth Avenue,
New York, New York 10011

93 92 91 90 89   5 4 3 2 1

Library of Congress Cataloging in Publication Data

Daniels, Doris, 1931–
Always a sister : the feminism of Lillian D. Wald /
Doris Groshen Daniels
p.   cm.
Bibliography: p.
Includes index.
ISBN 0–935312–90–0 : $24.95
1. Wald, Lillian D., 1867–1940. 2. Feminists—New York (N.Y.)—
Biography. 3. Women social reformers—New York (N.Y.)—Biography.
I. Title.
HQ1413.W34D36   1989
305.4'2'0924—dc19
[B]   89–1065
CIP

Text design: Paula Martinac

*This publication is made possible, in part, by public
funds from the New York State Council on the Arts.*

Printed in the United States of America on acid-free paper
by McNaughton & Gunn, Inc.

Dedicated to the memory of my parents,
Jack and Clara Groshen,
for a lifetime of love and encouragement

Contents

Preface

My parents were two of the vast number of Eastern Europeans who came to the United States and settled first on the Lower East Side of Manhattan. They met at a lecture given at the Educational Alliance, a settlement house, and stories of their courtship and their lives on Henry Street, East Broadway, and other streets of lower New York were part of my childhood. I heard also of my mother's first days in a sweater factory, of her introduction to trade unionism and the picket line within weeks of her arrival in America, and of her attempts to become a "Yankee." I am sure that these tales were the impetus for my professional interest in the immigrant experience.

Another dimension was added when I started to study and later to teach women's history. The most prominent woman on the East Side in the first four decades of the twentieth century was Lillian Wald and yet so little is known about her today. I decided to use her life as the subject of a research project and at the same time to satisfy my continuing curiosity about the lives of women like my mother.

The presence of the Wald papers in the New York Public Library and at Columbia University offered the opportunity to examine the career of this remarkable woman. I was also fortunate in that some of the people who knew Wald were willing to speak to me about her. Each interview dealt with Wald's personality and charm, but each mentioned her use of power and methods of achieving success for her favored project. It became clear to me that Wald was as much a political creature as she was a "do-gooder."

Despite the great changes that she helped to inaugurate, she has not been the subject of many studies. Nor has a satisfactory interpretative biography of this woman been published. Wald wrote two books of reminiscences, *The House on Henry Street* and *Windows on Henry Street,* and in 1938, two years before her death, she cooperated with newspaper writer R. L. Duffus on *Lillian Wald: Neighbor and Crusader,* an uncritical study of her contribution to reform. Since her death, Wald has figured in a number of works geared to young people or dealing with isolated aspects of her life.

I started to do a full-length biography that would include a section on Wald's participation in the feminist movement. I found, however, that her feminism motivated many of her reform activities and could not be separated from them. My work then went in a different direction. First, I wanted to write a selective biography of Wald, concentrating upon her role in local and national politics, trade unionism, the peace movement, the work of settlements, the suffrage movement, and the determination of public policies in the area of social welfare. Second, I wanted to illustrate the extent to which Wald's interest in female equality was a guiding philosophy in her personal and public life.

Help for this work has come to me from so many sources. My thanks go to the librarians at the New York Public Library, Columbia University, Swarthmore College, the Schlesinger Library, and Nassau Community College, all of whom were unfailingly helpful and gracious. My friend and colleague Martha Robbins read this manuscript in an early form and offered valuable suggestions. As important, she spent years as my office mate and tolerated my complaints and frustrations.

The Visiting Nurse Service of New York permitted me to use the Wald manuscript material and to publish from their photograph collection. I am grateful for this and to their staff which went out of its way to assist me.

I am indebted to Joanne O'Hare, my editor at The Feminist Press, whose guidance made work so much easier and more pleasant than it could have been. My thanks too to Wendell Tripp, editor of *New York History,* for publishing the chapter on suffrage in an earlier version.

Lastly, to my family—Shep, Jessica, and Leslie—my gratitude for enriching my life.

*Always
a Sister*

Introduction

*L*illian D. Wald espoused two related but at times distinct movements which hoped to effect profound change in American life. Her place among Progressives is easily documented, for there was hardly an organization for liberal reform with which she was not associated. Diverse crusaders asked for her help, at times having to settle for only the use of her name. By the end of her public career, she complained to a friend, "I just cannot join in on another thing! I know that my only value consists of the fact that I do keep up with the things with which my name is associated, but I have reached the saturation point."[1] Wald lobbied and propagandized for better housing, labor legislation, better health care, and every other measure that sought to solve the twentieth-century problems caused by immigration, urbanization, and industrialization. When the liberal impulse declined after the first World War, she was one of the pre-war Progressives who kept her objectives alive and helped train a new generation which came into its own during the New Deal.

The second movement in which Wald participated was the drive for sexual equality. Feminists sought to improve women's status and to redefine their traditional roles. They had an image of themselves outside the accepted sphere of marriage and family. To be a feminist, according to an advocate in 1914, implied an "instinct for sex-loyalty," a consciousness of membership in a group that was denied equality. It meant taking part in a struggle "to bring about the removal of all artificial barriers to the physical, mental, moral and economic development of the female half of the race."[2]

The study of women's history is still in its infancy and disputes abound as to approach, methodology, and periodization. There has been, however, much interest and research in the stage of the women's movement that paralleled Wald's public life. In the 1890s, the feminist drive gathered momentum, later attracted great popular support in the suffrage fight, and then faced increased hostility in the 1920s and during the Great Depression when the organized movement declined. But there is little consensus among historians that women as a group in this period advanced in status or gained significantly in freedom. Some of the disagreement stems from the very diversity of the movement. It was multifaceted and multidimensional as well as headed by people of widely divergent personalities and goals. A victory for one group was not necessarily applauded by others. Still another area of debate is the level of feminist activity after 1920. An examination of Wald's life provides clues to help form an understanding of her era.

This book is not meant to be a traditional biography of Lillian Wald. While it deals with her life, it does so topically rather than chronologically, in order to show that her major work as a social reformer was rarely separated from her desire to improve the position of women. Wald's role as a feminist is generally ignored. She is usually linked with Jane Addams and categorized by some historians as a "social feminist" who sought equality for women generally and suffrage in particular as a means to other social goals rather than as an end in itself.[3] Evidence indicates that such an analysis may be too simplistic and in need of modification.

Wald's belief in the need for equal rights for women was a vital ingredient of her thinking and a part of her belief in social reforms. For nearly forty years, she participated in almost every aspect of the feminist movement. The Visiting Nurse Service and the Henry Street Settlement, which Wald founded in 1893, served as the sources of her power and prestige and she did not hesitate to mobilize the goodwill generated by these two institutions into support for her work to elevate the status of her sex.

As a young girl, Wald received an orthodox middle-class education, but like many of her future colleagues, she found this training for marriage and motherhood to be unsatisfying. Her decision to enter the new profession of nursing was the expression of her discontent with women's traditional role. Nurse training was Wald's introduction to a world of activist women. Her "old girls'" network came to include working women, settlement workers, labor organizers, and revolutionaries. They were able and ambitious women who cared for each other and were proud of their female leaders and their accomplishments in forging a new place for women in society.

If nursing offered one set of opportunities for Wald, the settlement house movement offered another. The scheme whereby young, well educated, upper-class people live among the poor as neighbors had its start in England in 1884 when a group of university males started Toynbee Hall in a London slum. Americans, particularly college educated women, were attracted to the idea because it provided them a channel for their social reform impulses. They soon established settlements in major cities in the United States and lived side by side with the immigrant and the industrial worker. The plan called for the social classes to come to know each other, to educate each other and to work together for the improvement of the neighborhood. The settlement idea also offered a special benefit for women, who came to dominate the movement in the United States, since it made it possible for them to rise to positions of leadership and to set a "women's agenda" for reform.

When Wald started the settlement on Henry Street, the house had nurse residents whose salaries were paid by private contributions. She was the Head Worker, the first among equals. In time, the scope of settlement activities expanded and lay workers, both male and female, came to live at or to work at Henry Street. Wald retained the title of Head Worker, but she now was the chief executive of a vast social welfare agency.

Any study of Wald must have as its point of departure an understanding of her personality and methods of operation. Early in her career, an experienced politician told her that her "friends don't play the game intelligently. You got to begin early and stick to it."[4] Wald never forgot this lesson. To all her work she brought executive talents for organization and skills in the use of power and influence. George Alger, her old friend, described Wald as a "great executive" who had "a native gift which grew with her as the need for it developed." She knew how to organize her work and to choose the right people from the hundreds who would do anything to help her projects. Alger remembered being apprehensive about introducing Wald to Loton Horton, the head of the "milk trust," because Horton claimed to hate "uplifters," but the meeting was a success. The Sheffield Farms executive judged that Wald "was just as practical as he was." She talked sense and was running a big business, too.[5]

Lillian Wald could be described as a practical idealist who saw conditions as they really existed while at the same time envisioning a better world. Given her pragmatic turn of mind, it would follow that Wald could not be harshly militant in her methods. Success, she wrote to a friend, resulted from developing "a practical workable project,"[6] and then employing the tactics of organization, flexibility, persuasion, and conciliation. Getting along with people, even those of differing viewpoints, was essential, for as soon as they were disarmed, she could use her skills of argument. If her charm and logic did not prevail, Wald did not hesitate to call upon her powerful friends to use their influence. Proper timing was another ingredient of success and the reformer cautioned her more impetuous friends to wait for change and to submit their plans to the "test of common sense"[7] even though it seemed at times that advancement was a process of "one step ahead and two steps back."[8]

Even where Wald recognized the need for radical change, she adopted the methods and timing that took into account the differences in people.[9] She accepted that reform could be accomplished only when attitudes were changed; therefore, it was her function to reshape the thinking of the public through propaganda and publicity. Using the personnel power and the forum provided by the Henry Street Settlement and the Visiting Nurse Service, she worked toward creating and forming "public opinion" for "progressive, reasonable and right projects."[10] In *The House on Henry Street,* she wrote that she set out to give "such publicity as was in our power to the conditions we found, not disdaining to stir emotionally by our 'stories' when dry and impersonal statistics failed to impress."[11] By the close of her career, Wald considered herself to be primarily a publicist. Much of her work was unspectacular—writing, phoning, and speaking to the powerful—and it was not always visible to the public, which may explain why she is less recognized today than other women leaders.

In *Windows on Henry Street,* Wald described the public meetings, contacts with the press, petition drives, and the hard fight of a small group "against powerful business, financial and political strongholds" that constituted a typical campaign effort.[12] She used these same tactics whether she worked to keep the "El" loop off Delancey Street or to get support for the passage of protective legislation for working women. Since "Lillian Wald never gave her faith exclusively to any one kind of work or believed that any one activity could be a cure" for all of the ills of society,[13] she worked with many groups and often was unable to keep up with the demands upon her time. She would then volunteer Henry Street as a meeting place or use its personnel in her stead. Most often, she permitted her name and prestige to be used for various committees whose cause she supported. Wald believed, in fact, that she was most effective on an individual basis and frequently gave up active membership in an organization after its initial work was done. She then operated with the leadership to lobby for the cause in New York's City Hall, in Albany, or in Washington.

Wald's aversion to radicalism and militancy was very much rooted in her personality and temperament, but it also had a practical aspect. She early understood the sources of her influence: Henry

Street and the Visiting Nurses. To maintain these bases in an age before public funding, she had to avoid open breaks with her wealthy supporters, many of whom did not endorse her ideas for change. For four decades, she raised money for her work and at the same time learned to be circumspect in her dealings with her patrons. A letter written to a benefactor, not noted for his feminist views, offers an illustration of her technique. Wald told of a meeting with President Woodrow Wilson and then added, "a very interesting interview it was too. I presided and introduced the men speakers, which I hope does not shock you."[14] It was better to avoid a clash, to be conciliatory, and to attempt to educate when the time was right.

An accurate analysis of Lillian Wald and evaluation of her role as a social reformer and feminist requires viewing her not only as an idealist crusader, but as a "tough-minded realist who understood how the political system operated."[15] Power and prestige properly used brought public support; Wald employed both to achieve social reform and also to remove the barriers to the development of women, the fundamental change in American society that she thought was essential.

ONE

What Are Feminists Made Of?

Lillian D. Wald "came out of an environment far removed from the tumult of Henry Street" and from the public world she was to occupy as an adult.[1] Little evidence exists to indicate what influenced her to abandon the traditional role for women in the late nineteenth century, that of wife and mother, and to become a public figure. Unlike other prominent women of the time, she was not given to introspection and never wrote an analysis of her early life, family relations, and motivations. Throughout her career she was reticent about discussing her personal life in her speeches and writings, and for a time, as she noted in a letter to attorney Louis Marshall, had "a rule of abstaining from the papers" at all.[2]

She resisted pressure to write an autobiography and described her books as biographies of the Henry Street Settlement rather than of its founder. Nor would she permit her life story to be written by another, threatening to "hant" [sic] the person who attempted such a work. She did relent a few years before her death and assisted R. L. Duffus in writing her story. But Wald was very ill by then and, according to Helen Hall who succeeded her as head of the Settlement, Duffus was reluctant to probe too deeply.[3] To further complicate the task of reconstructing the reformer's early life, a fire destroyed her childhood family home and household goods in Rochester and, through carelessness, her "records of the first ten years [at Henry Street] seem to be lost."[4] Therefore, Wald's early life must be deduced from the bits and pieces of information she dropped over the years in personal letters and interviews. It would appear, however, that the motivations to work for reform traditionally ascribed to Progressives by historians do not apply to Wald in the first step of her career. Neither loss of family status, nor religion, nor firsthand knowledge of urban poverty appear to have played a part.

The future reformer was born in Cincinnati, Ohio on March 10, 1867 to a family whose background was German, French, and Polish. Her parents, Max D. and Minnie Schwarz Wald, were the "descendents of many generations of rabbis, merchants and professional men." Wahl was the original family name and then de Wald until Max dropped the "de" in the United States, however, retaining "the letter 'D' as a middle initial . . . for sentimental reasons." A folk legend persisted about the family which claimed that one of their ancestors was King of Poland for a day because he was good and was needed until the rightful heir appeared. Lillian once asked Felix Warburg, the banker, if he knew "anybody who delves into Jewish legends of the people, and if he—I suppose it would be a 'he'—would let me know" if there is any truth in the story. There is no record that Lillian Wald was able to substantiate her link to royalty.[5]

Max D. Wald was born in Germany in 1838 to a family that was "more German than Jewish in their culture. . . . They were cosmopolitan without being sophisticated, seasoned in more than one national culture over and above their Hebraic substratum." At the age of ten years, he migrated to the United States hoping to find greater economic opportunity and a less restricted political and social environment. The immigrant's expectations were realized and Wald, who became a dealer in optical wares, and his wife were able to provide their children, Alfred, Julia, Lillian, and Gus, with a happy, affluent childhood.[6]

The relation of most potential feminists to their families is of considerable importance and the more influential parent in terms of emotional involvement is usually the father.[7] This generalization does not hold true in Lillian Wald's case. Max was a self-effacing quiet man, "so kind, so thoughtful, so unselfish that the children took him for granted." When they were older, his children "often felt that they had not appraised him at his real worth."[8] It is possible, nonetheless, that at least a part of Wald's practical nature was a legacy from her father.

Wald's maternal relations had more color and dash. She "remembered with affection a benevolent grandfather who told stories and an uncle who declaimed endlessly out of the Psalms, Marcus Aurelius and Shakespeare."[9] Both Grandfather Goodman Schwarz, called "Favey" by the children, and Uncle Samuel Schwarz introduced the youngsters to the theater, music, and literature, spoiled them with elaborate toys and ponies, and did all this with a flourish. Minnie Wald was perhaps the star of the family, and "it would be difficult to imagine Lillian Wald without such a mother," a woman of trusting nature, generous impulses, and warmth. She was "beautiful and loved beauty" in her surroundings. It was she who taught her children to love good works, good books, and good talk.[10] Minnie was an indulgent older sister as well and Samuel grew accustomed to her care. Lillian inherited this charge and over the years lent him and his children both moral support and money.[11]

Wald admired her mother and enjoyed hearing that she looked like her but felt that "she could never be as good-looking."[12] After Max Wald's death in 1891, Minnie moved into the home of her elder daughter, Julia Barry, and then later lived in the house on Henry Street. In 1919, her daughter Lillian observed in a letter to Uncle Samuel that "she is remarkable for her age, and not easy to 'manage' but the children all love her, and she is young in heart and young in speech, too. In fact, I do not think that she has changed at all."[13] Wald was disconsolate when in 1923, her mother died. "The world seemed to change . . . and though other affections remained, there was of course none like her." Mother "was very dear . . . and had a genius for loving and sympathy that was extraordinary" and to Lillian her death made the "world seem poorer for having so much love and sweetness removed from it." A decade after Minnie Wald died, her daughter still mourned her passing for she had not "forgotten what it meant when the dear mother departed."[14]

Max Wald's optical business took the family from Cincinnati to Dayton and eventually to Rochester, New York, which Lillian always regarded as her home town even after the family had scattered to other places. The city was growing rapidly and its industrial poor were suffering from the effects of low wages and long hours, but there is no indication that Wald was much aware of their misery. She frequently read newspapers aloud to her mother and so it may be assumed was at least familiar with current events. Later developments demonstrate, however, that the young girl was unaffected by social problems.

By 1870, the German-Jewish community in Rochester was the fourth largest ethnic group in the city. The Civil War had played an Americanizing role, although through the 1880s, German was still spoken in most Jewish homes. In most ways the Jews were considered much like the native-born Yankees; they voted Republican, took lavish vacations, and joined social clubs like the Harmony and the Phoenix.

As early as 1848, the first synagogue, Berith Kodesh, was formed in Rochester. By the time the Walds moved to the city, the congregation had abandoned the traditional adherence to Talmudic law and the Orthodox service. It had adopted instead the Reform ritual in an effort to modernize and identify with Protestant America. Reform Judaism, which was influenced by the Enlightenment, evolved in Germany when Jews of the upper class altered their rituals to make them closer to the forms of other western religious services. Among the innovations to traditional Judaism was the introduction of the sermon, which in Rochester was delivered in both English and German. The congregation also agreed to alter the Kol Nidre prayer for Yom Kippur (the highest of Holy Days), to use English instead of the historic Hebrew, and to drop the bar mitzvah ceremony for the custom of confirmation. For a time, a Sunday service was considered in lieu of the traditional Sabbath. Berith Kodesh installed an organ and did away with the separation of men and women in the synagogue. Women were permitted to take an active part in the life of the congregation, although most did not receive any religious training. There is little wonder that Wald's education in traditional Judaism began after she left Rochester for Henry Street.[15]

Wald's attitude toward her own Jewishness was ambivalent. It may be presumed that her family belonged to the Berith Kodesh congregation since she, her brother, and parents are buried in the temple's cemetary, and she never denied her heritage.[16] On one occasion, when informed that a hotel was restricted, Wald wrote asking if it was true "that Jews are not welcome. I am of that race, and . . . want to understand the situation clearly."[17] And at another time, she sought to investigate discrimination against Jews in sororities at Swarthmore College.[18] On the other hand, she identified with Felix Adler and the Ethical Culture Society after going to New York City, and always emphasized the fact that her works and interests were "non sectarian and non creedal."[19] She went so far as to disclaim the right to be included in a study of work done by women as Jews, asking the authors to look instead into the careers of Rose Schneiderman and Miriam Finn Scott.[20] It was only with the rise of Hitler and German anti-Semitism that she publically proclaimed a sense of kinship with the persecuted. "Poor, poor Jews!" she wrote in a letter to friends. "They appear to be necessary to furnish an objective."[21] But even this shows her detachment from her co-religionists as she refers to "they" rather than "we."

It would seem unlikely, therefore, that for Lillian Wald religion motivated her work. She was probably a non-believer. Lavinia Dock, her closest nurse friend, chided her once on "that strange allusion of yours to God—you don't believe there is such a person do you? If so, then Margaret Brown and I are the only unbelievers left."[22] For some of her fellow workers, religion was a dominant influence; it did not dominate Wald. It was only after she had begun her life's work that she joined the Ethical Culture movement, with its emphasis on good works. Whatever Wald herself felt about her religion, she was clearly identified by the East Side immigrants as a Jew. Her knowledge of German was an asset, for most of the immigrants understood both Yiddish and German. Her background also provided her with a link to German Jews like the Loebs, Schiffs, and Warburgs, who would help her found the Henry Street Settlement.

The Jewish community in Rochester experienced great changes during the years of Wald's adolescence. The early settlers established a clothing industry in the 1840s which within a generation employed more than fifteen hundred people, a large portion of whom were Jews from Eastern Europe. With the influx of Poles, Russians, and Austrians in the 1880s, clothing became one of the two largest industries in Rochester. The established Jewish community at first welcomed the newcomers and assumed responsibility for their welfare; they organized the United Jewish Charities Association when the problems of assimilation became too great to be handled by the old benevolent societies. A Young Men's Jewish Association was also formed to permit the ghetto Jews to mingle with their German coreligionists. It was, perhaps, the first experiment in Rochester in settlement work.[23]

As the numbers of Russo-Poles migrating to Rochester increased, the attitude of the established Jewish community changed. In religion, the Orthodox Eastern Jews considered the members of the Reform congregation as apostates. The immigrants formed their own synagogue and bought a separate cemetary. They arrived with little or no money and usually boarded in small flats until they could afford better living accommodations. They spoke Yiddish. Many were unskilled, and to the better-assimilated Jews, uncouth and uncivilized in the western sense. Most important, the East European Jews arrived in such large numbers that by 1900 their population surpassed that of the Germans, who felt that their position as assimilated Americans was jeopardized by identification with the newcomers. In 1893, the Rochester United Jewish Charities Association wrote to an emigrant society in Europe asking them to stop the flow of immigration from Eastern Europe.

An additional source of friction was the economic relations between the two groups since the majority of the clothing workrooms were owned by German Jews, who were frightened and antagonized by the weapons adopted by the Eastern Jews in the constant labor conflicts. The establishment of unions and the Socialist Labor Party seemed to be direct threats to the older Jewish community.[24]

Emma Goldman, whose life and Wald's crossed many times, worked in Rochester after migrating to the United States. The two women were friendly philosophical antagonists, but nothing in their future lives illustrated their differences as much as their memories of the "Flower City." To Goldman, it was a dull provincial city where she worked in a "model factory" by day and then endured evenings that were "dreary and meaningless." Her recollections of the time are an interesting contrast to Wald's girlhood.

> Now I was in America, in the Flower City . . . as I was told. Certainly, Garson's clothingworks were a vast improvement on the glove factory [in Russia]. The rooms were large, bright, and airy. One had elbow space. There were none of those ill-smelling odours that used to nauseate me. . . . Yet the work here was harder, and the day, with only half an hour for lunch, seemed endless. The iron discipline . . . and the constant surveillance of the foreman weighed like stone on my heart. The end of each day found me sapped. . . . This continued with deadly monotony week after week.[25]

It is probable that Lillian Wald knew little or nothing of the life of the immigrant poor. "She was unbelievably innocent of the real world. She did not know what a sweatshop was until she saw one" in New York City. Max Wald, unlike some family members, was not involved in the garment industry, and understandably the membership of the Reform temple did not welcome criticism of labor conditions. Wald's social conscience did not develop as a reaction to an intimate knowledge of poverty and working-class problems in Rochester.[26]

Lillian Wald's memories of her childhood were of a happy home on Rochester's East Avenue. While her parents performed acts of private charity, they were not involved in social causes and devoted their time and energies to their family. Life for the Wald children was happy, normal, and uneventful. A spoiled and indulged child, Wald could recall being punished only once. It was a life "of storytelling, of housekeeping with all things in miniature that grown-ups use" and other "games and stories" that "reflected the protective care" of her elders.[27]

With her older sister, Julia, Lillian maintained a good relationship even through the rivalries and differences of girlhood. As they grew older, their concern for and friendship with one another grew. To Julia's children and later her grandchildren, Wald was the beloved Aunt Lillian who wrote affectionate notes, offered help, sent presents, and gave advice that she did not always expect to be heeded.[28] Gus, the youngest of the Wald children, became Lillian's special charge. He continued in this role even when both were grown, and when his health failed in later years, Wald helped him financially. After he died in 1924, she wrote to a friend that "we feel very much broken. . . . It draws our family circle very close. Nobody is left now but my sister and myself."[29]

While she was close to both Julia and Gus Wald, her special favorite was her older brother, Alfred. He was the object of her love and admiration; they played together when children and shared plans for adulthood when they grew older. Alfred Wald dreamed of college and medical school but the implementing of these plans had to be postponed because he had to oversee Samuel Schwarz's business in California while his uncle sought a health cure in Europe. After almost two years, Alfred was freed of this family obligation, but by this time he had changed his mind about entering medicine. Soon after, in 1885, just before his twenty-fifth birthday, Alfred Wald was drowned. The family never recovered from this tragedy, the circumstances of which are still a mystery, and Lillian Wald, who had shared and envied her brother's dreams, was perhaps the most influenced by his premature death.[30] Years later, when asked to name her favorite children's book, she replied:

> Strange as it may seem to you, aside from fairy tales, the first book that I remember and have remembered for years and years is George Eliot's "Mill on the Floss." . . . I do not know why that book should have made such a deep impression excepting that I had something of the same kind of a relationship with a brother that existed between Tom and Meg.[31]

If Wald's memories were accurate and she can be compared to Meg, the great passion of her childhood was her love for her brother. She was content to follow him everywhere asking in return only that he reciprocate her love and admire her.[32] The breech that came between Tom and Meg Tulliver had no parallel in Lillian and Alfred Wald's relationship. She looked to him always as someone to adore. The drowning deaths of both of the Tullivers at the conclusion of *The Mill on the Floss* has a particular interest in the light of Alfred's accident. Lillian Wald could identify with a woman who tried to "save" her brother. She would be touched by Eliot's description of Tom Tulliver calling his sister by her childhood nickname and then "brother and sister" going "down in an embrace never to be parted: living through again in one supreme moment the days when they clasped their hands in love and roamed the daisied fields. . . . In their death they were not divided."[33]

Wald's relationship with her brother influenced her life in several ways. Most likely her love for Alfred was mixed with some envy. His childhood prospects were great while hers were limited. His choices of life career were broad while hers were restricted. It would have been impossible for Wald not to have made these comparisons and equally impossible not to have resented the limitations placed upon her because of her sex. It may be that subconsciously she sought a means to adopt her brother's dreams after his death. She would be the child to fulfill the family's expectations for success.

Wald attended private schools, including Miss Martha Crutten-den's "English and French Boarding and Day School for Young Ladies and Little Girls," which aimed to "make scholarly women and womanly scholars." While the curriculum included languages, trigonometry, astronomy, physics, and chemistry, its goal, unlike that of boarding schools for boys, was not to prepare its students for college or for careers. Rather, Miss Cruttenden's hoped to transform the girls into elegant young ladies.[34] After she left school, Wald wrote:

> I may say that I have had advantage of what might be called a good education, knowing Latin, and able to speak both French and German. . . . My life . . . has been—I presume—a type of modern American young womanhood, days devoted to society, study and house keeping duties such as practical mothers consider essential to a daughter's education.[35]

Wald had no plans of a career and fully expected eventually to follow the path of her sister Julia into marriage. She was, nevertheless, dissatisfied and wanted the advantage of more education. At sixteen, she decided to leave Miss Cruttenden's school and to apply for admission to Vassar College. Her idea to attend a new school surprised her family, which held the traditional sex-typed concepts of women's education, but long accustomed to indulging their children, Max and Minnie Wald deferred to their daughter's decision. Vassar, only a dozen years old, did admit students at fifteen years of age so long as they fulfilled the entrance requirements, which included Latin Grammar and French. In Wald's case, however, President James Monroe Taylor rejected her application. He thought that she was too young for entrance and suggested that she reapply in a year or two.[36]

The next years were for Wald a time of waiting and increasing restlessness despite the fact that she returned to her studies at Miss Cruttenden's. She wore the elegant clothes her mother provided for her and entered the life of the "stylish young lady" with the unspoken purpose of meeting a man and marrying.[37] Her friend, the lawyer George Alger, speculated many years later that "she must have been a very good-looking girl" when she was young. She was tall, five feet seven inches, with typical brunette coloring, and brown eyes and hair.[38] Her appearance and personality insured popularity with members of both sexes. When both were adults, a classmate would recall to Wald:

> I remember you . . . with a streamlined figure . . . how stun-. ning you were when going out. I especially remember a blue satin, with your evening coat and party bag. We thought you the most beautiful girl we had ever seen.[39]

Throughout her life, Wald was vain about her appearance and maintained an interest in dress and style. In middle age she was particularly upset by pictures of herself that she considered to be unflattering. She believed that she was unphotogenic—"an unsatisfactory subject for photography"—and tried, where possible, to substitute copies of a painting "which on the whole has been less objectionable than the attempts of the photographers."[40] George Alger was appointed on one occasion to carry out the work of destroying the negatives of a picture that she claimed made her look like an "inebriated washer-woman."[41] When she grew older, she complained that some photos made her appear "as if she were Barnum's fat lady,"[42] and with some humor accused Arthur Brisbane of the *New York Times* of employing an artist to touch up a photograph "to give me a double chin." She insisted that "I really haven't got one! I am sure your artist thought I ought to have one or he would not have done it!"[43] Approaching her sixty-fifth birthday, she still refused to accept the camera's view and complained that "I have no notion of being middle-aged ever, and certainly not now. That picture is a libel."[44] Two years later, she grudgingly admitted that perhaps "it is not the camera's fault," but she decided that she would never again allow it "to have a shot at me. I had rather have a real shot."[45]

Wald, therefore, was unlike what some thought a feminist should be. She believed that appearance was important, and that "femininity" and beauty were weapons that she could legitimately employ to gain converts to her work. Her co-workers recognized this trait when they wrote on the day of her departure to a conference in Europe:

> The book, the eye, the safety pin—
>   The feminine array—
> Must verily all perfect be
>   When our Lady sails away.
>
> She goes to sit in Councils wise
>   But wiser yet is she
> She knows man gives a closer ear
>   To one gowned perfectly.[46]

Pretty clothing, husband hunting, and the social whirl did not entirely satisfy the young Lillian Wald. While she had fun and enjoyed attention, she was bored and wanted to venture out into the world. Yet she could think of nothing to do. Middle-class young women in Rochester society, especially Jewish ones, did not look for jobs; indeed, none existed in business in the 1880s. She might have reapplied to Vassar or gone to another women's college or she could have taken courses at the University in Rochester, but she chose instead to study on her own. Her father helped her to gain the position of correspondent for the Bradstreet Company. It was paperwork that she could do at home and while it was socially acceptable, it apparently was not satisfying to her needs.[47]

Seemingly, Wald was somewhat aware that other young women were similarly discontented. Looking back in 1914, she commented that her education in Rochester had given her little stimulus and only a vague knowledge of the "forces blazing paths for the women of today."[48] The American feminist movement originated in western New York State and shortly after the Walds moved to the city, Rochester became the focus of activity when a number of women attempted first to register and then to vote in the 1872 election. These actions culminated in the widely publicized trial of Susan B. Anthony. The following year, led by Mary Anthony, a Woman Taxpayers' Association was formed to give strength to an equally unsuccessful attempt to gain suffrage. When Wald was eleven years old, the National Suffrage Association held its annual meeting in Rochester with Frederick Douglass, the Anthonys, Lucretia Mott, and Elizabeth Cady Stanton in attendance. Throughout the last three decades of the nineteenth century, women in Rochester organized into clubs, including a Women's Political Club, and took part in and voted at school meetings. There were other feminist campaigns, including one to open the University of Rochester to women. In the latter endeavor, the Jewish women of the Reform Congregation including the rabbi's wife, Mrs. Max Landsberg, took part. While a few young women did attend the University between 1875 and 1893, it was not until the end of the century that they were officially welcomed.[49]

Women, by the 1880s, had made promising gains in higher education; women's colleges were developing standards as high as those attended by men and many institutions, particularly in the western half of the nation, were coeducational. But many graduates echoed Vita Scudder's sentiments that "college years had been years of inbreeding and cultivated introspection" and when "they were over, we women of twenty-two felt as if all life could offer had been exhausted and left behind." Educated women had few outlets for their training and powers and were left adrift, their schooling frequently causing them to feel more alienated by their stereotpyed roles than before. Individuals made inroads into the professions, but only after combatting vigorous opposition. Most women were too timid to attempt so independent a course.[50] As a rule, as sociologist David Reisman points out, the college-educated woman "waited vicariously on the men's table, feeling frustrated because of an inability to deploy talents she was not actually sure she possessed."[51]

Wald was fortunate, for an avenue for her talents was presented to her. Much as she might have liked to fulfill her older brother's dreams, she was, at this stage, too much a product of her parents and Miss Cruttenden's training to study medicine, a "man's profession." She needed something that would stay within her definition of "femininity" and yet free her from its constraints. She found a profession for "a gifted and naturally endowed" woman, "who clung to the old tradition and yet accepted new obligations."[52]

Wald was visiting her pregnant sister, Julia Barry, when Julia became ill and needed a doctor. The physician, not wishing to leave his patient without care, called in a trained nurse. The woman was a Bellevue Hospital graduate and the first member of the profession that Lillian Wald had ever met. "The experience was" for her "the opening of a window on a new world." Nursing could provide a way to satisfy her desire to do more, to overcome her restlessness, and to get out into the world.[53]

Nursing was for Wald a means of escaping the role that was prescribed for women in the nineteenth century, and the profession would be throughout her public career a major vehicle of her feminist thinking. She called her decision to enter the field "an irresistible impulse,"[54] but she never claimed to have experienced a "call" or to have been possessed by a "youthful instinct for self-sacrifice."[55] She could agree with a colleague, Isabel Stewart, who was a nurse educator, that few of the early nurses were so inspired. Rather nursing offered "a pioneering kind of job"—a new profession—where "there was a chance to see life in all its aspects." In an era when few careers were open to women, nursing appealed to the "restless," to those who "wanted to see more of life, wanted to see different kinds of people, wanted to travel, wanted to do things." It appealed to those who wanted a career. "Marriage was just an ordinary type of thing that everybody could do." Perhaps "weak sisters" would marry, but "not the free woman" who wanted more, who possessed a talent and wanted to exert an influence.[56]

In the summer of 1889, Wald applied for admission to New York Hospital's School of Nursing. Her family did not approve of her plan, but they came to accept her decision. Wald later wrote, "Mothers and daughters have from time immemorial occasionally been in conflict with each other, often because of the devotion that would spare the loved ones the hard knocks of life." While the commandment to honor one's parents has come down through ages,

"Honor thy daughter and thy son is a commandment no less impera-
tive . . . that the wings of their idealism may not be clipped because
of the fear of the hardships they may encounter.[57] Wald could have
studied nursing in Rochester, but decided instead to go to New York
City where she had no "social ties . . . that might interfere with earnest uninterrupted work." In her letter of application to nursing
school, she wrote of her life and education and explained that:

> This does not satisfy me now, I feel the need of serious, defi-
> nite work. A need perhaps more apparent since the desire to
> become a professional nurse has had birth. I choose this profes-
> sion because I feel a natural aptitude for it and because it
> has . . . appeared to me womanly, congenial work, work that I
> love and which I think I could do well.[58]

Wald's girlhood indicates that neither religious urge nor class
anxiety nor sense of mission was an important factor in her decision to enter nursing. Also, while it is unlikely that she was as socially naive and poorly informed as a girl as she pretended after
she achieved fame, it is implausible that empathy with the poor and
oppressed of society motivated her to abandon the traditional life of
the middle-class lady. Wald's drive came from her personal needs.
She had to express herself, to use her talents, and to do something
important. She could not have met these needs if she had remained
in her parents' home and lived the life that was expected of her.

TWO

The Nursing Sisters

When Wald entered New York Hospital Training School in the summer of 1889, nursing was acknowledged to be a woman's occupation, and in many cases, femininity was defined in terms of the nurture of the young and the care of the sick. Professional nursing, however, was not as yet considered to be a field acceptable for well-bred "ladies" and was only in the beginning of the process of recognition as a profession.

From 1873, when the first schools were established, to about 1900, nursing skills grew to be respected and the women could insist on some degree of independence.[1] For Lillian Wald and many of her coworkers, this period of transition presented unparalleled opportunities to exercise pioneering leadership. Because of the lowly status of the occupation, men played little part and young women were able to move rapidly to positions of command. It seemed to Wald that if young women really wanted "to amount to anything in life," there was "but one way open to them." Nursing could be satisfying to women of ability for it permitted the development of intellectual, organizational, administrative, and executive powers.[2]

After the turn of the century, there was a clash of interests between the female nurses and the male hospital managers and physicians. The sexist attitudes and paternalism of the men as they attempted to exert authority created deep resentment on the part of the nurses. Wald and many others in the vocation came to consider that "the nurse question had become the woman question."[3] The position a woman could hold in a civilization, her independence, and the kind of work she could do were reflected in the nurse's position in that society. Organized nursing was "a gauge and an unseparable part" of the "eternal woman movement," the movement to elevate women by training them to perform better in the world.[4] It seemed to Lavinia Dock in 1929 that those who worked to uplift the cause of nurses were also doing a "genuine 'bit' in the wider world of . . . feminism."[5]

Nursing, until the mid-nineteenth century, was in the hands of women in charitable religious orders or was carried out by untrained women who worked in hospitals or came into the home to care for the sick for wages that "did not exceed thirty-five cents per day."[6] Nurses were regarded as little better than lower-class housemaids and no "respectable" woman would stoop to such work. The popular image of the nurse was not too far from the satirical portrait painted by Charles Dickens in *Martin Chuzzlewit*. Both Sairey Gamp and Betsy Prig were sloppy, gabby, careless old women whose indifference to the plight of their patients caused greatly increased suffering. In one episode, a patient complained to Mrs. Gamp that Betsy had put soap into his mouth while he was being washed.

> "Couldn't you keep it shut then?" retorted Mrs. Prig. "Who do think's to wash one feater and miss another, and wear one's eyes out with all manner of fine-work of that description, for half-a-crown a day!"[7]

War, however, inevitably creates a demand for better nursing care and the Crimean and American Civil Wars in conjunction with the medical advances of the late nineteenth century worked to bring to a close the dark period in nursing depicted by Dickens.

The dominant figure in the earliest development of professional nursing was Florence Nightingale, a woman of exceptional organizational ability who captured the imagination of the public and changed the image of the nurse. She called for specialized education and training because "nursing is an art . . . [and] training is necessary for this as for any other art." This training was to be conducted in a hospital under the supervision of a woman superintendent who had her own jurisdiction in the hospital.[8] Nightingale's plan featured, according to nurse historians, "the positive mandate that the entire control of the nursing staff, its discipline and instruction, was to be taken out of the hands of men and lodged in those of a woman."[9] The majority of medical men were hostile to the Nightingale system; they liked having nurses on the plane of domestic servants. In the opinion of one physician, "A nurse is a confidential servant; but still only a servant. She should be middle-aged when she begins nursing; and somewhat tamed by marriage and the troubles of a family."[10] Nurses had to overcome these attitudes in order to gain control over their own education and standards.

The new system of training was exported to the United States in 1873, when the Bellevue School in New York City opened despite the objections of many doctors, who were convinced that the high standard for entrance would not be met because conscientious, intelligent young women of good education would not be willing to do nursing work. The Bellevue experiment was a success and led to the establishment of other schools including the New York Hospital Training School in 1877. Women who entered nursing in those early years were taught under an apprenticeship system that was designed to provide care to patients in addition to clinical experience for the students. Though the training was arduous and financially rewarding only to the hospitals, many young women believed they were "blessed with exceptional opportunity" for they were pioneering a profession. Years later, one graduate of the New York Hospital remembered:

> Hours were long and work was very hard in those days. . . . Besides the care of the patients, there was much cleaning of wards, washing of dishes and polishing of brasses, of which the hospital had a super-abundant supply, and withal, most indifferent food. Despite all this, many of the nurses of that first decade have repeatedly spoken and written most enthusiastically of their great enjoyment and happy content during those years.[11]

Irene Sutliffe, an alumnae of the New York Hospital Training School, took charge of nurses there in 1885, only five years after her own graduation. She was "a woman touched with a genius for sympathy" and an understanding of "youthful heroics,"[12] and was fully able to impose discipline and organization upon "the young probationer from Rochester, Lillian Wald" who entered the hospital with "abounding energy of mind and body and . . . overflowing goodwill."[13] Another of Sutliffe's students wrote, "I look back upon those years at New York Hospital as the happiest of my life. Undoubtedly the most important factor was the superintendent of nurses, Irene Sutliffe."[14]

Sutliffe was to be only the first of the group of extraordinary women that Wald would meet over the years in nursing. They were, she said, women of above average "intellectual equipment," of "exceptional character, mentality and scholarship."[15] They called each other "sister" after the fashion of the British nurses and in many ways they regarded themselves as members of a family—a family of similar interests and expectations, if not similar temperaments. It would be extraordinary if differences of approach to the solution of problems did not appear. These differences, however, were never as important as the commonly held goals. One nurse urged that they "grow in the belief of the sisterhood of women, and help each other by appreciation. . . . learning to work together in a noble harmony."[16] The women did learn to work together and, as one wrote, "to help and strengthen" each other by "moral support and by professional union."[17]

Some also learned to fight together. "Nurses have always had to fight. That is not perhaps in their character, but that is what they've had to do." And according to one veteran, Isabel Stewart, "Most got pretty well started on our militant career before we finished our training."[18] It was a battle to convince the public and the medical establishment that nursing education and training were essential to patient care. It was a fight to enable the female nurses to develop the formal requirements of this education and to leave their administration in the hands of these same women. The nurses had to struggle to get proper equipment, libraries, laboratories, and classrooms for their schools and then to have these schools rated on the basis of standards of excellence in training and performance that the nurses themselves would set. It was a battle to remove the stigma from nurses and to elevate them from scrubbers and housemaids to the legal status of professionals. Intertwined always was the belief that "nursing could not advance more rapidly" until "women could advance their status and . . . their education."[19] The nurses, therefore, were interested in anything that had to do with the elevation of women, and giving them the tools with which to work, and with anything that gave them the opportunity to develop their minds. The "leaders . . . were quietly yet determinedly Feminist" according to Lavinia Dock, and her opinion is echoed by both Wald and Isabel Stewart, who claimed that they were able to remember only one or two nurses who stressed femininity rather than feminism.[20]

Wald was part of that leadership of nurses that emerged in the last two decades of the nineteenth century. Many of the women were her closest friends and all were "sisters" and "dearest comrades." "Ah the nurses!" she said, "like the old agnostic, I might say, 'they make me almost believe in God.' "[21] As a group, the women presented a great contrast in styles, temperaments, and methods, but they shared attitudes and goals and complemented each other's work. Together, Wald claimed, they "helped to open up opportunities in the professions,—not as special privileges, but to individual woman that her natural gifts might come to full fruition, and not for her, the individual, but for all womankind."[22]

The most overtly militant of Wald's friends was Lavinia L. Dock. She, perhaps more than any other early nursing leader, continually demonstrated how closely the development of modern nursing was tied up with the movement to secure the emancipation of women. Her views are of more than academic interest in any study of Lillian Wald because it was known that Dock "did a great deal of writing for Miss Wald and helped her in many ways."[23]

Dock was a scholar whose interest in languages, music, and the arts was well known. She coauthored *A History of Nursing* and herself wrote *Materia Medica for Nurses,* one of the first textbooks in the field, as well as countless articles. She grew up in a Quaker family of the Hicksite branch that held liberal views and undoubtedly nurtured the strong feelings Dock held for the underdog. The years she lived at the Henry Street Settlement were the happiest in her life. She never considered it to be a burden; rather, service was an opportunity. When she was studying in Europe in 1898, she wrote Wald of her sadness at being away from the Settlement, but then added that, "I am more fortunate than I deserve in having had so much of it."[24]

No two people could have been more different in temperament than Dock and Wald yet their affection for each other endured and grew over the more than four decades of their friendship. To Dock, Wald was the "Dear dear Leading Lady" who would "shine on everyone with warmth like the sun." And to Wald, Dock, was "Dockie dearest," who always brought enthusiasm, humor, and idealism to any project. Wald never stopped missing her feisty friend after Dock was forced by family pressures to leave Henry Street.[25]

Unlike the diplomatic Wald, Dock never felt the need to temper her language or to suppress her feelings on issues. She fought for years to gain autonomy for the nurses and to set criteria for education, licensing, and fees. The enemy was clear to Dock—the medical man. To one doctor she wrote:

> It seems to me particularly unseemly and ungrateful for physicians to talk about "fighting" nurses. Why, you owe seventenths of your success and prestige to nurses. And here you are trying to beat down . . . the very women on whom your success depends. If you do not think that is shabby, I do.

Dock went on to call the doctors both selfish and stupid for failing to recognize what was in their own best interests. If physicians did not permit good education for nursing women, "it will only take . . . twenty-five years to get back to a state of general degradation." The demand for good women of superior qualifications was more than could be filled and "no one wants women of the servant class, except for a few doctors."[26]

In the midst of a battle over the licensing of nurses, Dock wrote to her friend at Henry Street:

> I am afraid we are done for. There is some deep laid villainy—it means, body, soul and mind under the doctor's heels if it goes through. . . . We had better compromise and admit a couple of physicians to our Board and keep it under the Regents rather than have it all into the hands of vipers and pigs.[27]

Lavinia Dock became a heroine to younger nurses because of her vivid personality and intellect. Isabel Stewart, reminiscing on the first time they met, said:

> I'd never seen Miss Dock, but I'd studied her materia medica. I was sure that I'd know her when I met her, because she'd be tall and angular and intellectual.
> Who should turn up at the door but this small, short sort of roly-poly little person with curly hair. She'd just been at a suffrage meeting and she had "Votes for Women" across her hat and . . . across her chest.

Dock had been invited to lecture student nurses about the state of the profession in Europe. " 'Oh,' she said, 'very bad. It'll not be any better till I get to suffrage. I'll talk about suffrage.' " When Stewart reminded her of the selected topic for the day, Dock said, " 'Well, I'll tell them a little about that,' " too.[28]

Dock's collaborator on *A History of Nursing* was M. Adelaide Nutting. A graduate of Johns Hopkins, she was instrumental in organizing the American Society of Superintendents of Training Schools for Nurses. Nutting was primarily an educator whose goal was to improve on the apprenticeship system of nurse training and to promote uniformity in curricula and methods of teaching. Nurses had to be educated and skilled workers, she said, for "the day for saying, 'Be good sweet maid and let who will be clever' has passed in this as in other women's vocations. Rather must we continuously urge here the moral obligation to be intelligent."[29]

Nutting helped to establish the Hospital Economic Course at Teachers College, Columbia University and later took charge of it as Professor of Nurses' Education. The program was geared to graduate nurses; it permitted them to work for a B.S. degree in order to qualify to teach. At first, the Society of Superintendents carried the economic burden of supporting the course work at Columbia. This came to an end in 1909, when Lillian Wald convinced Mrs. Helen Hartley Jenkins, a well-known philanthropist, to donate $200,000 to endow the nursing department. A new program was developed to include special training in all the new areas of social service including public health nursing. Practice work was done at Henry Street and Wald, for a time, lectured at the college. Wald always admired Nutting for her intellect and warmth, writing that "The first precious contact with Adelaide Nutting has developed into a friendship that has grown closer and more tender through the years that have followed." What was important to the teacher was "to have women, and particularly women who are nurses, intellectualize and think about their responsibilities and their progress."[30]

Nutting's interest in nursing extended beyond education to all aspects of the profession. She worked with Josephine Goldmark and Florence Kelley on the Committee for the Study of Nursing Education to produce the famous Goldmark Report which recommended shorter work days and weeks and a longer period of training for nurses. Nutting and Wald also lobbied to educate medical men as to the role of nurses in public health work, fought for registration, organized the women into professional groups, and agitated for the appointment of females to executive posts.[31]

For many years, Wald's close associate at Henry Street was Annie W. Goodrich. The ties between the two women went back to their days at New York Hospital. Of their meeting, Wald wrote:

> Annie Goodrich started her nursing profession in Ward G, New York Hospital when I was head nurse there. She was fond of reminding me through the many years that her first bed making had been under my immediate direction. . . . I have never forgotten the amusing, brilliant, well bred young probationer."[32]

Goodrich remained always Wald's "Comrade Annie W. G.," who would lay down her life to gain recognition for her profession. And the younger woman regarded her mentor as the "Madonna of the Slums," a woman who had a special something even in their training days, a creative drive that made it possible for her to work hard and inspire an extra effort in others.[33]

Wald came to recognize Goodrich's leadership in training nurses for the public health field. Goodrich was a member of the faculty at Teachers College and became director of nursing at Henry Street when Wald's interests and duties became too large for her to supervise the day-by-day operations of the Visiting Nurse Service that operated from the Settlement. After World War I, Goodrich was named head of the school of nursing at Yale University, an appointment that realized the dream of pioneer professional nurses—a full four-year college education for nurses.[34]

These women and others like Yssabelle Waters, Harriet Knight, Jane Hitchcock, Lina Rogers, and Rebecca Shatz of Henry Street formed an "old girl network" of nursing. Sometimes, membership in the network came by recommendation, as when Lavinia Dock wrote, "This is to introduce Mrs. Kempler. . . . just the kind of Sister exactly that you will all like."[35] But the real requirements for membership were talent, personality, adaptability, and spirit, qualities that the women believed they possessed and looked for in others. Younger women, like Naomi Deutsch, were added to the group and the network spread through the country, but for Wald, the "old girls," who tried to pioneer a profession for nurses, would always receive special love and loyalty.[36]

Wald was considered a member of modern nursing's "triumvirate." Nutting and Goodrich were the educators; Wald was the practitioner concerned with the products of the nursing schools. She was never an innovator or original thinker; rather, she was able to analyze contemporary needs and adapt existing ideas to these needs, which she claimed was the wisdom to see. If Florence Nightingale created the idea of scientific nursing, then Wald "took the next interpretation in the relation of the nurse to the public rather than the individual or ward."[37] She was not the first to put district nurses into the field (there were about twenty visiting nurses when she began), but her system was nonsectarian where previously nurses were available only through religious organizations or free dispensaries. Her organization was original, she believed, and "based on the independence of the nurses' service." Moreover, she "did originate the term 'Public Health Nurse.'"[38]

The establishment of this form of social service was considered by many of Wald's supporters to be her greatest single contribution. Her visiting nurses cared for the ill at home, which was less expensive for the patients, and also left beds in the hospitals for the critically ill. More important, the patients benefitted for they were more at ease in familiar surroundings and families were able to remain together. The nurse became a teacher to the poor through her personal contact as well as a healer. Since protection of the dignity of the patient was all-important, a token fee was charged for all nursing services even though these payments never covered costs. The nurses functioned independently and answered calls from both patients and physicians. Wald—a superb administrator—divided the neighborhoods to be serviced into territories and then subdivided these into districts. Student nurses from Columbia assisted graduates and received their training in the field. Wald believed in tight organization although she permitted the individual nurses autonomy on each call.[39]

Since each nurse enjoyed a large degree of independence, Wald favored generalized education in many fields rather than specialized training. Because her needs were different from those of her friends who were interested in establishing curricula, Wald was often in disagreement with others in the profession. After one debate, she wrote to Adelaide Nutting, "Sister dear, Take down your tomahawk. I wanted to make the point the other night that sick people were still to be nursed and my plea was for a balance." Wald did not in any way favor less education, but she wanted the educators to remember that general patient care was most important.

> You know of course that there is a great amount of people going into homes advising and educating and that it is possible that even if all of them were nurses, the patient might not get the bath, might not have the wound dressed. That was the point I was trying to make. Not at all that they needed less education.[40]

Wald's concept of public health nursing spread around the world and Henry Street became "one of the great work centers of nursing education." Through the years, more than two thousand women graduate nurses of all nations gained experience in New York and then left to teach others in their own countries. From Japan, China, the Philippines, "wherever the public health idea begins to develop, people turned to Henry Street for advice, for leaders and for equipment."[41] Wald introduced other innovations in nursing. A national visiting nurse system, the Red Cross Town and Country service for rural communities, was established with the financial assistance of the Schiff family. The first American public school nurses came out of Henry Street but it was the visiting nurse concept that was most important in guaranteeing Wald fame as a humanitarian. It, along with the Settlement, formed the two major sources of her power and prestige. A pragmatic thinker, she took care to polish the image of the Henry Street Settlement and keep it in the public eye.

Isabel Stewart called Wald "a great promoter . . . very much interested in public opinion, and the value of getting the right people to back whatever you were interested in, and [she] had tremendous influence."[42] Wald helped causes she espoused by publicity, and by the pressure she exerted in person or in writing on her ever growing number of influential "connections." She was well aware of her power and if an official did not "do his duty," she did not hesitate to "put a little more pressure on him."[43] Through the years, she continually used her position to benefit her profession and individuals within it. When a nursing friend, like Adelaide Nutting, needed help, she reminded Wald that "a word from you would be of great value," and Wald spread the word to her "many men and women friends" who were willing "to be informed and helpful."[44]

She also lost no opportunity to give informal speeches. Though she gave countless formal addresses, she believed that her technique was best suited for small groups where she could use her ability to influence by what she termed sound arguments and thoughtful presentation. Usually she concentrated on people of wealth and power who could help her most. A friend who knew her well, Paul Kellogg, editor of *Survey,* remarked that her greatest asset "was the life long friendships with men and women whose confidence in Miss Wald was grounded in mutual experience and respect."[45]

Wald never did her best work in committee or as part of a group or organization. She lost patience with sessions where "I am sure that we will meet, listen, be photographed and adjourn."[46] She believed strongly in the need for nursing organizations so that the leaders of the various movements of the profession could get to know each other in order to work together and she was instrumental in forming a number of professional groups. However, she served as an active officer of only one, the National Organization of Public Health Nursing, and that for just one year, 1912 to 1913. Wald generally preferred to be a letterhead member, one whose name was included as honorary president or vice president or member of the board in order to give the group greater prestige and at the same time make it possible for her to avoid many meetings. She stayed in contact with every organization and lobbied for it, but always as an individual and outside the structure of the group. Lavinia Dock, who knew her so well and understood her talent, wrote Wald, "You . . . are essentially a woman of action and intuition. . . . Keep on with your active work and let those who are already sitting behind desks" do theirs.[47]

A high priority issue for nurses throughout Wald's career was maintenance of their autonomy. Resentment of the medical profession was a consistent theme in letters and speeches, as was the desire to remove the physicians' influence upon the organization of nursing schools, the discipline of nurses, or their registration. The doctors' claim that too much education caused nurses to lose their womanly qualities was countered by the nurses' assertion that the medical establishment had "made a mess of nursing" and was not to be trusted.[48] Many women echoed Wald's sentiment when she wrote that "when medicine gained control, almost complete control of the nursing orders and organization, it did not reflect credit on either branch of the healing art."[49]

Wald was especially vulnerable in the fight for self-rule because the public health nurse operated in the field without the supervision that existed in hospitals, although she worked under a doctor in most cases. Dock warned her of the "opposition to you and your work in this question of the nurses and the doctors." There was, on the part of the physicians, "strong disapproval" because Wald's "nurses carried ointments in their bags" and even "gave pills." Dock cautioned her that the medical establishment believed

> it was quite wrong for district nursing to be done in any way except under the strict control of the physicians—the nurses ought not to go to cases except on their orders—doctors ought to be in charge of district nursing associations—no nursing ought to be done in any other method.

Wald had to take care because complaints from the medical society might make it difficult to raise funds for her work.[50]

Wald did not back down. She carried her message to the public by speeches and articles extolling the virtues of her nurses, encouraging people to send for a nurse when ill because "there are many cases where skillful nursing is of greater value in preserving human life than the best medical advice." Anyone familiar with the work of the visiting nurses would be impressed, she believed, with the quality of their work and initiative. They carried the "findings of the scientists and laboratories to the people" and made them intelligible. "What a change . . . from the priestly secrecy of the . . . medical practitioner." Any woman with a commitment to the profession understood that the nurses had to stay in control. While Wald recognized that "there may be some souls so humble and so meek that the old time position of women nurses,—namely that of blind obedience in the treadmill—is all that they desire," she and most other women wanted more. They were not going to be left behind or be dictated to by the men in the medical profession whose arrogance excluded women from any control of their work and caused the nursing profession to deteriorate.[51]

The pioneers of nursing realized early that there was a need to gain legal status for the profession and in the 1890s the drive began for registration. The only way to maintain high standards was to license practitioners, and the criteria for qualification were to be set by examining boards staffed by nurses. The first registration act was passed in New Zealand in 1901, and within the next five years other nations enacted similar legislation. American women frequently played a part in securing these registration laws in accordance with the belief in nurses as members of an international sisterhood. Lavinia Dock went to Europe to help and to report on progress to her colleagues in the United States. While overseas, she wrote to Wald to recruit her into the drive. "If you have the time . . . , speak of the registration movement—it is more or less acute in Great Britain, Holland, and Denmark, Belgium, and Australia."[52] Wald quoted her friend frequently as she went from place to place speaking for the professionalization of nursing and linking it with the women's movement for better living conditions. Everywhere, she said, women nurses were bitter over their exploitation and lack of recognition.[53]

State-by-state registration in the United States began with North Carolina, spreading then to New York, New Jersey, and Virginia. Other states followed in fairly rapid succession and by 1923, all states had some form of nurse practice legislation. Even while the registration campaigns were being conducted, many women realized that the battle would have to be repeated because these initial licensing requirements reflected not the highest professional standards, but the lowest. Dock observed in 1900 that "restrictive legislation affecting the professions, then, is not to be gained once and forever. . . . It does not mean just one effort, but continuous efforts for the rest of time."[54]

The attempts to raise standards above the voluntary minimum levels set in 1903 were no easier than the campaigns for the original measures. Wald played a part in each of them. To educate women for six months and then to consider them to be trained was to pull down the standards for all nurses and, more important, it was detrimental to their patients. To the governor of New York, William Sulzer, she wrote of her interest in the Nurse Practice Bill of 1913:

> It has been reported out of committee, and we are very desirous of having the State extend its protection of the people who employ the nurse, and who do not understand how the correspondence schools and other centers of quack and inadequate "training" mislead.

She went on to mention the millionaire Jacob Schiff's support of her position and that Schiff had sent her the governor's "cordial response to him." She concluded, "This is only a reminder, for I am sure from your letter to him that you will do what you can to get the measure enacted into law."[55]

Above all, Wald publicized the cause of the nurses. Believing the profession needed a spokesperson because it had not been accorded the place it deserved and its splendid work was rarely mentioned, she undertook the task of raising the image of her "sisters." Wald tried to get articles about the nurses and "their work and their devotion" into such magazines as the *New Republic* and commended those publications that showed the proper appreciation for the profession. If a public figure neglected to mention or praise the nurses, Wald was quick to point up the omission.[56] She expected one of her coworkers to be included in all public events that stressed social welfare. Writing to the president of the American Academy of Political and Social Science in 1921, she expressed amazement that the "instrument of service—the public health nurse" had not been included in a program on child welfare. "It looks as if you had a man, and a man only get up your program!"[57] On other occasions she wrote letters to emphasize the need for advertising so that the nurses would not be overlooked. An example:

> Would it not be advisable for the Red Cross to have a great deal of publicity upon the training of nurses for public health work? Their last pamphlet . . . is excellent, but I should say that the nursing world, training schools and so forth ought to get the benefit of the Red Cross publicity experts. The main facts would be to advertise.[58]

Her work in publicizing the nurses paid practical dividends, and the service she established at the Henry Street Settlement grew larger. Unfortunately, Wald had to devote much of her time to fundraising from the public, which was a task she disliked but one in which she excelled. In later years, the nursing organization was underwritten in part by public funds and Wald was sure to carry her message to sympathetic politicians at budget meetings.

Her work and reputation gave Wald the opportunity to meet political officials from New York City Mayor Seth Low to Franklin D. Roosevelt and to remind them of the work of the nurses. Al Smith, an old neighbor on the East Side, heard from her frequently when he was in Albany. Sometimes, Wald urged him to favor a particular piece of legislation that would benefit the nurses, but more frequently, she wrote just to remind him of their work. She sent Settlement reports and calendars with the Henry Street nurse pictured—"the girl in blue guarding you and your desk"—so that he would not forget if an opportunity arose to help. Smith acted as a fundraiser for the nurses when he left public office.[59]

Another source of influence was that formidable mother, Mrs. James Roosevelt, who was named General Chairman of the Visiting Nurse Fund when her son became president. Sarah and Eleanor Roosevelt were both friends to Wald and Henry Street, and when letters to Franklin Roosevelt did not produce the desired endorsements, his mother was pressed into service. Sarah wrote to Marvin McIntyre, the president's secretary, "Please see that my son sends a nice message to Miss Wald. *I* shall be at the dinner and shall hear it read!" The president sent the telegram.[60] Wald also enlisted the assistance of Eleanor Roosevelt in her unsuccessful attempt "to have a stamp for the nurses" since they had been "unflatteringly ignored as far as Government recognition is concerned."[61]

Wald's fame as a reformer, settlement worker, and statesman caused people to forget she was a nurse. She, however, always remembered that nursing was her first love and though she developed many other interests in her long public life, she never stopped her support of the "sisters." "I feel that as long as I have vocal powers I ought to make it clear that the nurse must stand as recognized authority in her field," she wrote in 1935, more than forty-five years after she entered the New York Hospital nurse training school.[62] Nor did she forget "the old girls" with whom she had worked over the years to improve the status of the nursing profession and through it, the status of all women.

THREE

The Education
of a Reformer

Lillian Wald began her public career after she was graduated from
the New York Hospital Training School in March 1891. She immediately thereafter took a job at the Juvenile Asylum in New York
City. This early work experience forever embittered her toward in-
stitutional care for children and she stayed at the Asylum for only a
year. Perhaps because she did not wish to compete in the over-
crowded, poorly paid world of the private duty nurse, or because she
felt hospital duty too confining or because she wanted to fulfill her
brother Alfred's dream, she enrolled in the Women's Medical College
of the New York Infirmary. She elected to get her education in "one
of those schools founded in protest against the exclusive attitude
adopted by the men's medical colleges." All of the teachers were
women, and the emeritus professor of hygiene was Dr. Elizabeth
Blackwell, America's first woman doctor. Wald must have realized
that a medical degree would not guarantee sexual equality, for female physicians were obliged to expend much of their energies in
combatting prejudice in the profession.[1]

Long after she had abandoned any thought of practicing medicine, Wald supported the rights of female doctors. In 1928, she
wrote to the editor of the *New York Times* to defend the New York
Infirmary for Women and Children. It had been established to "give
greater opportunities for practicing physicians who are women" and
the original reasons for creating the hospital had "not been greatly
altered."

It is true that the prejudice against women on ambulances has disappeared in theory at least, and occasionally in fact, and one no longer hears the Victorian objections against their service in hospitals and in clinics. But, as a matter of fact, analysis of the appointment of women on staffs of hospitals throughout the city shows that the equal opportunities granted to women are to a larger extent theoretical.

Women, Wald continued, were rarely given "positions of authority in hospitals," and it was especially difficult for female surgeons to gain appointment in prestigious medical centers. "Were such appointments not very unusual, it would give conclusive evidence of the recognition of merit, irrespective of sex." There had to be a place for competent women practitioners and their patients, Wald declared. Therefore, she supported the maintenance of the Infirmary. Its existence, however, "should in no way diminish the very just insistence on the part of the public to give women their share in the great medical institutions."[2]

Lillian Wald was not destined to remain for long at medical school. She heard of a school for immigrants that met on Henry Street on the East Side of lower Manhattan. The school was financed by Mrs. Sophia Loeb and its original purpose was to select potential candidates for nurses' training. Wald was admittedly ignorant of East Side life, but when a friend asked her to teach a course in home nursing, she agreed. She soon discovered that her pupils were not ready for professional training and really needed basic instruction in housekeeping and hygiene.[3]

As she grew older and more prominent, Wald loved to relate the experience that changed her life. One day, a child asked her to look in on her sick mother, a Mrs. Lipsky, who was a member of Wald's class. The nurse was willing to help and asked the child to lead her to the patient. Wald recalled:

> Over broken asphalt, over dirty mattresses and heaps of refuse we went. The tall houses reeked with rubbish. . . . I will not attempt to describe the place, the filth, the smell or the sanitary conditions, which were too foul for words. . . . There were two rooms and a family of seven not only lived here but shared their quarters with boarders.

After cleaning the rooms, the nurse made Mrs. Lipsky comfortable and then fed the children. When she was finished, "that poor woman kissed my hands." Wald was embarrassed and

> ashamed of being part of a society that permitted such conditions to exist.

That morning's experience was my baptism of fire. That day
I left the laboratory and the college. What I had seen had
shown me where my path lay.[4]

No one had ever told Wald that such suffering and poverty existed.
She was not repelled by what she saw, only amazed. It is characteristic of her naivete and ignorance that she believed that the poverty
she had discovered was generally unknown to the public and would
be removed if people were informed and aroused.[5]

Wald invited Mary Brewster, a friend from nurse training school,
to share in the new venture. "We were," she explained in *The
House on Henry Street,* "to live in the neighborhood as nurses and
identify ourselves with it socially."[6] As nurses, they were in a
unique position to become part of the community and to establish
relationships with the people of the East Side, who recognized their
own helplessness among the conditions that surrounded them. Wald
believed that the people were eager to learn how to live better lives
and that she could help. She admitted that she did not know how,
and that she and Brewster "were both quite ignorant, but this we
did know, . . . we cared for these neighbors."[7]

They quickly began to overcome their ignorance when someone
introduced them to two very good men who, it was said, knew all
about the East Side—Charles Stover and Edward King, founders of
the University Settlement. King, the author of "the outstanding
novel of the Russian immigration" was a "kind of patriarchal uncle"
to a large number of the Eastern Jewish intelligentsia.[8] Both Stover and King had wide-ranging interests and held a Tolstoian philosophy about conditions of life of the poor that Wald would
partially adopt. The men became her guides and entrée to the East
Side and East Siders. They took her on walking tours of the neighborhood and the streets served as an informal classroom. Among
the people Wald met through King and Stover was Ernest Crosby,
the first president of the Social Reform Club.

The Social Reform Club was a discussion group whose membership included Mary Simkhovich (later the founder of Greenwich
House), Felix Adler of the Ethical Culture Society, and Leonora
O'Reilly. O'Reilly, a working-class woman who impressed everyone
with her intellect and speaking ability, became a resident at the
Henry Street Settlement and in later years worked with Wald on a
model garment-workers' cooperative. The experimental factory was
short-lived, but not the friendship between the two women. The
Club was primarily concerned with improving labor conditions in
New York and encouraging trade unionism. Other critical issues,
also, came under discussion—housing, tenement problems, immigration. Many of the measures that Wald would endorse throughout

her life had their origin during the debates at the Social Reform Club.[9]

Charles Stover made still another contribution to Wald's education. It was at their first meeting that he suggested that she and Mary Brewster live with "those nice girls at 95 Rivington Street" until something suitable and permanent could be found. The two nurses became residents for several months at the College Settlement, "in stimulating comradeship with serious women, who were also the fortunate possessors of a saving sense of humor."[10]

Before she lived at 95 Rivington Street, Wald had never heard of a settlement house. The College Settlement, which anticipated Hull House in Chicago by a few weeks, was the product of an attempt by a number of graduates of the young women's colleges, such as Dr. Jane Robbins and Vida Scudder, "to shape an independent life." To Scudder, the new life permitted a sharing of mind and heart with all people, an escape from the prison of class to a different life that was closer to reality. Most of all, it was a chance to see life at first hand. Though she was one of its founders, Scudder had reservations about what settlements could accomplish for the poor, but she was convinced of their value as a vehicle of enlightenment for women.[11] Another settlement house woman told Ramsay MacDonald, future prime minister of England, that she was part of "the revolt of the daughters . . . the revolt against a conventional existence" and the life that "the majority of well-to-do American women have to live." The women wanted new and more challenging roles to play.[12]

The College Settlement women were, like the nurses, a new kind of woman and Wald easily identified with them. They moved into many different fields and their lives and work were in the public sphere rather than confined to the domestic. They were women who might not articulate feminist slogans, but they were women who enjoyed personal freedom, who were young, modern, and dedicated.

Early in 1893, Wald met the man who would have the greatest impact upon the course of her life. When she first had the idea of living and working on the East Side, she took her vague plans to Mrs. Solomon Loeb, wife of the New York banker. Nina Loeb Warburg recalled the day her mother came home saying:

> An extraordinary young woman has called upon me. I don't know whether she is a genius or whether she is mad. She wants to start a visiting nurse service on the lower east side and would like me to help her. I prefer to think she is a genius, so I am going to ask your uncle Jacob [Schiff] to help me give this young woman her chance.[13]

A formal introduction was arranged and this gave Wald an opportunity to interest Schiff in her project. About a week later, he and Mrs. Loeb decided to accept the responsibility for the two nurses. The bond between the banker-philanthropist and Wald that was formed at this first meeting lasted until Schiff's death and then extended to his children and grandchildren. Wald claimed that he responded whenever he was called, no matter how busy he was, and perhaps more important, supported her work even when his conservatism kept him from agreeing with her views. For her friend's biography, she wrote:

> More than a quarter of a century has passed since a mutual friend provided the opportunity for me to meet Mr. Schiff. . . . Immediately did this busy banker respond. . . , and thereby started a fellowship in friendship and social interest. . . . Money help was given and without conditions. . . . What was perhaps more valuable than even the material aid was the support of measures of vital importance to the people . . . but often strange and remote from the experience, the interest, and the traditions of Mr. Schiff and his associates.[14]

Jacob Schiff's background was similar to that of Wald's parents. He was born in Frankfurt, Germany in 1847 to a family of rabbis, scientific men, and merchants. Schiff attended the school of the Jewish Religious Society until the age of fourteen when he was apprenticed to a businessman. He emigrated to the United States while still a teenager, and after some indecision, entered the investment banking firm of Kuhn, Loeb and Company. His marriage to Theresa Loeb, daughter of one of the company's founders, helped to ensure his success. Bruno Lasker, a social worker, remembered Schiff as "a great philanthropist, of course," but also a "wonderful promoter." He did many small personal things to help people and without him and his wife, "Wald could not have functioned as well as she did." Schiff and his family "were people of the old type, who had transplanted to New York something of the sense of civic responsibility which you find in the most refined circles of Jewish people in Europe."[15]

Schiff was raised as an Orthodox Jew, and though he joined a Reformed congregation in New York, he maintained his belief in the old religious practice of *tzdakah,* the care of the Jewish community by those able to provide aid. It is a concept that combines charity and justice, a tradition that "may have come out of the ancient ethnic instinct for survival that placed value of the whole community above the value of particular classes or individuals."[16]

Tzdakah, therefore, was both charity and civic responsibility. It was a religious duty that had to be performed during the giver's lifetime since the wealthy were considered only temporary custodians of their fortunes. Schiff described his sentiments as to social service and philanthropy when he wrote:

> The word of God heard in the Synagogue becomes of value only if it is carried into everyday life. This is so well understood. . . . And still how few in daily life practice this! How few stop to consider how egotistical are their lives. . . .
> There is, perhaps, no more cruel principle, . . . than . . . "the survival of the fittest." Because of this, we should feel that duty calls us to step in and be of help to those who are left behind in the race by reason of this inexorable rule.
> In this large community how many need us, to how many can we be useful!

Schiff continued by urging service "to the dependent classes" like the immigrant, the tenement dwellers, the sick, and the delinquent.[17]

Schiff's contribution to Wald's work and personal development was inestimable. She learned executive and administrative skills from him and she heeded his advice on the necessity for efficiency and thoroughness as ingredients of success in any venture. Schiff also taught his protégé of the value of the right friends. He was a "hero worshipper," who despite his own high position enjoyed associating with people of ability and success, and Wald adopted the Schiff practice of attending to small matters for friends. She learned that little acts of kindness such as taking time to remember important days, choosing appropriate gifts, performing favors, and answering letters promptly would result in great devotion to her and her work.[18]

The banker followed several principles in his philanthropy. He gave money to Wald so that she might enjoy personal financial security, and he also supported Henry Street and the Visiting Nurses. He did not, however, believe in bearing all the costs. He was willing to start a fund and perhaps buy a building, but was unwilling to support any work in its entirety. An individual should not be identified with any charity, he believed, "since the time might come when the institution would be in need of larger funds, and the public would not have been trained to support it."[19]

Wald's letters to the Loeb-Schiff-Warburg clan were always entertaining and chatty, with a manner that was deferential but never servile. Most interestingly, the letters show Wald's development from an inexperienced and unsure young woman, anxious for assurance and advice, to a leader of a vast enterprise that had gained worldwide recognition. As the years passed, her deferential tone remained, but she was clearly in command.

The earliest letters from Wald to her benefactor reflected her dismay over "the tragic condition of our neighbors" and their "wretched lives." She despaired that she could, with all her efforts, relieve the misery of only a comparative few, but was gratified for the opportunity to "make some small gleams of light these dark days" even for the few. She related the details of individual cases, always attempting to give a favorable picture of the people, and sometimes received small sums from Schiff for those in special need. At times, Wald complained of the "unlovable" qualities of some of the "unfortunates" with whom she had to deal and eagerly sought Schiff's advice on how to handle them. The banker recommended sources of support, both financial and service, which she inevitably explored. Wald kept careful financial records, as well as case studies, even in the first years when the Visiting Nurse Service had only two workers, herself and Mary Brewster. She dutifully sent these records to Schiff in her monthly reports to him.[20]

Schiff responded to Wald's letters with sympathy, advice, and encouragement. On one occasion, he wrote:

> I am almost afraid to think of the misery which surrounds us here on all sides, but I know you always feel as I do, and perhaps more so, that those whose lot it has become to help their unfortunate fellow beings are more to be envied than those who have a quiet and easy life and know nothing of the misfortune which exists in the world.[21]

As Wald gained confidence, the roles reversed and she became more Schiff's teacher than his pupil since through her, he came in close and personal contact with the East Siders and their problems. When Lavinia Dock heard of Schiff's death, she wrote to Wald, "I have been remembering back to the afternoon when we sat in the old dining room while you persuaded him to be in sympathy with the garment workers' strike."[22] Wald conveyed to her uptown friend her enthusiasm for her profession and he donated a building for the Visiting Nurses at 99 Park Avenue in New York City and gave vast sums of money to the Red Cross. Immigrants, working people, nurses, and reformers grew accustomed to seeing and talking to the investment banker across the dining table at Henry Street. Some, like Jacob Riis, the writer and reformer, came to consider Schiff a source of support and a friend.[23]

Despite his support of Wald and her work, Schiff was a conservative in his thinking about women. He acted as treasurer of the group established to found Barnard College and donated money to the fund, but endorsed higher education only because it would better fit women for the duties of married life. Wald applauded his support of Barnard but secretly wished he were "equally lavish with some nursing project."[24] Additionally, she hoped to see Schiff more concerned with the plight of the poor woman and tried to educate him as to the problems of brutal husbands, sickly children, and low-wage work.[25] While they did not always agree, Wald and Schiff grew closer over the years and she became his "Dear Miss Wald, dearest friend." He paid tribute to her organizing abilities and wrote that he and Mrs. Schiff could not help but admire her and her associates for their unselfishness. Finally he thanked her "for the opportunities you made for us to cooperate."[26]

The next generation of the Schiff family recognized Wald's position as expert, leader, and friend. Paul Warburg and his brother Felix took charge of the Henry Street Settlement investments, but Paul playfully thought it necessary to seek Wald's permission to call "each other by our Christian or rather Jewish names."[27] Wald reacted to the millionaire brothers with a combination of flattering friendship and coyness. "I have not a doubt . . . that you are making real sacrifices," she wrote to them in a request for funds, "but if you have any pennies to spare," it would help.[28] To Jacob Schiff's grandson, John, Wald was the dowager aunt, issuing instruction and advice and fully expecting that he would share his family's interest in the welfare of the Henry Street Settlement.[29]

While Wald absorbed and utilized most of Jacob Schiff's recommendations as to administration and promotion of the Visiting Nurse Service and the Henry Street Settlement, she chose to overlook his views as to growth and incorporation. In 1902, he wrote of his fears that incorporation would make her work seem like that of any other society, "and the interest of some, at least, in the Settlement, its work, and its influence may be lost, or at least diminished." Moreover, he added:

> It is . . . not at all unlikely that some of the earnest young ladies who now come to the Settlement, to work in it and with it, are to some extent attracted to it "just because it is a family," and that a society, even if this feature be kept in the background, would be less of an attraction to many a young woman who would otherwise like to engage in the great work which unites you and the other members "of the family."[30]

In some respects, Schiff's fears were realized. With each year of operation, both nursing and nonnursing expenditures increased. In 1902, Wald and her associates treated over 3,000 patients; ten years later, the number was multiplied seven times over. By 1917, a staff of 134 nurses was giving care to nearly 33,000 patients. In the same year, the Social Service Departments of the Settlement were spending $43,000, and it cost over $50,000 to administer the city and country properties.[31] Since Wald and her work were intertwined in the minds of the public, she was forced to do most of the fundraising personally. Persuading people to contribute money became her essential passion, even at the expense of all other interests. In the hundreds of letters she wrote to friends lamenting her problems in funding her work, one thing is clear. She considered the effort to be "the only sacrifice she made in her career."[32]

A list of Henry Street's supporters reads like a Who's Who in American business and banking. Morgenthaus, Lewisohns, Rockefellers, Lehmans, and Morgans were invited to the Settlement to be educated and to be persuaded to donate money. Always the approach was personal and tailored to the personality (and prejudices) of the individual.

Herbert Lehman, for example, visited Henry Street for the first time in the 1890s, while still a college student. As the child of a wealthy family, he had never before been exposed to the poverty, filth, and bleakness of slum life. The visit had a lasting impression on him, as did the "vigor" and "radiance" of Lillian Wald. At her suggestion, he became a club leader at the Settlement. The boys in the "Patriots" soon outgrew the club, but Lehman maintained his friendship with Wald throughout her life and credited her "with a large part in introducing him to social problems and hence to public affairs."[33]

As Lehman became more powerful and wealthy, even after he was elected governor of New York, the Head Worker appealed to him often. In 1928, when she hoped to add to the Settlement, she wrote, "If in your wide contacts you find anybody who has had good fortune in money making and who may be looking for investments in altruism, would you bear in mind our great desire to have a nursery school?" Wald denied that this was to be taken as an appeal to Lehman for she would "have to hang my head in shame" if she failed to remember how much help he had already extended to her. Despite these protestations, two weeks later, Wald mailed her friend a five-page memo detailing her plans for the school. To those who cared for her, and so many did, a Wald appeal was difficult to resist.[34]

Wald was often asked what she would do when her wealthy "uptown friends" died or stopped giving her money. She replied that she had faith that the boys and girls who frequented the Settlement and "whom I feel to be my sons and daughters," would remain faithful to her. In time, many did make their fortunes and support her work by donating money and serving on the Board of the Settlement. Former East Siders—realtors, bankers, attorneys—such as

Hyman Schroeder, Leon R. Spear, Benjamin Schoenfein, Aaron Rabinowitz, and Louis Abrons fulfilled her expectations.[35]

It is sometimes forgotten in the rhetoric of reform that Wald and the other women who played important public roles in the Progressive period were as much hard-headed businesswomen as "angels of mercy" and altruists. The historian Allen Davis, in a biography of Jane Addams, attributed the success of Hull House to the ability of its founder to get on with the strong willed and aristocratic.[36] Both Wald and Addams learned that as their enterprises grew in size and influence, so did their obligations to support and administer them.

In September 1893, with the help of their new friends, Wald and Mary Brewster found living quarters on Jefferson Street. The young women lived there for the next two years and as Wald remembered:

> Naturally objections to two young women living alone in New York under these conditions had to be met, and some assurance as to our material comfort was given to the anxious, though at heart sympathetic families by compromising on good furniture, a Baltimore heater for cheer, and simple but adequate household appurtenances.[37]

That first winter spent on the East Side remained etched in Wald's memory. The Panic of 1893 exacerbated the usual conditions of poverty and the nurses were "plunged . . . into abysses of need and helplessness never dreamed of." Reminiscing during the 1929 depression, Wald wrote:

> In the early morning, before we had time to put the kettle on, people began their tramp up our five flights; and the procession continued after our nursing rounds were ended till the last minute of the night, before we sank into fatigued sleep. They came begging us to help them find work, or at least to give them a ticket entitling them to a few days of the "made work" which was being provided as a relief measure.[38]

Perhaps, Wald wrote, this introduction to suffering, pain, and poverty was in the long run an advantage. Being so busy "left neither place nor time for self analysis and consequent self consciousness, so prone to hinder and dwarf wholesome instincts." Instead, the two nurses worked hard and established friendly relations with their neighbors. The young nurses did not have the time to be nervous about walking about in "unsafe neighborhoods" and into tenement apartments unaccompanied. Though friends warned of dangers, no one, even the most rowdy, ever bothered them.[39] Indeed, the good behavior of the poor, particularly at this time of unemployment, amazed Wald even years later. The more she realized the poverty of the Lower East Side, the more she "couldn't help" but "wish that the victims would show protest."[40]

The poor were not alone in climbing the five long flights of stairs to the apartment on Jefferson Street. Many "uptowners" came as well. One sympathetic visitor who stayed to run errands and to help promote the cause was Josephine Shaw Lowell. Mrs. Lowell, a founder of the Women Worker's Society, was one of the first to urge female wage earners to organize "to assist in the removal of the unjust features of the present labor system." Wage-earning women and women of the community such as Lowell had to join together to get fair wages and working conditions. The Consumers' League, which attempted to educate the public as to labor conditions and to influence legislation, was a direct outgrowth of the Society, as was the idea for the Women's Trade Union League.[41]

Within a short time Jacob Schiff offered to buy Wald and Brewster a suitable "house either in Henry or Madison Street," sites that Wald considered most suitable for a Settlement house. Wald found the perfect place at 265 Henry Street and Schiff provided the funds for repair and restoration. The nurses' new headquarters was situated in what in the past had been a good residential section and the women hoped that they could save something beautiful from an older New York. Mary Brewster was denied the pleasure of watching her dream materialize because before too long, overwork endangered her health and she was forced to abandon nursing.[42]

The settlement house established on Henry Street (at first called the Nurses' Settlement) evolved along the lines of others founded for the poor in the last two decades of the nineteenth century. Its most unique feature was the Visiting Nurse Service. But, in most other respects, it followed the same patterns and developed the same range of activities as other houses—music, art, and dance classes and club work. It was Wald's belief that beauty was essential to well being, as much so as any other necessity of life. The emphasis on the arts was perhaps best expressed in the establishment of the Neighborhood Playhouse under the direction of Irene and Alice Lewisohn. The Playhouse was the showpiece of the Settlement for years and was often a visitor's first introduction to Henry Street.

Social settlements have been subject to much criticism over the years. Conservatives equated social work with radicalism while radicals suggested that social workers attempted "to paint the wound of poverty with a camel's hair brush dipped in a weak solution of Ruskin, Prince Kropotkin and Florence Nightingale."[43] Emma

Goldman "dismissed settlement work as 'teaching the poor to eat with a fork.' "[44] Even friends of the settlement movement, like Bruno Lasker, faulted it for scattering energies in too many directions in the beginning and for settling into accepted routines in later years. Lasker believed that the real function of the settlements, aside from any of the other things they might do, was to bridge cultures.[45] And in this function, Henry Street was a success. Wald established the Settlement to help the immigrant Russian and Polish Jews who made up a majority of the population of the Lower East Side, and her reputation as friend to the immigrant is well documented. Her efforts to prevent exploitation and to get state and federal governments to extend protection to the newcomers were unceasing. She fought devices to curtail immigration such as the imposition of literacy restrictions, even when other social workers turned their backs on the foreigners.[46] At all times, she hoped to help immigrant women who faced prejudice both because of their gender and their foreign birth.

Yet Wald initially failed to understand her neighbors in one of her earliest projects to help young immigrant women. She encouraged them to leave factory jobs and to go into domestic service. This endeavor met with little success. For many young women, life in service was more oppressive than life in the sweatshop. Wald had to learn that Jewish girls regarded housework outside of their own homes as degrading. They preferred living with their own families, no matter how poor the conditions. Moreover, she did not realize that Eastern Jews deeply feared the Gentile world and she could not comprehend the reluctance of parents to permit their daughters to live in Christian homes. Wald and her coworkers needed time to understand the attitudes of young Jewish women whose desire for independence could easily be interpreted as disrespect and impertinence and whose immigrant ways could be equated with lack of refinement.[47]

Some Jews would always mistrust the settlements, including Henry Street, because they did not stand for Jewish values and ideals. Nevertheless, Wald, despite her initial misunderstanding of the Eastern Jews, became a valued friend. She never exhibited the prejudices of some social reformers or some German Jews. She learned from the East Siders because, as one woman recalled, "I was sure of one thing, that Miss Wald would listen to me patiently and try to get to the bottom of what I was saying."[48]

All settlements had a special relationship with women and children because these represented the two groups most served by the clubs and programs of the houses. This generalization was particularly true of Henry Street, for the Eastern Jewish immigrant population included a disproportionately large number of women and children, more than any other immigrant group.[49] For the young boys and girls of the East Side, Henry Street was a refuge, a place that provided fun and a world of "firsts"—circuses, train rides, summer camp, plays, and organized sports. Whatever was needed for fun in childhood was to be found at the Settlement. Even after the young were forced into factories to help with family support, they returned to Henry Street to find their recreation in evening classes, music, lectures, and clubs.[50]

Rose Cohen, a devoted alumna of Henry Street, described the influence of Lillian Wald and Henry Street in her book, *Out of the Shadow*. She remembered being ill as a child and her mother calling for a nurse.

> I opened my eyes and saw a woman, a stranger, sitting beside the couch. Neither in looks nor in dress had I ever seen one like her. . . . She was . . . beautiful and distinguished.
>
> She spoke to mother in German, gave her a card and went away. I spelled out the printed name on the card, Lillian D. Wald, 265 Henry Street.

Cohen kept a diary as a young girl and quoted from it:

> Miss Wald comes to our house, and a new world opens for us. We recommend to her all our neighbors who are in need. The children join clubs . . . and I spend a great deal of time there. Miss Wald and Miss Brewster treat me with affectionate kindness. I am to be sent to the country for health, for education.

The Settlement encouraged the youngsters to aspire and to achieve. It inspired some to step outside the boundaries of the East Side.[51]

Life was particularly difficult for the immigrant women who remained in the home and came to feel that their husbands and children were growing beyond them. The men learned American ways at work and the children spoke English in the schools. Though Eastern European Jewish women enjoyed a degree of independence in the European *Shtetl*, by the end of the nineteenth century, in America, the women found they were frequently regarded as alien, old fashioned, and an embarrassment. Wald attempted to help these women in two ways. The first was to give dignity and recognition to their old world handicrafts, culture, and customs. The second way was to assist and accelerate their acculturation. She believed that all women had to be trained in motherhood and housekeeping methods for they were not innate skills. "It is never to be forgotten," she said, "that they [women] are the executives in the home, placed there without training, but literally directing and controlling the incidents of family life." The alien women, in particular, needed help in adopting new methods. To meet this need, lessons in child care, proper nutrition, and homemaking were given at Henry Street and in a model apartment rented by the Settlement.[52]

A Mother's Club was formed in order to give women a chance to expand their interests and to learn the things that their children and husbands absorbed outside of the home. It is interesting to note that Wald, while she endorsed the idea of the club, hated its name. She wrote to the man in charge of these groups:

> Thank you for all the various reports. And please dig someone for insisting on calling the Women's Clubs, *Mother's* Clubs! I notice in the Board Delegates Meetings that every reference is to the *Mother's* Clubs. You know my sentiments about the right of a woman to be something *besides* a mother.[53]

Most important to the immigrant women was their contact with the Henry Street nurses. The residents of the Settlement represented a new kind of woman—emancipated and useful in public activities. The immigrants learned English, removed their wigs (*sheitels*) and kerchiefs, and attempted to emulate their American teachers.

FOUR
Winning Friends and Influencing Politicos

*L*illian Wald's experiences "in one small East Side section, a block perhaps, . . . led to the next contact, and a next, in widening circles, until . . . community relations came to include the city, the state, the national government, and the world at large."[1] Contact with her Henry Street neighbors over a forty-year period pointed up the need for play areas and parks, clean streets, and better housing. Children required trade schools, school nurses, ungraded classes, and scholarship money. Working people needed a meeting and social hall and protective legislation to guarantee them a degree of security. Some of Wald's attempts to meet these needs were nonproductive, some were piecemeal, and some were superficial, but she undertook all with a dedication to and a conviction of the importance of social reform.

Wald moved energetically from one activity to another. At times her pace was almost frantic as she tried to fulfill her commitments. Her friend Lavinia Dock regarded her with awe and confessed that she could not keep up with the Head Worker. Once, after receiving a gift from Wald for her birthday, Dock commented that it looked as if it had come from Egypt. "Have you been over there and come back? Some one told me you were going. Did you just drop in there between committee meetings etc. on the way as it were? You are indeed a wonder."[2] Wald, in a rare moment of self-analysis, wrote to another friend, Elsa Herrman, that she had discovered "someone who must have been as busy as I." While visiting Russia, Wald learned about Catherine the Great, who "might easily have lived on Henry Street. She seems to have had the capacity for busyness."[3]

In all of her activities, Wald employed the same techniques and tactics that she used in gaining support for the nurses. When she was convinced of the need for reform in some area of life, she learned the facts and set out to gain converts to the cause, especially those with political and or financial power. She wrote letters to influential politicians and got others to do the same. It was rare for her to miss an opportunity to plead before boards of health, boards of estimate, legislatures, and special investigating commissions. Her statements were artful and replete with anecdotes designed to stir the emotions. Herbert Lehman was fascinated by Wald's "combination of gentleness and power" and noted that she had influence not only with idealistic reform groups, but with "hard-bitten sachems of Tammany Hall" who "consulted her, and knowing she was an effective crusader, gave weight to her desires."[4]

Frances Perkins, who would later become secretary of labor in Franklin Roosevelt's cabinet, described a typical Wald performance at the hearings called to investigate the Triangle Shirtwaist Company fire in 1911. Wald was at the height of her influence and when she was called to testify, it created a hush in the chamber.

> Miss Wald was going to speak. Everybody came and listened. Miss Wald didn't know anything about fire prevention, but she was known as a person whose heart was always in the right place and was greatly respected because she was loved.[5]

When organizations were formed with others of aroused social conscience, Wald withdrew to a less active position. She usually maintained contact with and membership in the group, but was not involved in day-by-day policy decisions. For example, she took great pride in her part in the establishment of the Federal Children's Bureau and the organization of the National Association for the Advancement of Colored People, but with each group, other activities demanded her attention after her initial interest.

Wald frequently related the story of the origin of the Children's Bureau. Her experience on Henry Street made clear to her the need to protect the working child. In addition, her interest in the working woman could be served with the elimination of child labor, since it would be possible to upgrade the position and wages of women in the labor market if there were no competition from children. Wald was a lifelong member of the New York Child Labor Committee (NYCLC), an amalgam of social workers, academicians, and a few wealthy bankers such as Jacob Schiff and Paul Warburg, which grew out of the University Settlement. She also belonged to the National Child Labor Committee (NCLC), which was founded by Felix Adler and had the same general membership. Both groups were committed to a program that advocated legislation to prevent child labor.

Questions directed to both the NYCLC and the NCLC illustrated the need for a governmental agency to collect and provide concrete information on children—births, diseases, accidents, delinquency, and dangerous occupations. Wald wrote:

> Toward the close of President [Theodore] Roosevelt's adminis-
> tration, a colleague [Florence Kelley] and I called upon him to
> present my plea for the creation of this bureau. On that day the
> Secretary of Agriculture had gone South to ascertain what dan-
> ger to the community lurked in the appearance of the boll wee-
> vil. This gave point to our argument that nothing that might
> have happened to the children of the nation could have called
> forth governmental inquiry.

The NCLC became the "sponsor for the necessary propaganda" for the creation of the Children's Bureau, which was a step toward governmental responsibility for child welfare.[6]

Wald worked without cease for the establishment of the bureau, even stepping down as supervisor of nursing at Henry Street in favor of Annie Goodrich, in order to have more time. From 1906 to 1912, when the bill establishing the bureau in the Department of Labor was passed, she testified, spoke before interested groups, and wrote letters.[7] Nevertheless when President Taft offered her the job of chief of the bureau, she declined. Writing to a friend, she declared that "conceited as it may seem, I think I am more useful in New York and at my post."[8] It was a realization that her value lay in publicizing causes.

For Wald and other feminists, the establishment of the bureau was a women's victory in that they had supplied "the generals, the diplomats, ammunition, and a vast army" for the campaign.[9] The *Woman Voter,* the official organ of the Woman Suffrage Party, hailed the passage of the Children's Bureau in an editorial.

> Since the movement was originated by women, has been sup-
> ported by women and will deal with children through the co-
> operation of teachers, social workers and others, chiefly women,
> who are in touch with the younger generation, not even the
> most ardent anti-suffragist could deny that management of this
> Bureau is strictly within woman's sphere.[10]

Julia Lathrop was named as head of the Children's Bureau and it was the first time a national agency was directed by a woman. His-torians believe that the bureau's history "is inseparable from the history of a group of strong, ambitious women" such as Florence Kelley and Wald. It became "a focal point of the newly emerging career woman and the professional and social leverage for which women were striving."[11]

Wald maintained her interest in the child labor issue, but by the early 1920s she had involved herself in so many other matters that she was no longer active in the cause. When Owen Lovejoy of the NCLC asked her to join the Speaker's Bureau for the Amendment to the Constitution that would bar child labor, she acceded to his request but doubted that she had the time to speak because she was so busy and all her time was pledged to other causes. She did, however, contact such friends as Al Smith for support.[12]

Wald was back in the fight in the mid 1920s when attempts to emasculate the Children's Bureau, the conservative leadership of the NCLC, and the difficulties encountered by supporters of the amendment forced her into active participation in the war against child labor. A major reason for her renewed interest was the pressure exerted on her by old friends such as Florence Kelley of the National Consumers' League and Grace Abbott, chief of the Children's Bureau. Both chided her for permitting Wiley Swift, the head of the NCLC, to obstruct the Child Labor Amendment. It was time, Kelley argued, for her old colleague to discontinue lending her name to the NCLC (which they had both helped to organize), or if Wald chose not to resign then she was under a moral obligation to use her influence with the board to get it to abandon its conservative policies. She urged Wald to attend meetings and to bring her "far famed and sorily [sic] needed ingenuity!"[13]

For the next few years, Wald again battled actively to eliminate child labor. She attended conferences, gave speeches, and wrote to her political contacts, newspapers, and influential friends, while at the same time she helped to maneuver Wiley Swift out of the NCLC. In the 1930s Wald accelerated her efforts for the children, especially for the Child Labor Amendment. Now in semiretirement, she applied pressure to her allies to intensify their efforts by using the argument that the abolition of child labor would increase adult employment during the depression.[14]

Throughout her battle for children's rights, Wald believed that she was working within the women's movement. "Women," she said in a 1932 speech, "from the first sensed the significance" and importance of the abolition of child labor and the need for information about child health.[15]

A second illustration of Wald's approach to reform is her relations with black Americans. The historian Allen Davis has pointed out that settlement workers as a group were not "free of the prejudice, bigotry and racist ideas that were so widespread" in the early twentieth century. But they were among the few groups of northern whites that had any sustained contact with urban blacks, and this contact gave them "a greater sympathy for the lot of the Negro . . . and a better understanding of . . . [their] needs . . . than most of their generation."[16] Wald recognized that the difficulties encountered by the ordinary person in the labor market were intensified for blacks. In *The House on Henry Street,* she related the story of the day a black woman called at the Settlement and challenged Wald to face the race problem. The nurse responded by opening Henry Street to blacks and by establishing a branch, Lincoln House, on the West Side of New York City to service the black community. At the same time, Wald sought out trained and efficient black nurses to staff the new settlement and encouraged a program adapted to neighborhood needs.[17]

In 1909, a group that included Mary Ovington, Henry Moskowitz, William English Walling, Oswald Garrison Villard, Florence Kelley, Charles Edward Russell, and Wald met to form an organization to work for the cause of black people. Early meetings of the group, the NAACP, were devoted to publicity, fundraising, and membership. When it was decided to hold a national conference on the status of black people, the reception was to be held at the Henry Street Settlement, one of the few places in the city that would accept an interracial group. Wald and her friends, however, did have misgivings about the bad publicity that would result from people of different races sitting down to dine together. Fearing the newspaper stories, even some of the organizing committee members opposed the idea. The problem was solved when two hundred people agreed to attend the conference and Wald estimated that Henry Street was too small for everyone to have a sit-down dinner, therefore all the guests would have to eat standing up. She declared the party a success. When the NAACP was firmly established, Wald characteristically withdrew from active membership claiming lack of time. She did maintain contact with the group through Florence Kelley, who was regarded as the Henry Street representative.[18]

By present-day standards, Wald was not free from bigotry. She believed that lack of economic opportunity for blacks discouraged them and "reacted unfavorably on character and ability."[19] Also, she resisted the efforts of Bruno Lasker to integrate the dining room operated by the Visiting Nurses and questioned his attempts to encourage blacks to move to the East Side neighborhood, which she believed was "not suited to them."[20] Wald likewise minimized the difficulties faced by the American Indians. Even after educating herself as to their problems, she declined an invitation to help the American Indian Defense Association.[21] Despite these shortcomings, she did try to raise money for black social workers and to petition friends for justice and jobs for the black people. Wald was ahead, yet still part of her time.

It may be claimed that Wald assisted the black woman more than the race as a whole, and that the aid was given behind the scenes rather than overtly and through a formal organization.[22] At her memorial service, the Reverend John Johnson said:

> Perhaps more important than anything else was Miss Wald's contribution to colored women. She gave the impetus to seek their place in the nursing profession, and Henry Street was the first organization of its kind to take them on equal terms.[23]

Wald's involvement in the campaigns for children's rights and the NAACP were typical of her activities. She played similar roles in various pacifist organizations, the Women's Trade Union League, women's suffrage groups, and a variety of other associations formed to promote reform. Her methods and thinking were the same in all areas, and in most cases she sought to advance the position of women.

Wald's strongest asset was her "dynamic personality" backed by the prestige she enjoyed as founder of the Henry Street Settlement and the Visiting Nurse Service. She was able to communicate her beliefs to others in a manner "very gentle, but very forceful, with an unusual amount of determination."[24] One young nurse on meeting her, claimed that Wald "generated an enthusiasm that was 'almost religious fervor,'"[25] and reminiscences of Wald never fail to comment upon her exuberance, charm, and warmth. She had such a reputation for humor and a love of gaiety and conversational banter that George Alger claimed that she was never one of the reformers of "rueful countenance." Instead, "she carried the healing power of generous laughter."[26] If Henry Street became a place that attracted all kinds of people—elected officials, bankers, labor leaders, lawyers, and newspaper editors—then Wald was the magnet that drew them. The dinner table was her battlefield. Tales circulated about her powers of persuasion and it is said that it was expensive to be Miss Wald's dinner partner.[27] Felix Warburg loved to tell the story of meeting a businessman who was angry at something Wald wanted and was going to see her about the matter. "No," Warburg had said, "don't do that. If you're sure you're right you'd better write her a letter. If you see her," and he shrugged his shoulders expressively, "you might change your mind. I have."[28]

The dining room at Henry Street was also used for educational purposes. Schiffs and Rockefellers were introduced to the problems of the East Side and political novices were persuaded to side with the reformers. Frances Perkins recalled the time that Mrs. Borden Harriman was appointed by President Wilson to a committee on industrial relations. Wald decided that she had to educate the "amateur" and invited her to Henry Street for a dinner party whose guest list included Florence Kelley, Paul Kellogg, Perkins, and Rose Schneiderman of the Women's Trade Union League. The pros gave their pupil a picture of working conditions, economics, and living standards of the poor and Daisy Harriman proved to be a useful member of the committee.[29]

It was rare for Wald to offend anyone either by her importunities for money or by the stands she took on issues in the years prior to World War I. Like Jane Addams, she had the "gift of imaginative sympathy" which made it "impossible for her to have toward either party in a conflict the cold hostility which either party has for the other." She was able to see both sides in a conflict and even though one side was wrong, she tried to understand why its partisans believed in it.[30]

She was "one of the most loved of the great women of our time," said a friend, and "love was an essential element of the life she led. . . . There is no use trying to understand Lillian Wald unless you understand that inordinate capacity for loving people of all sorts." This talent for caring and making others love her was Wald's special strength.[31] But it may be suggested that it was also a factor that made her cautious and careful not to offend. It may have prevented her from taking more radical positions on issues as well. Her strength was at times the source of her weakness.

While Wald needed the rich to lend financial and moral support to her work, she needed elected officials to aid with legislative programs. Most settlement workers learned to recognize the areas of joint interest that they held with politicians. Certainly the reformers came to respect the power of the bosses and to understand the reasons for that power. In turn, the politicos learned that the settlement workers represented a factor they had to deal with.

By the end of her career, Wald was a recognized political power. While she usually supported reform administrations, she got on "harmoniously with almost all politicians." Tammany Hall leaders constantly consulted with her and candidates of all parties sought her endorsement. A *New Yorker* magazine profile of Wald described her as an instinctively political animal who "could have gone far in politics on her own" had she been born in a different era.[32] She learned quickly the realities of political life—when to use pressure, when to use publicity, when to use the power of an influential friend, and when to mobilize the numbers available at Henry Street.

Wald eschewed formal connections with any party. Though born to a Republican family, she always proclaimed her independence.

She campaigned for Democrat, Republican, Independent, Fusion, and Progressive candidates, depending upon the issues and the influence she had upon the individual politician. She was also a frequent supporter of the Socialist party, which had great popularity among Jewish workers on the East Side as well as with women, many of whom viewed socialism as the only means to sexual equality.

Wald's introduction to politics came early in her career. She recalled that when she and Mary Brewster started their work, they believed that "politics concerned itself with matters outside their realm and experience,"[33] but it did not take long for Wald "to realize that when I was working in the interest of those babies . . . , I was really in politics."[34] She discovered how powerful the political control was on the individual and the collective life of the neighborhood. As a rule, Wald participated in the campaigns of reform candidates and those that involved "moral issues." But her decision to support an individual was also predicated upon his attitude toward women and his utilization of women and their experience in government.[35] She did not hesitate to play the role of political boss during an election and would mobilize the members of the Henry Street household and clubs to distribute literature, speak at meetings, and act as poll watchers.

In New York City, reform movements were basically anti-Tammany Hall campaigns and Wald's first experience in a mayoralty election was supporting Seth Low in 1901. Two members of her staff, one a young club member and the second a nurse, wrote of their campaign experiences in the Henry Street *Settlement Journal:*

> Surely the mind's eye must see Miss Wald in the blue checked dress giving final instructions to her corps of assistants and sending them forth with the printed sheets that were to help secure a clean mayoralty for our great city.[36]

It is characteristic of Wald's humor that her own memory of the election centered on the rental of a meeting hall that was normally used by pro-Tammany politicians and was owned by a "machine" regular. The reformers, who had sold out the meeting, discovered that the hall owner had rented them a room without chairs and had planted hecklers in the audience. "Never was there a sadder failure," Wald recalled. The next day when the Henry Streeters went to hear the election returns, they saw signs and banners held by the Tammany crowd reading, "To Hell With Reform."[37] Wald's support of subsequent mayoralty candidates was more sophisticated—invitations to dinner, use of the house personnel, and some speech making—but no less energetic.

Whether or not she had supported an official for election did not matter to Wald when she decided that she needed assistance. She pressed for all manner of causes, from more posts for women in government to the night-time removal of garbage on the East Side. Her campaigns usually brought results, although at times she had to use powerful "connections" as extra ammunition "to coax opportunities" for pet projects. When Alice and Irene Lewisohn needed tax benefits and permits for the Neighborhood Theater, "the influence and rapport of Lillian Wald with the city departments paved the way to the cooperation of the department chiefs in the building of this . . . enterprise."[38]

In the same way, she put pressure on city leaders to make greater use of the womanpower in the community. Her strong commitment to the cause of women in public office may be seen in her work to have Katherine Davis appointed to a post in the New York City Bureau of Preventable Diseases. She first led a delegation to see Mayor John Hylan and later wrote to him:

> Women and girls constitute a large proportion of the employees [of factories] and therefore, the protection of the female worker is an important function of the Government, and female sanitary inspectors and female physicians would be of the utmost value in the work.[39]

Women were qualified for office by both personality and experience, Wald believed, therefore had to be given greater opportunities in public life. She recommended the appointment of females to a variety of posts, mostly in areas usually identified with women such as education and child welfare. But she also suggested that women be named to posts of fire and police commissioner, jobs that were usually associated only with men.[40]

When Wald's interests expanded beyond municipal boundaries, her campaign activities followed. Governors Charles Evans Hughes, Alfred Smith, Franklin Roosevelt, and Herbert Lehman were all friends and supporters and Wald tried to educate them all on social issues. She was especially proud of her role in instructing Hughes on immigration, child labor, and trade unionism and she made sure that he recognized Henry Street's part in his election. The Settlement formed a League of Independent Voters for neighborhood campaigning, which Wald claimed in a letter to Hughes was "extremely effective" in vote getting and in interpretation of the issues.[41] When Hughes created a Commission on Immigration, "to make a full inquiry, examination, and investigation into the condition, welfare and industrial opportunities of aliens in the State of

New York," Wald and Frances Kellor were the two women on the committee of nine members. Kellor was later named chief of the Immigration Division of the Department of Labor when that bureau was created.[42] Hughes utilized other women in his administration, including the feminist Crystal Eastman, who was appointed to the New York State Employer's Liability Commission.[43]

National politics was for Wald a natural progression of interests. The first president with whom she enjoyed good relations was Theodore Roosevelt, a man she first met when he was police commissioner in New York City. Social workers, she wrote, could go to him and suggest projects, as she had done with the Children's Bureau, or talk to him about social problems like the shirtwaist makers' strikes, "and we felt that he considered himself a social worker in the truest sense of that term." Roosevelt was a sounding board for the reformers and she believed that was what a president was supposed to be.[44]

The election of 1912 was a difficult one for Wald. The platform of the Progressive party was in large part inspired by social workers and many believed with Henry Moskowitz, of the University Settlement, that Theodore Roosevelt's speech at the Chicago convention was the best one dealing "with social and individual justice" ever uttered.[45] To Jane Addams, it seemed that the new party represented "the action and passion of the times." It would make social reform a national political issue.[46] Wald's feminist friends were particularly entranced with the Bull Moose program and party since the Progressives encouraged women's participation and sought "to draw upon the great reservoir of their moral energy so long undesired and unutilized in practical politics."[47] Most important, the Progressives formally endorsed the vote for women.

From the start, there was tremendous pressure upon Wald to support Roosevelt, whose platform, according to Mary Dreier of the Woman's Trade Union League, held all of the things that social workers had struggled for.[48] Even her friend, Rabbi Stephen Wise, who was anxious for Wald to support Woodrow Wilson, admitted to her that the "Roosevelt platform is tremendously attractive. It embodies nearly all the dreams and aspirations which have been a large part of our lives."[49] Wald applauded the social justice sections and the equal suffrage plank of the Bull Moose platform, but believed that her friends had to surrender too much to get these provisions. Unlike Jane Addams, who understood her friend's dilemma, Wald could not "swallow those two battleships," which the platform advocated building each year, nor accept the fortification of the Panama Canal.[50] While she encouraged men like Henry Moskowitz to run on the ticket and supported local Progressive candidates, Wald refused to take an active part in the campaign on behalf of the Progressives.

Democrats, nevertheless, feared that Wald would follow Addams into the new party. Rabbi Wise suggested that the Henry Streeter be part of a group to press Wilson to abandon some of his conservative supporters.[51] At the same time, Henry Morgenthau, an old friend of the Settlement, wrote her saying that as Jane Addams's "connection with the Bull Moose Party has received so much publicity," it would be important for the Democrats to try to counteract it by publishing a letter from Wald espousing Wilson. Morgenthau then suggested that she allow herself to be placed "on some committee which would not entail any work on your part, to give us the benefit of your name and influence."[52]

Wald decided not to support the Democrats because they did not endorse women's suffrage. It was hoped that she would become president of the Woman's National Wilson and Marshall Committee, but she refused the post. In letters explaining her action to Morgenthau and Mrs. Borden Harriman, she wrote that while she could approve Wilson's record in social reform and believed the party was moving toward progressivism and while she was concerned lest the liberals divide their forces and reactionaries unite for Taft, she could not support the Democratic platform. She fully expected all the parties to endorse votes for women and it was, to her, illogical "to assume even a minor responsibility for a platform that has no suffrage plank." She continued:

> The question of suffrage is an issue and it seems to me that it no longer admits of academic discussion. Those of us who care for it should have a right to ask [for] a plank in the political platform that we support.
>
> I do not know where Governor Wilson stands on suffrage. If he is for it, his advisors should tell him that one and a half million women will vote for president.[53]

Wald was relatively quiet during the election, but after 1912, she joined the permanent legislative committee of the New York State Convention of the National Progressive party. In 1916, she abandoned the party when she and Jane Addams supported Wilson on the peace issue.

When New York State convened a constitutional convention in 1914, Wald was selected as one of the delegates-at-large. She became involved because she wanted women represented at the convention, a viewpoint shared by Theodore Roosevelt. The former president hoped that the Progressives would insist upon the election of women delegates to the meeting to write a new state constitution and pointed to at least fifty women who were qualified because of their experience on various state boards and in charity work.[54] Wald, as chairwoman of the Women's Temporary Committee of the State of New York for Representation in the Constitutional Convention, hoped to elect at least five female delegates, although neither of the major parties was anxious to assist. She worked to publicize the accomplishments of women like Frances Kellor and Josephine Goldmark, the social investigator and author, so that sympathetic men would support their nomination and that of other women. Wald's value was great as the representative of her sex, for she showed that she could organize and function among tough-minded politicians. Although females in New York State did not have the vote, she set an example of what they could do when they were granted suffrage.[55]

Considering Wald's anti-Tammany history, it is interesting that one of her great political friends was a Tammany product. But Alfred E. Smith met Wald's two criteria for support. He shared her social convictions and recognized, if reluctantly, women's right to a place in public life and to the vote. Wald supported Smith in each of his bids for governor and arranged for him to meet the heads of other settlements. All though his career, she (often accompanied by Florence Kelley) made frequent trips to Albany to insure passage of reform legislation. To Wald, Smith had a true understanding of the living conditions of the poor and said and did the right things to alleviate them. He was an inspiration for young East Siders.

Smith developed strong friendships with many women in social work after his introduction to them as the result of the Triangle Shirtwaist Fire. Mary Dreier, Frances Perkins, Wald, Kelley, and Belle Moskowitz greatly influenced his thinking not only in social legislation, but also on the place of women in public office. Wald lobbied to have Smith appoint Perkins to the State Industrial Commission and then worked to gain support for his choice. A letter to a friend written by Wald's secretary illustrated the social worker's activities.

> Miss Wald asked me to let you know that she took immediate steps to bring about support for Governor Smith in his appointment of Miss Frances Perkins. She herself telegraphed . . . him; she and Mrs. Walter Rauschenbusch wired . . . ; and she asked Mr. Hall of the N.Y. Child Labor Committee and Mr. John B. Andrews to get what support they could throughout the state.[56]

Wald and other women were particularly excited by the success achieved by Perkins because the governor had sought out a woman who knew the field rather than someone's wife or daughter.[57] It seemed to Wald "that any working woman who failed to support Smith was almost guilty of treason."[58]

She abandoned her usual cautious approach in the election of 1928, when she came out forcefully for Smith despite his stand on the repeal of prohibition. She acted as an individual, hoping to spare Henry Street and the Visiting Nurses from criticism. Her endorsement, however, resulted in a break with most other social workers, prohibitionists, and some feminists and women trade unionists who favored Hoover's position on women's rights. Wald joined with John L. Elliott of the Hudson Guild Settlement in sending a letter to welfare workers throughout the United States asking for support for Smith. They called the Democrat a "social statesman" who worked for the "preservation of great power for the use of women who wash, and women who iron, as well as for the great manufacture[r]s."[59] In a personal note to Jane Addams, Wald explained her position. She acknowledged that Smith's record as a "wet" conflicted with her professed support of prohibition, but Wald believed that the governor was so good in other ways that she had to support him.[60]

The Wald-Elliott circular letter stressed Smith's record on humanitarian issues and his understanding of the nature and value of social work. Wald never anticipated "the perfect Niagara of mail" she was to receive in response.[61] Some old friends, like Addams, Grace Abbott, Graham Taylor of the Chicago Commons Settlement, and Sophonisba Breckinridge, though unable to support Smith, assured Wald of their affection and respect for her.[62] A few colleagues, like Paul Kellogg, agreed with her position,[63] but most people used the occasion to attack Wald and her candidate. The bigotry expressed surprised and offended her. It was as if "a poison gas had spread over us."[64] She interpreted much of the abuse not as a question of Smith's position on prohibition, since he had promised to enforce the Eighteenth Amendment, but as an expression of "irrepressible prejudice against a Catholic."[65] The great number of letters she received from Protestant clergymen convinced her of the argument. Despite the criticism she received, which in some cases meant the loss of money for the Settlement and the nurses, Wald vowed to continue to campaign for Smith.[66]

If Wald suffered a political defeat with her support of Smith's candidacy, the 1928 vote did accomplish the election of an old friend, Herbert Lehman (as lieutenant governor of New York) and of a new one, Franklin Roosevelt (to the governorship), both of whom she strongly endorsed. Lehman was, she wrote him, "a light shining in the midst of discouragements" and she hoped that Henry Street had played a part in this.[67] Her devotion to her one time pupil was important to him four years later when Wald assisted

Smith and Roosevelt in pushing Lehman into the gubernatorial race. Tammany leaders opposed her protégé and Wald helped to overcome this opposition by letters to friends in politics, visits to Boss John F. Curry and publicity threatening to withhold her support of the national ticket unless Lehman were assured the nomination.[68]

In 1932, Wald supported Democrat Robert Wagner for the Senate and Morris Hillquit, the Socialist candidate, for mayor. Her major interest aside from Lehman, however, was the presidential race; the Hoover administration had to end. She felt sorry for the "inept" president. "Poor thing, he continues to do everything on Friday and with his left hand."[69] She was sympathetic with the goals of Socialist Norman Thomas, but a visit to Hyde Park with Jane Addams assured Wald that FDR was a fine man "who wants to do the right thing."[70] Addams was less impressed and voted for Hoover again.

While Wald applauded FDR and quoted newspaper columnist Dorothy Thompson's remark that "people must understand that . . . Roosevelt thinks as Jane Addams and Lillian Wald think,"[71] it sometimes seemed to a few of her friends that she was more enthusiastic about Eleanor than her husband. Wald probably met the future first lady when she worked at the College Settlement and with the Consumers' League before her marriage, but the two women became close friends during the 1928 election. In that year Wald wrote Lehman, "the conjunction of Mr. Roosevelt and you and Mrs. Roosevelt augers [sic] well not only for the State but for the whole country."[72]

Certainly Mrs. Roosevelt figured large in many of Wald's political letters in 1932 and 1933. In notes describing the new president and the first lady to Ramsay MacDonald in England, she wrote, "I have faith that Mr. Roosevelt and more importantly, Mrs. Roosevelt will keep the White House human and accessible." They were a "splendid pair." "The President-Elect is a very fair man, emotionally suggestive, and his wife who has real knowledge and real convictions, is in his entire confidence."[73]

Wald was not alone in her attitude of favoring Eleanor Roosevelt. Apparently Molly Dewson of the Consumers' League, who later played a large role in the New Deal as head of the Women's Division of the Democratic Party, stressed his wife rather than Franklin to her associates. A friend wrote Dewson, "As to Roosevelt, I sometimes wonder if once in a while you forget you are electing *Mr.,* not *Mrs.* Roosevelt. If you clear this confusion up, and elect *Mrs.* R.— why of course I'll vote for her gladly." Otherwise, her vote would go to Hoover.[74]

Wald was always optimistic as to the inevitability of social change if only people were informed. The New Deal, therefore, seemed to her the culmination of forty years of work as a publicist. Economist A. A. Berle, who had been a resident of the Settlement, confirmed her thinking when he said that the seed of the New Deal was to be found in Henry Street and in the principles behind the work of the Visiting Nurses.[75] Wald's pet projects, such as the Children's Bureau, were left intact or expanded. Ideas that she had endorsed over the years—unemployment insurance, old age pensions, and the recognition of the Soviet Union—were adopted. More important, Roosevelt drew upon skilled professionals, including women, for social welfare programs. She delighted in the presence of Henry Streeters—A. A. Berle, "little Henry" Morgenthau—influential in the administration. Wald's visit to the White House at the invitation of the Roosevelts was a source of great satisfaction, as was FDR's willingness to listen to her ideas.[76] With Lehman in Albany and "that vigorous, unmatched, fiery Mayor" Fiorello La-Guardia in New York, she believed that the experiences of her life were being utilized by government.[77]

Equally important to her was the recognition of female talent in public life. The appointment of colleagues Maud Swartz, Molly Dewson, Frances Perkins, Caroline O'Day, Rose Schneiderman, Clara Beyer, and Josephine Roche to governmental and political posts was testimony to Wald of New Deal interest in the women's causes. In 1936, Wald as co-chairman of the Good Neighbor League said:

> Though the extreme feminists do not claim me, I rejoice that the President's vision is broad enough for him to see good servants and potentially great servants among the women. He has found them capable from membership in his cabinet and emissaries abroad, down to the least conspicuous office.[78]

Wald's refusal to be identified as an "extreme feminist" must be understood in the light of her times. She and many other activists of the 1920s and 1930s "consciously shied away from that label . . . using it in a fairly narrow . . . sense." The "term was reserved for members of the National Women's Party" and not for all women who worked to remove the disabilities placed before members of their sex.[79]

Wald's health did not permit her to participate in an election campaign after 1936. For forty years she had worked in the political arena to promote her causes. Her greatest accomplishment in this area was in the education of politicos to social reform and women's rights. Hughes and Smith offer examples of two of her more apt pupils, the latter moving from being antisuffrage to acknowledging women's right to a role in public life. While some historians, including Arthur Schlesinger, question Smith's conversion to the cause of women in politics, Wald never did.[80]

To accomplish her aims, Wald frequently broke with old friends and coworkers. They had the same goals, yet, to use one example, she and Jane Addams often took different paths. Most students of the women of the early twentieth century lump all of the social reformers into one category and describe their activities by using Addams as a model. Yet the two most prominent women of the time differed in approach in the three most important elections (1912, 1928, and 1932) of the period.

FIVE

A Women's World

*P*eople of all nations, economic backgrounds, and professions came
to Henry Street and Wald had ties to men in the financial, political,
settlement, and medical worlds. Yet in many ways, Wald's world
was a women's world. They were her comrades; she lived and worked
with and for them. She could say about many women, as she did
about Mrs. Belle Moskowitz, that they were "more than friends."
They understood each other and cared for the things that they
"held in common."[1] Wald's relations with others of her sex were var-
ied. To some, she was a social friend, to some, a colleague in common works, and to others, a kind of mother figure in the family
that the Settlement had become. To one, Mary Dreier, "Sister Wald"
was "big sister and little sister and above all beloved sister to all
the eager and hungry and unhappy and striving folks in all the
world."[2]

The wives of the wealthy, such as Nina Warburg, provided Wald
with diversion and she considered time spent with them "playing
hookey" from "serious matters." She welcomed the distracting
change in at least one instance for she was "tired of being good."[3]
Wald enjoyed "the many good times . . . , the gay parties and the
fun" and, as she explained to socialite Maude Nathan of the Consumers' League, believed she needed them in order to live a "sane
and balanced" life.[4] She and Nathan were members of a "special"
Tuesday night group of game players. When in 1932 Wald was hospitalized and had to miss the sessions, Mrs. Jacob Schiff sent her a
backgammon board and a contribution for Henry Street. Wald
thanked her saying:

I am going to have your check recorded as a tribute from Mr.
Backgammon Board. No apology for not feminizing it, when
anything as stiff as a board ought not to be called a lady! I am
sure you'll agree with me about its gender.[5]

Though she relied upon her wealthy friends for fun and relaxation,
Wald expected them to have feelings and emotional and intellectual
range. She was not interested in people who were content to devote
their lives to being named in society columns.[6]

The family at Henry Street was all female at first, both nurses
and later lay workers as well. In a brief time, it became apparent
that male residents were needed to attract boys and men to the
Settlement. Graham Wallis, John Crosby Brown, and Raymond B.
Fosdick moved into 265 Henry Street in short order and by 1926,
Wald could describe the family as "larger and properly balanced
with more men than before."[7] The pervasive female influence pre-
vailed, however, and may be seen in the following letter written by
Wald to describe the head of the Boys' Clubs in 1910:

Dr. Shoemaker is . . . a very pure hearted man and has the devotion of the boys. We count ourselves fortunate in that . . . [he]
possesses certain qualities of goodness that might be regarded
the peculiar property of women in the minds of the boys were it
not that such "damaging" qualities are counteracted by a very
fine physique and skills in athletics that wins the admiration of
the boys.[8]

So dominant was the nurse-female influence in the Settlement in
the early years that Yssabella Waters felt obliged to write Wald to
ask for permission to include the men at a Christmas dinner. Of
course, Waters explained, the males would have to "understand that
they can't stay afterward," but it would appear "heathenish to shut
them out in a night like this when they have no home to go to, and
this stands for their home."[9]

Many young women traveled to the East Side, and for some
daughters of wealthy American Jews, work at Henry Street was
considered a form of finishing school.[10] Included in this group were
the Lewisohn sisters, heiresses to a copper fortune. Alice Lewisohn
Crowley recorded her initial impression of the Settlement and its
Head Worker.

The Leading Lady . . . led . . . us up to the dining room where
the starched and happy company, the Settlement's Visiting
Nurses and their co-workers were waiting. . . . Lively spirits
sparred across the table, and presiding at its head, Lillian Wald
played not one part, but innumerably changing characters. In

her role as hostess, work automatically as she mixed the . . . salad . . . , while she clarified some problem about unions, interlarding her conversation with whimsical stories.

Crowley viewed Wald as a statesman of a new order that would function through a "Great Mother—instead of through the rigidity of a patriarchal system."[11] The concept of Wald as matriarch was not limited to Crowley. On the Head Worker's sixty-first birthday, she was honored with a poem entitled, "Mother of Henry Street."[12]

Two other sisters, Ethel Frankau and Aline Frankau Bernstein were attracted to the Settlement and Lillian Wald. Together, the sisters worked to create scenic designs, costumes, and props for the drama clubs and for pageants produced by the Settlement to celebrate the rich heritage of the immigrants. In 1913, Wald suggested that the Lewisohns, Rita Morgenthau, and the Frankau sisters develop a program to commemorate Henry Street's twentieth anniversary. The enormous success of this endeavor inspired the Lewisohns to build a permanent theater. Helen Arthur, a lawyer, and Agnes Morgan, who had production talents, joined the other women in the project, now called the Neighborhood Playhouse. This "women's theater" opened in February 1915, and newspapers reporting its progress announced that "No man has anything whatsoever to do with it except by invitation." The Playhouse was, from the start, a success, for its experimental nature attracted major playwrights and professional performers to the East Side.[13]

Henry Street was a women's world with a woman at its head. It was their own; they weren't just taking a part in it. They had the exhilarating sense of belonging to a special circle that gave them opportunities for the realization of their talents and powers. Freed of the usual divisive competition for men and the usual competition from men, the women of Henry Street developed a feeling of camaraderie and commitment to cause. They enjoyed an autonomy of action that was unique for females of their time and so considered themselves extremely fortunate. Lillian Wald was to one of them "the Leading Lady," the dear sister, who made Henry Street home.[14]

The Settlement provided an intense community life like that of an exclusive sorority. The women worked hard and then took time to play, often staging home entertainments—usually frivolous skits and plays with new lyrics to popular music. The words expressed their delight with life at Henry Street and their pride in the recognition they and Wald received from the public. One piece, "At Last," had Wald elected mayor of New York City and choosing her cabinet from among the nurses. To achieve "this happy state," they wrote,

Talk suffrage loud and suffrage long,
At every chance you get
If you persist in suffrage now,
We *will* have suffragette.[15]

Common interests and goals and the fact of womanhood rather than common ideology and class were the criteria for entrance into the "family." Sisterhood was not limited to nurses; instead it extended to all kindred spirits. While the majority were middle class and associated with settlement work, such working-class women as Leonora O'Reilly were included. In a study of O'Reilly, Ellen Lagemann claims that the "colleagueship" of Wald, Lavinia Dock, and the other women of Henry Street "nurtured the sense of sisterhood that Leonora, among others, would eventually seek to institutionalize in the Women's Trade Union League."[16] "Sisters" were activists and leaders; they were special; they accomplished. Frances Perkins, reflecting on the era, claimed that her great memory was of good friends who worked without competitiveness, with great spirit toward common ends.[17]

For Wald, the feeling of sisterhood extended, of course, to the nurses—Lavinia Dock, Yssabella Waters, Adelaide Nutting, Harriett Knight—and to the other women of Henry Street with whom she lived, worked, and vacationed. It also extended, however, to women in other professions and other nations. Most were feminists and together they formed a women's network that was mutually supportive. They provided for each other the uncritical acceptance and encouragement that is usually given by family members.

Jane Addams in Chicago and Lillian Wald in New York were the loci of the network and both Hull House and Henry Street were opened for their friends. The Chicagoan stayed with the nurses who "were so heavenly good to her" during her frequent trips to the east. And Wald, in turn, was assured a welcome at Hull House, where her visits with kindred spirits refreshed her soul. "You may not believe me," Wald wrote to Mary Smith of the Chicago settlement after returning from a visit, "but these few days with you meant a great deal. They steadied and strengthened me."[18] This sentiment was echoed by labor leader Mary Kenny O'Sullivan after a stay at Henry Street. She wrote Wald of the pleasure of seeing "so many of the real people together."[19]

Like members of a family, the women performed favors for one another. They ran errands, purchased gifts, tried to help blood relatives, and they accepted the people sent to them by other women friends. They worried about each other's health and their letters are filled with news of medical problems. Dr. Alice Hamilton, a physician, and Wald represented the sources of professional advice and were often consulted on health care. And they gloried in their achievements. "We swell the mighty chorus of rejoicing over your success," Wald wrote to Florence Allen when she became a judge.[20] At the news of Hamilton's appointment to the faculty of the Harvard Medical School, Wald sent congratulations: "Hurrah! I had no idea that old Harvard had so much judgement."[21] And in an introductory letter about Hamilton, written years later, Wald said:

> She is the only woman on the Harvard faculty, and I suppose they couldn't avoid her appointment whatever the sex discriminations may be, because she is undoubtedly the first authority on Industrial Hygiene. . . . I think she would disarm any antifeminist.[22]

As in Alice Hamilton's case, pleasure increased when "mere females" were able to secure desirable positions.[23] Wald and her friends willingly participated in dinners and tributes to one another. If there was any resentment at another's success, it was not apparent in their writings. Certainly there was no hesitation in recommending a kindred spirit to a job. For one woman, Wald wrote to Mayor James Walker:

> I am not asking for Miss . . . Phillip's appointment . . . because she is a woman, but because I think her well qualified both by training, experience and an effective personality to hold the position. I cannot deny that women would be pleased to find that her sex was not a handicap.[24]

Occasionally, Wald and her contemporaries waged massive campaigns to gain recognition for "the younger generation" of women. In 1921, Wald mobilized support for Grace Abbott to succeed Julia Lathrop as head of the Children's Bureau. Nine years later, at a meeting of social workers, a resolution was adopted urging President Hoover to appoint Abbott as secretary of labor and Wald played an active part in the campaign that followed. She asked Hoover to give "evidence that women who have shown their ability and suitability are eligible for high office without prejudice of sex."[25] But she had little faith in the president. "I suspect that his prejudice is against the idea of a woman, but no man measures up to Grace Abbott in training, personality and ability," she wrote to a friend.[26] Activity on behalf of Abbott's candidacy failed. Letters to the influential did not bring enough pressure upon Hoover to break with precedent and appoint a woman to the cabinet. Abbott remained at the Children's Bureau and to Katherine Lenroot, her successor, continued to be "the hero and the pride of women who were just beginning to find a place in public affairs."[27]

Wald and her friends were more successful in pushing the career of Frances Perkins, first to the post of industrial commissioner in New York and then for secretary of labor in Franklin Roosevelt's cabinet. For this second appointment, Wald wrote to Perkins asking her not to object and to stand back while Henry Street mobilized "the nurses and the settlement people into action."[28] Wald then wrote a general letter emphasizing Perkins's training and experience and stressing that it was time to have a woman in the cabinet.[29] She also sent a personal appeal to FDR expressing "the hope that you in your wisdom will think the time has come for a woman in the cabinet when an outstanding woman has appeared."[30] To reinforce the pressure, Wald wrote friends to remind Roosevelt of his "good intentions" during the campaign and to "tactfully" stress the argument that the AFL people supported Perkins and were "insisting that the Labor Department . . . [be] feminized."[31]

Of all the women of her generation with whom Wald was associated, two stand out clearly as having had the greatest influence. The first, Jane Addams, she recognized as "the incomparable leader," the woman who "affected the morals of her generation." Wald admired her friend's pragmatism, her ability to articulate her social philosophy, and her intellectual integrity. Addams had the capacity to be "in the struggle and yet above it" so she was able to see things more clearly than most. The "Beloved Lady" from Chicago was a model for all women to follow.[32]

The Wald-Addams letters tend to be more reserved than Wald's letters to other female friends. Addams's nephew claimed that Addams's letters did not give a clue to her personality; her warmth did not emerge in messages that were "strictly business."[33] Mary R. Smith, Addams's companion of many years, seemed to provide the personal contact with the female network. Wald and the Hull House founder worked together through the years on scores of projects, but each respected the right of the other to dissent. Their common goals did not require them to walk identical paths. In addition to political differences, they parted on the issue of attendance at the Hague Peace Conference in 1915. Also, Addams, in 1920, asked Wald to become a member of the American Commission on Ireland, pointing out that the group provided a "chance of real usefulness." Wald responded that "It's just terrible not to telegraph 'Yes,' for you know without my telling you that I would go to the end of the earth with my hand in yours and not care to peep over the horizon." But, again she had to refuse membership and joining with Addams in the cause.[34]

The second great influence on Wald was Florence Kelley, who was as close personally as she was professionally. Nevertheless observers of the pair delighted in pointing up the differences in their personalities and temperaments. One recalled that while both fought for the same principles, seeing them in action brought "the fable of the sun and the wind . . . to mind. Miss Wald won her points by her forebearance [sic] and understanding of her opponents, whereas Mrs. Kelley practically demolished them."[35] George Alger, a friend and admirer of both women, believed that Kelley "knew what needed to be done in a practical way perhaps better than Miss Wald did many times," but Kelley didn't have the other's political qualities and "wasn't anywhere so efficient in the process of getting them done. She made enemies where Miss Wald made friends." Alger gave specific examples of their techniques and concluded:

> The two of them together . . . worked out perfectly for years. Mrs. Kelley . . . was a great admirer of Miss Wald, but I think Mrs. Kelley hated not to be able to tell what she thought about people she thought were doing wrong. To deprive her of that would be too much for her.[36]

The two friends regarded their differing qualities with amusement. In one exchange, Kelley wrote the nurse:

> I have made a New Year's resolution for this my 49th year. In order to form the habit for the remaining century . . . , I am starting at noon today to be nice, and say only agreeable things especially about the absent. This is due to the force of your example.[37]

At times, however, Wald's behavior unnerved the more volatile woman who complained, "when I revile her, she merely smiles and leaves everything as it is."[38]

Wald's tributes to Kelley's intensity and "inspirational influence" were many. She was the prod, the "dedicated one who made us think." Kelley's wit and brilliance made her intolerant of inaction and she could be a terrifying opponent. Wald loved to tell of the time she tried to apologize for a woman who had disappointed those who had expected much of her. The Henry Streeter defended her saying, "Well, she has an open mind." "That's what I object to," flashed Florence Kelley, "It's open top and bottom."[39]

Her father, William "Pig Iron" Kelley (a Pennsylvania Congressman), guided her haphazard education until she entered Cornell University, and after graduation, the Law School of Zurich. Kelley's fellow students in Switzerland ignited her mind, which was like "tinder awaiting a match," with socialist philosophy. It seemed to her to be the answer to the problems of industrialism that she had viewed while traveling with her father. Kelley's American pragmatism was distrusted by her colleagues, however, and she was expelled from the party.[40] Once many years later, while watching a parade of socialist workers, Kelley said, "I belong there, but they put me out because I could speak English."[41] While she maintained ties to socialism all her life, Kelley came to accept the fact that social reform came with "drudgery and delay—spade work with or without a harvest." She never learned to compromise, but she did try to reconcile differences and she did learn to operate within the system.[42]

Kelley was unique among the women in that she was personally familiar with the problems of the working mother. While in Zurich she had married a Russian physician, Lazare Wischnewetsky, and had three children before the couple were divorced. Kelley went to live at Hull House and entrusted her children first to the care of the Henry Demarest Lloyds and later to boarding schools. Her letters to her children are evidence of her loneliness for them as well as her constant concern: "This separation is only of the body, for whenever you fix your mind on your loving old Ma, you know that you are the light of her eyes, and the joy of her heart, and the hope that cheers her hours of absence.[43]

Governor John Peter Altgeld appointed Kelley to the post of Illinois chief inspector of factories. As the first woman to hold such a position, she set the standards for the enforcement of child labor and anti-sweatshop legislation. Her salary was too small to support her children adequately and her life would have been even more difficult were it not for the generosity of Mary Smith and other friends who bought clothes and paid the tuition for her daughter Margaret. The Kelley children were always welcome at Hull House and often stayed there when their mother was away. The women in Chicago and later at the Henry Street Settlement became surrogate parents to Kelley's children.[44] The ties between the Henry Street people and the Kelleys lasted through the lives of all the principals. Nicholas Kelley became a member of the Executive Committee of Henry Street and chairman of the Board of Directors of the National Consumers' League, while Hyman Schroeder, an alumnus of Henry Street and financial advisor to Ward, was treasurer of the National Consumers League (NCL).

When the Altgeld administration was voted out of office, Kelley was not reappointed by his successor because, as Maud Nathan noted, "She had enforced the factory laws so fairly and impartially that a protest went up from the manufacturers." Kelley's friends, like Wald, Jane Addams, and Nathan worked to secure a job for her in Albany where Theodore Roosevelt was governor. Roosevelt refused, saying that the time was not ripe to appoint a woman as factory inspector. In 1899, Kelley moved to Henry Street and took over the post of general secretary of the NCL and remained its driving force for the rest of her life. Through most of this time, she was a resident of the Settlement and worked closely with Wald and the nurses whom she called on for firsthand evidence of the home conditions of industrial workers. In 1923, looking for a quieter place, Kelley moved from Henry Street, but she never relinquished her friendship with its founder.[45]

The bonds of love that existed between Addams, Wald, and Kelley are documented by their correspondence. The support they provided one another, even when they differed, should never be underestimated. Wald was the politician, Kelley the passion, and Addams the philosopher and symbol of the women of the Progressive period. Their qualities complemented each other and their common goals drew them together.

Other women, too, enriched Wald's life as she did theirs. Leonora O'Reilly's early diaries illustrate the interplay between the Henry Street residents and the working girl. One of O'Reilly's pupils was Rose Cohen, the immigrant girl who was helped by Wald's nursing. Later, Cohen's memoir, *Out of the Shadows*, was used to educate the public on the trials of work in a sweatshop. In a different category, but still a sister, was Catherine Breshkovsky (Babushka). She became a heroine to Wald, Addams, suffragist Alice Stone Blackwell, Emma Goldman, and American working women because of her bravery in pre-revolutionary Russia and was a welcome visitor at Henry Street and Hull House during her periods of exile. The social workers' endorsement of the Leninist revolution and Wald's push for recognition of the Soviet Union, which Breshkovsky opposed, believing it was as repressive as Czarist Russia, caused a split in the ranks. But the women continued to worry about her and support her despite the rift.[46]

Englishwoman Margaret Bondfield, Labor Secretary in the Ramsay MacDonald cabinet, was another of the "old pals" and a frequent guest of Wald's. Bondfield was for the women in the United States a perfect example of a talented female who was permitted to achieve high public office. Perhaps a clue to the camaraderie the women enjoyed with one another can be found in a letter Wald wrote to Mary Dreier.

> I liked the picture of you in the paper so very much. And I liked the idea of your playing with Eleanor Roosevelt in that happy, carefree way.
>
> Margaret Bondfield is here and she is fine, fine! She is so fair, and fair to the people with whom she doesn't agree. I think she has grown in two ways—in avoirdupois and mentality.[47]

Emma Goldman and Wald were not really friends, but these two knew each other so well that they trusted and respected one another. A frequent critic of settlements, Goldman believed that Wald was "genuinely concerned with the people of the East Side" and "felt an interest in the economic condition of the masses." Despite the sincerity, however, Wald's work was palliative and was, on balance, "doing more harm than good."[48] Nevertheless, Goldman valued the social worker's opinion, sent her copies of *Mother Earth,* and felt free to call upon her for help with social and personal matters.[49] Wald was sympathetic to Goldman and recognized that she was "seriously devoted to the causes that she espoused."[50] In only one instance did Wald refuse her help. The radical hoped that Wald would support her fight to place ads in the nurses' *Journal.* Goldman wished to represent herself as a "Vienna Scalp and Face Specialist," a claim that offended Wald's professionalism.[51] Wald did donate money to a fund set up to permit Goldman the time to write her autobiography after she was deported from the United States. Her contribution, Wald was assured, "tickled" Red Emma.[52] The easy relationship between the women is evidenced by the following note sent to Henry Street after Lavinia Dock was arrested in a suffrage march. Goldman wrote: "Please remember me to Miss Dock and Miss [Yssabella] Waters. Tell Miss Dock, I welcome her as a fellow convict now that she too has tasted the sweets of the station house."[53]

Questions have been raised by modern historians as to the nature of the friendships enjoyed by the feminist women. An article by James R. McGovern about Anna Howard Shaw, the suffragist leader, claimed that many of the females "were critical of men and lacked any sustained pleasurable contact with them." These negative attitudes toward men did not, however, prevent the women from adopting characteristics—toughness, fondness for power and hard work—that are usually associated with the male sex. Further, McGovern maintained that many, if not most of the women, maintained relationships of an "intimate personal" nature with other women.[54] In *American Heroine,* Allen Davis attempted to define the relationship between Jane Addams and Ellen Gates Starr when both were young women and the historian concluded that "the Victorians' conception of love between those of the same sex cannot be fairly understood by an age steeped in Freud—where they saw only beautiful friendship, the modern reader suspects perversion."[55] In the same vein, Doris Faber's *The Life of Lorena Hickok* alluded to a possible lesbian relationship between Eleanor Roosevelt and Hickok.[56] While Wald never had a permanent woman companion, Blanche Wiesen Cook, in expanding the traditionally accepted definition of lesbianism to "Women who love women, who choose women to nurture and support and to create a living environment in which to work creatively and independently" regardless of sexual behavior, concluded that Wald was a lesbian.[57] Another historian, Gerda Lerner, would agree that there may need to be a new definition of lesbianism. She writes that women who lived "all or part of their lives without emotional attachments to men or any single man" and who "derived their emotional and affective sustenance from close association with networks of women and with one or more women" may have been what "Victorian 'lesbians' looked like." Perhaps, it was possible for middle-class women to be "homo-erotic" in this earlier age without losing respectability.[58]

These are provocative arguments, but they do raise certain troubling questions for historians. Is it not possible for heterosexual women to love other women and to seek emotional support from them? Do all intimate relationships between women have a sexual component and should such relationships be called lesbian if that erotic dimension is absent or unprovable?

The claims of the historians that the relationships between settlement women were not "genteel" is based on evidence that comes largely from their sentimental and emotional personal letters. There is no doubt that Wald received and sent huge numbers of letters that imply intimacy. Women friends were addressed as "Beloved" (Mary Smith, Jane Hitchcock, Grace Abbott, Lavinia Dock) and "Dearest Angel Child" (Mary Dreier) even when the content of the letter pertained to business or casual gossip. Intimacy and affection run through the messages. Emily Balch wrote Wald:

> I would give anything to be able to fly up to New York and see you and J. A. tomorrow but I *can't*.
> I long to see you personally and to give you a good old-fashioned smacking kiss to show you how glad I am to see you after so long.[59]

and Wald communicated to "Sister" Yssabella Waters that

> It seems too odd to have you an up-towner. I cannot visualize you in the dining room of the hotel, though it is not so hard to see you in a bedroom there.
> You may be sure that I know how fatigued and strained you are, and I wish to heavens that it were in my power to give you refreshment of soul and body.[60]

Even the indomitable "Sister" Kelley was told that the news of her return from a trip "made my heart go quite pit-a-pat."[61] The closing lines of Wald's letters frequently expressed "dear love to you always and always,"[62] and "you know how dearly I love you."[63]

Letters to Wald from coworkers and friends at Henry Street were written in words even more effusively loving and sentimental. Attorney Helen Arthur wrote:

> I think so often of the hundred who remember you with affection and the tens who openly adore you . . . and I'm grateful to think that your arms have been close around me and you did once upon a time, kiss me good night and even good morning.[64]

Wald received similar notes from Mary Brown, Mabel Kittredge, and other female friends.[65]

Superficially, it might appear that overt lesbian activity was not uncommon at Henry Street. Such an interpretation would overlook the fact that the majority of Wald's letters to males and females were written in the flowery style of her time. As evidence, a message written to a young boy, Glenn Koenig, told him that she was glad to have him as her "boy friend." Wald continued, "I've liked you a great deal from the first time I saw you and I thought that you flirted a little with me too."[66] It is inconceivable that she had a sexual relationship with all the women (and men) Wald addressed with terms of romantic love. A more likely explanation is that she enjoyed giving and getting affection and this character trait is expressed in her correspondence. R. L. Duffus and Wald went through her papers for the preparation of her 1938 biography, and, given her concern with her reputation, her position, and the importance of her work, it is logical to assume that she would have destroyed letters that she considered in any way to be damaging or embarrassing. Apparently Wald believed that the correspondence was innocent and would not be interpreted in any other way.[67]

It must be remembered that it was common for women reared in the Victorian era and who were kindred spirits to love one another with a feeling of sisterly fellowship and to gain emotional support from one another. The erotic could, but did not have to intrude upon intimate relations. Carroll Smith-Rosenberg, in "The Female World of Love and Ritual: Relations between Women in Nineteenth-Century America," cautions modern readers to view the ties between women in the light of the general cultural patterns of the period. The focus would then shift "from a concern with deviance to that of . . . legitimate norms and options." The love of these women for one another "appears to have been both sensual and platonic" and "both socially acceptable and fully compatible with heterosexual marriage."[68]

In 1963, Allen Davis had the opportunity to interview Dr. Alice Hamilton, then in her nineties, about the relationship of women to other women in the settlement houses.

> She denied that there was any open lesbian activity involving
> Hull House residents, but agreed that the close relationship of
> the women involved an unconscious sexuality. Because it was
> unconscious it was unimportant she argued. Then she added
> with a smile that the very fact that I would bring the subject up
> was an indication of the separation between my generation and
> her.[69]

Two contemporaries of Wald, George Alger and Helen Hall, also deny any hint of sexual activity. Alger maintained that Wald "seemed to have the lower passions . . . thoroughly under control,"[70] and Hall, who succeeded Wald as overall Head of Henry Street, said that she never heard of any talk about the women and she was sure that she would have, if there was any rumor of "irregularity."[71]

Since the major goal in women's lives is supposed to be marriage, twentieth-century women are commonly considered to be competitors and therefore incapable of sustaining genuine friendship. Wald and her peers seem to disprove this thinking. Apparently some could sublimate their sexuality in favor of other interests. Vida Scudder, who so often articulated the thoughts of her contemporaries, wrote that while most people believed that "life devoid of sexual experience lacks fulfillment," she found that "sex is not the only clue to human behavior." The absence of this aspect of life "need not mean dearth of romance or of significant personal relations."[72] It is meaningful that her next chapter title in *On Journey* was entitled "Friends."

Wald may have raised sexual feelings in some. She was undoubtedly a mother figure to others, but to most women, she was a friend and an inspiration. Mabel Kittredge, an early Henry Street resident wrote:

> I am getting altogether too close to you—Lady Wald—or is it
> your life and all those doors that you have pushed open for
> me—half open—dear—just half open—and then I come up here
> and grow hungry for more knowledge.[73]

She and others loved Wald for herself, for the work she did and for opening new worlds to them.

In the last analysis, the question arises as to whether Wald's sexual preferences are essential to an understanding of her public career in social reform and feminism. It may be that the final words must go to Emma Goldman, who in discussing another woman, said that her "service to humanity and her great work of social liberation are such that they can be neither enlarged nor reduced, whatever her sexual habits were."[74]

Lillian Wald in her student nurse uniform, New York Hospital, ca. 1890. Courtesy of the Visiting Nurse Service of New York.

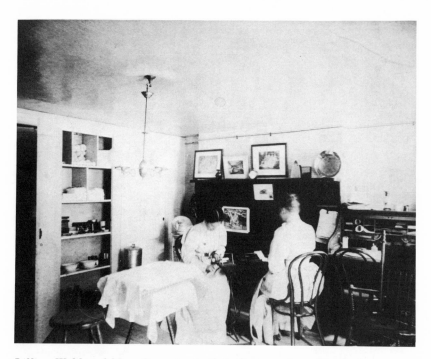

Lillian Wald and Mary Brewster in their first nursing office in the basement of 265 Henry St., ca. 1895. Courtesy of the Visiting Nurse Service of New York.

The Henry Street Settlement "family" in 1905. Standing left to right: Jane Hitchcock, Sue Foote, Jeanne Travis. Seated: Mary Magoun Brown, Lavinia Dock, Lillian Wald, Yssabella Waters, Henrietta Van Cleft. The children in the front row: "Little Sammy" Brofsky and "Florrie" Long, the cook's daughter and the "baby of the house." Courtesy of the Visiting Nurse Service of New York.

Lower East Side Apartment, 1910. Courtesy of the Visiting Nurse Service of New York.

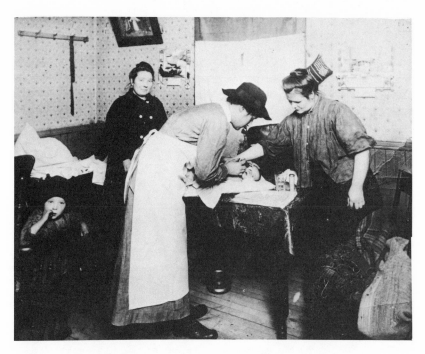

A Henry Street Visiting nurse at work during a home visit, ca. 1907. Courtesy of the Visiting Nurse Service of New York.

Jacob Schiff. Courtesy of the Library of Congress.

Lillian Wald at the height of her career, ca. 1910. Courtesy of the Visiting Nurse Service of New York.

*Lavinia Dock (third from left), holding a "Votes for Women" staff, 1913.
Courtesy of the Library of Congress.*

*Florence Kelley. Courtesy of
the Library of Congress.*

Henry Street nurses and neighborhood children, 1920. Courtesy of the Visiting Nurse Service of New York.

Henry Street nurses in 1922 (probably used for publicity). Courtesy of the Visiting Nurse Service of New York.

Left to right: Jane Addams, Mary Rozet Smith, Lillian Wald, Elena Landazuri vacationing in Mexico, 1925. Courtesy of Swarthmore College Peace Collection.

Lillian Wald at home in Westport, Connecticut in 1938. Courtesy of the Visiting Nurse Service of New York.

Lillian Wald in 1940, the year of her death at age seventy-three. Courtesy of the Visiting Nurse Service of New York.

SIX

A Woman's Mind

*L*illian Wald's reluctance and/or inability to analyze her work and to develop a comprehensive, consistent philosophy extended to feminism. Her pragmatic nature did not permit her to take a doctrinaire stand. Moreover, she believed that too much thought on a subject inhibited action. Describing her early days on the East Side to Albert Kennedy, she wrote that she "did not do much introspecting in those days" because she "did not want to be an idler."[1] Added to this was her unwillingness to articulate principles that might offend those whose acceptance and affection she needed both personally and professionally. When she took stands that were unpopular, she preferred to explain them to people in the dining room of Henry Street rather than on the lecture platform or in print. One other factor complicates the task of analyzing Wald's philosophy. She frequently called upon friends to help her with speeches. She corrected and added to the suggestions of such "experts" as Dock on nursing, Dreier, O'Reilly, and Gertrude Barnum on working women, and Emily Balch on the peace movement, but it may be suggested that much of what she said reflected the thinking of the source of her information.

Her writings, therefore, are sometimes contradictory as to the role and place of women in society. Generally, she tended to be more overtly feminist in her private letters to female friends than in her public utterances. To her credit, too, her views changed through the years. As a pragmatist, she was able to shape her thinking to changing times and new ideas on the role of women in society. Perhaps recognizing her own "radicalization" on the "Woman Question" in the last years of her career, she said in 1928, "it is needless to repeat, 'New occasions teach new duties. Time makes ancient good uncouth.' "[2]

Wald believed that while "new woman" and "feminist" described the position that women occupied, the business of being a woman was really unchanged. The age-old female desires—to cherish and dignify life—were simply being described in a new way. Women, she said, were "holding on to the things that are theirs, and ever have been and shall be." Wald referred to the description of the perfect woman in Biblical days and perceived her as a consumer, a business woman, a patron of the arts, and "plainly a social worker," for " 'She openeth her mouth with wisdom and in her tongue is the law of kindness.' " Just as society had evolved from an emphasis upon the individual, to the family, to the tribe, and then to an increased group consciousness, women had to expand their sphere of interests into the community. They could no longer engage in activity that concerned only the home. Wald credited her generation with being the first to take the great step toward increased social self-consciousness. Her contemporaries were part of the struggle of women toward social and political freedom. They were the pioneers who received the social training and education that was necessary to fulfill "the task of readapting the social interest . . . of [their] sex to a changed . . . environment."[3]

With the optimism of the liberal reformer, Wald anticipated that women's role in the public sector would continue to enlarge, slowly but inevitably. Well-intentioned people could not fail to recognize women's right to realize themselves as well as society's need for their talents.[4] Before the passage of the suffrage amendment, Wald tended to emphasize woman's traditional relationship to the home. In the 1920s and 1930s, however, she stressed more the right of "each one to decide for himself or herself what he or she wants to make of life,"[5] and the belief that "the professions, the vocations and avocations should be and ought to be the privilege of the individuals of the human race, irrespective of sex."[6]

Women like Wald herself, who had gained public acceptance, had an obligation to remove the barriers to the employment of other females.[7] For example, Wald insisted that the "indignities" that were visited upon women who sought government jobs had to be eliminated. Mary McDowell of Hull House asked her to intervene when the city of Chicago required vaginal examinations for nurses employed by the Health Department. The campaign waged against this practice caused McDowell to exclaim that "The . . . politicians have never known the kind of women we represent and are having a liberal education just now."[8] Further, though Wald understood the importance of appearance, she deplored, with her friend Adelaide

Nutting, the emphasis placed upon personal attractiveness that was "thrown into the scales as it seldom would be in considering the fitness of a man for a . . . post."[9]

Wald recognized still another obstacle to the full utilization of female talents. In *The House on Henry Street,* she related the story of the reaction of the inmates of a girls' reformatory to the women's movement. They disapproved of women voting as "unladylike" and clung to "orthodox ideals." In commenting, Wald wrote:

> I understand that I shocked one girl . . . , by advocating the appointment of women police. The probation officer who called upon her asked her opinion of my recommendation, which was then sufficiently novel to attract newspaper attention. "Oh," said the girl, "it's not right, women's place is in the home."[10]

With the freer admission of women to public and professional life and with more women in the marketplace supporting themselves, Wald believed that the time of the "restricted, secluded, non earning woman," the "clinging vine . . . who rejoiced in the place assigned to them" and needed the protection of the chivalrous male was past. Nothing good, she would add, was lost in this change. Both sexes, as good comrades, could now work together at "the task of organizing human happiness." It was a job that needed the active cooperation of men and women and could not be relegated to one half of the world.[11]

Wald never questioned sexual parity.

> I have been fond of saying, until I fear, it has become platitudinous, that men and women are equal but not identical and that the aptitudes and traditions of each mingled is absolutely necessary for high accomplishments.[12]

If men differed from women, Wald believed, "it is . . . [women's] never changing devotion to the home," but this difference was only a question of degree. For Wald accepted, as did most feminists, that the majority of human attributes were not gender related. She said, "In my heart of hearts I see no great disparity between the profoundest convictions of men and women on the most challenging questions of our times." Both have a stake in life and their sources of happiness and security are identical.[13]

In 1931, Wald wrote to old friends about their daughter, "I think you have been very generous parents to give her the freedom to work out her own desires and her own talents."[14] All young women had the right to choose, she believed, and in most cases, the choice had to be made between marriage and family or career. To Wald and her friends, public life was largely incompatible with the duties of motherhood. Margaret Bondfield proclaimed that "marriage, in the true sense, is the highest of vocations, but all are not called to it." For those women who were "not Called," those who chose public rather than private service, there was a duty to help the larger body of women. They had to transform their "sex energy . . . into social energy."[15]

"The most important employment in the world," wrote Wald, "is the care of the home and the protection of children."[16] The absence of the mother often meant the destruction of the family. She believed that the "efficient mother" was best employed in that capacity and that it was "a wasteful sacrifice to have her engaged in a less worthy occupation."[17] One means of maintaining the women at home was the visiting nurse, for in case of illness, home care was preferable to hospital care. More important, Wald advocated that the state, as opposed to private charity, assume responsibility in the event "there is no man in the family, or where the man is sick and unable to work." To preserve the family headed by a woman, she recommended and lobbied for aid to dependent children of widowed mothers. Women could never be content with the progress of their sex until they had equally assured the welfare of children.[18]

In at least one instance, Wald deviated from her support of the motherhood ethic. In 1912, the Board of Education of New York City began the practice of denying leaves of absence to pregnant teachers. Women's groups immediately opposed this decision, which discriminated against women on account of marriage and childbearing. The board ultimately relented, but later declared that it would grant only two maternity leaves. Wald, when interviewed on the subject, castigated the board, claiming that it had no right to set itself up as a birth control agency. The selection and retention of teachers, she said, should be based on their work and on the contribution they make and not on the number of children they bear.[19]

Wald's record on the controversial issues of sex education and birth control illustrates the tightrope she walked as she became a popular figure and identified in the public mind with the Visiting Nurses and Henry Street. As an enlightened nurse, she recognized the needs of the community, but as an executive dependent upon outside funding, she frequently could not be too vocal.

She favored instructing children in matters of sex and regretted the neglect of "this most serious question," and the false conventional attitudes of the community. Since most parents were, she discovered, ill-equipped to handle the subject, nurses could provide the solution to any problems. They had the education and the opportunity to "talk frankly on the subject of sanitary and moral Prophylaxis in sexual hygiene," and she believed they should be given the opportunity to do so. Wald was aware of the conflict her suggestions would elicit and hoped for changes in societal attitudes toward sex education.[20]

No worker among the poor could fail to observe the ramifications of unlimited family size. Nor could any nurse on the East Side overlook the ignorance of the immigrant woman in the area of contraception. Information made available to the middle-class woman by her physician did not exist for the poor.[21] Wald's sympathy with mothers who had more children than they could cope with is well documented. Further, she must have been aware of Emma Goldman's lectures, starting in 1900, on the subject of contraception and her "work for healthy motherhood and happy child-life."[22] Nevertheless, Wald did not leap into the fight for the dissemination of material on birth control.

She was, undoubtedly, loath to enter into combat with the medical fraternity on still another issue. Most doctors, as individuals and through their local societies, refused to endorse the distribution of birth control information because it would, they claimed, cause all manner of physical and mental illness, undermine morality, destroy the family, and lend support to the radicals who favored family limitation.[23] Some physicians like Adolphus Knopf, however, did advocate medical involvement in the fight for contraceptive rights and asked for Wald's help. She wrote to Knopf giving qualified support.

> I believe that there should be birth control, but I do not know whether I would be able to endorse your term "general" since that implies so many issues. I have taken the position that doctors should not be forbidden to give information to their patients. The rich have been able to obtain this information from their family physician.

She argued that doctors should have permission to give advice on contraception to all their "married" patients, lest this information "be used in ways not contemplated by the reformers."[24]

The restraints placed upon Wald by her position are more evident in her dealings with Margaret Sanger, the birth control pioneer. Wald followed the career on the Lower East Side of her sister nurse with great interest. When *Woman and the New Race* was published in 1920, Wald read this "interesting book" and wished that she were able to take "a leading part" in "this particular battle for married women's freedom." Yet she did not give free rein to her wishes. She wrote:

> However much I may cherish my individual liberty to say and do things, I am under obligation to the army of nurses affiliated with me on the staff, and less directly in other organizations. There is no question at all but that the nurses would be committed by inference to this propaganda, if I become prominently identified with it.

She believed that the gain to Sanger "would be too slight to warrant me taking a liberty with the nurses." The nursing profession had been too often singled out for criticism from physicians and the public on this issue.[25]

Wald modified her position somewhat the following year when she joined, or at least gave her name to, the committee to organize the first American Birth Control Conference.[26] Her decision to bow to Sanger's wishes drew the applause of at least one colleague, Lavinia Dock, who wrote that she was glad to see Wald on the committee. "I find most nurses have the true R.C. [Roman Catholic] 11th Century point of view about it—class it with the 'secret vice.' "[27] But support for Wald was not universal and she took care in subsequent actions on the National Committee on Federal Legislation for Birth Control, a lobbying organization, to point out that her endorsement of the dispersal of contraceptive information was "a personal, not a Henry Street matter." Many of the people in her organization, she maintained, had different ideas.[28]

Churchmen criticized Wald's position on birth control, and as a "public relations" person, she sought to quash the opposition with acceptable platitudes. To the Reverend Monsignor John Chedwick, she responded:

> I entirely agree with you that the integrity of the family is the very basis of our civilization, and any nurse "connected with Henry Street" must I am sure, understand that that is a fundamental conviction.
>
> I think you may rest assured that the nurses are not giving instruction themselves on birth control or contraceptive methods and that they are using all their power to discourage abortion.[29]

Wald's letter to the Monsignor was accurate, but it told only half the story. The Visiting Nurses did have a policy of referring Protestant and Jewish women to birth control clinics for contraceptive advice.[30]

Nurses were well aware that women who had no knowledge of contraception frequently resorted to abortion, despite the fact that it was considered a felony offense. That abortion was commonplace can be induced from a 1921 study that reported that half of all pregnancies did not reach term and of these, half were considered criminal abortions. These figures indicate that one-quarter of all pregnancies were deliberately terminated. Most of the women involved were married.[31] Emma Goldman, working on the East Side as a nurse and midwife was approached often, her biographer writes, and "reluctantly turned down the heart-rending pleas of involuntary mothers to perform abortions."[32] How many similar pleas were made to Henry Street nurses is impossible to ascertain and how many of these requests were granted is equally unknown. Despite Wald's denial to Father Chedwick, a letter to Herbert Lehman indicates that help might not have been uncommon in an era when abortion was a frequently used means of family limitation. Wald wrote her friend of a "Protestant Henry Street Nurse" who

> finding an harassed patient almost out of her wits because she had prevented the birth of a child (she had more than she could manage) found a priest who understood and she took her woman to the door of the Confessional and all is well.[33]

Wald's support of women's rights—to have knowledge (even if limited to married women) of contraceptive material, to find employment in fields normally associated with men, to have unlimited maternity leaves without penalty—did not transcend her emphasis upon women's role as mother. Although she felt that mothers "had other parts,"[34] motherhood ranked first. The focus Wald placed upon the beauties and obligations of the maternal life cast doubts that she thought women could function well in various roles, could combine motherhood and a career outside the home. Although she called for education for fatherhood and the Settlement had a father's club, she accepted the notion that child rearing and homemaking were women's obligations.

Historians generally agree that in ignoring these issues and by accepting Victorian stereotypes, most of the feminists of the early twentieth century severely limited the women's movement. Wald was not unique in her thinking, for only a few women, such as Charlotte Perkins Gilman and Henrietta Rodman, offered plans for alternate life styles within the traditional marriage, and this lack made Progressive women vulnerable to criticism from later feminists.

Perhaps the failure to explore nontraditional roles within marriage resulted from the fact that so many Progressive feminist leaders rejected the institution for themselves. They were, at times, even hostile to it, viewing it as a loss of independence and personal freedom. Wald, while acknowledging that she saw only extreme cases, related the incident of one woman who agonized over keeping from her husband the knowledge of her secret savings from her weekly food allowance. Wald concluded the tale with, "Nor was this our only encounter with the enslavement of womanhood by 'the master of the house.' "[35] Marriage for these emancipated women was "the cruelest of traps," claimed another feminist.[36] Only such women as Margaret Dreier Robins and Carrie Chapman Catt, who were childless and married to men of wealth, could continue to play leadership roles in the public sector. "Until I was thirty," wrote Vida Scudder, "I wanted terribly to fall in love." But as she grew older, she confessed, "married life looks to me often as I watch it terribly impoverished for women." Marriage meant for most of these women an end to a life-style they enjoyed, to a public position that they fought hard to attain, and most important, subordination after enjoying leadership. Matrimony was perhaps a fulfillment and an indulgence at first, Scudder wrote, but later "a discipline."[37]

Wald, "with much emotion," penned a note to a young friend on hearing of her marriage:

> It seems but yesterday that you were the lovely little Rosamond with a personality of your own. I wonder how much of it will be merged with your new life. I should like to know who your partner is and what will be your trend.[38]

Marriage, Wald wrote another woman, was identified with housework and "troubles" for it was "no easy thing to be married and a mother."[39] Choices had to be made between self-fulfillment and home. "I can give up the writing or the housework," complained Marion Kellogg, the wife of Wald's friend.[40] It was obvious to the women that she could not do both. Historian Carl Degler states in *At Odds* that "the equality of women and the institution of the family have long been at odds with each other." The modern family depends on a woman's subordination of her individual interests to those of her family, while feminism seeks autonomy and emancipation for women. This has created enduring tensions. "Philosophically and practically the family and women's individuality are difficult to reconcile." Many women feel that they cannot realize themselves and their talents within a family situation.[41] Wald and her friends recognized this reality three generations ago.

Ironically Lavinia Dock, who was the first to express shock when a coworker married and had to give up her career, was forced into retirement in 1922 when she had to care for an invalid sister.[42] The

Wald-Dock correspondence is meaningful evidence of the women's attitude toward a life that followed the housewife pattern. Dock admitted that she was "getting to like housekeeping" even though she was not very good at it. She was worried, however, because she regarded her interest "as a species of atavism and as such to be deplored."

> I do see though how a housekeeper can get so that there is no time or—worse yet—no zip for anything else.
> I consider it the life of a slave or at least of an ant.[43]

Wald commiserated with her friend, saying, "I can't bear to think of your gallant spirits held down to household drudgery. I feel like coming on and washing the dishes."[44]

Jane Addams, looking back at forty years of work at Hull House, wrote that women of her generation were faced with the alternative of marriage or a career. They could not have both. Men did not want to marry women with professional ambitions and women could not fulfill two functions. Addams did feel a change might come when new inventions made a new type of housekeeping possible and when "public opinion tolerated the double role." She went on to quote from a message she had received from Emily Greene Balch, economist and peace advocate, on the subject of the unmarried professional woman. Balch spoke for all when she pointed up the personal freedom of these modern females who could take risks because they were not hostages to families. The women "found a tingling zest in discovering" that they need not be (as they had been led to believe) "weaker and more cowardly, incapable of disinterested curiosity, unable to meet life." Could these women successfully substitute professional life for marriage and family? Balch claimed that most did believe that they had lost a "universally regarded" experience, but none of the women believed that she was abnormal as the "Freudian psychoanalysts of life" would claim. The women took pride in opening new opportunities to the next generation. They were part of and shared the experiences of a great experiment in female freedom. Balch concluded:

> If the educated unmarried women of the period between the Civil War and the World War represent a unique phase, it is one that has important implications which have not yet been adequately recognized by those who insist upon the imperious claims of sex.[45]

These were not women who were necessarily hostile to men. Rather, they condemned the life of the married woman in their private letters, while at the same time they romanticized the institution of marriage in public. Being wives and mothers, it seemed, was the natural state for all women, except themselves.

SEVEN

The Sisters Who Toil

I am a working woman and . . . however far I may have
fallen short of my vision of accomplishment, I have always felt
proud to be called a comrade and share in my small way with
efforts for organization and for the dignifying of the industrial
worker.[1]

Wald spoke these words in 1924, and they expressed a lifetime of
interest and endeavor on behalf of the laborer. She supported the
efforts of working people and especially of working women. For
them, part of the struggle for equality lay in gaining the right to
unionize and to utilize such weapons of organization as the strike
and the boycott. She also lobbied extensively for industrial reform
and spoke often urging the public to place human values above
property values. Dr. Alice Hamilton, who had been a Hull House
resident, claimed that settlement women "got into the labor movement as a matter of course, without realizing how or when."[2] At a
time when labor had few friends, most social workers offered genuine sympathetic support. Wald, with probable exaggeration, declared that she personally did not "know of one settlement worker
who has not, through the acquaintance of the wage earner, been
drawn into the labor movement."[3]

Wald credited many people with educating her—"making the
light penetrate"—on labor conditions. Supporters of the infant labor
movement such as Josephine Shaw Lowell, Leonora O'Reilly,
Charles Stover, Ernest Crosby, and Edward King often used the Social Reform Club as a forum to discuss labor conditions and they

convinced Wald that poverty would never be eradicated until the worker could be guaranteed fair wages and working conditions. A member of the club recalled many years later that most of the group favored social legislation and unions at a time when "both were under suspicion among the righteous and prosperous as forms of socialism."[4] Lowell and O'Reilly helped organize the Working Women's Society, which aimed to establish trade unions to increase pay and shorten hours. The Society encouraged the cooperation of the working woman, the middle-class woman, and the consumer and set the pattern and goals for the Consumers' League and the Women's Trade Union League (WTUL) which succeeded it.

Perhaps overstating her ignorance, Wald confessed that when she moved to the East Side, she was "totally unaware of the causes of social unrest among workers"; in fact, she said, "I did not know that there was unrest or a 'problem.' "[5] Some of the "deeper implications" of labor's problems were explained to her by a young girl who came to ask for help in organizing a trade union. Wald's aid was enlisted because she spoke English and might bring "respectability" to the venture. The nurse paid a hurried visit to the library the following day "for academic information on the subject of trade unions,"[6] and during the 1890s she helped to organize small women's unions of garment finishers and buttonhole makers.

Ample statistics and information documented the low wages and long hours of the female breadwinner, and the problems of marriage and motherhood exacerbated her sorry position. To get the federal government involved in this issue, Wald joined with Jane Addams and Mary McDowell to pressure President Theodore Roosevelt to recommend an investigation of the problems of women and children in industry. Congress authorized the money in 1907, and the nineteen-volume Commerce and Labor Department *Report on the Condition of Women and Child Wage-Earners in the United States* that resulted was used as the rationale for subsequent proposals for social legislation.[7]

Wald found that she had no need for formal reports. Daily, as she made her rounds, she saw and heard of the abuses to women. For example, Wald asked Leonora O'Reilly to find work for a woman "whose husband found the struggle for existence too much for him and so ended his life and left the burden of three children on the shoulders of his frail little wife." The women discussed this "peculiar piece of masculine philosophy," which left the widow with the difficulties of both family and sweatshop.[8] Rose Cohen, the immigrant girl to whom Wald always lent a sympathetic ear, also provided the social worker with a direct line to the factory. Bosses and foremen who took advantage of their young women employees particularly outraged Cohen, who claimed that "Keep your hands off, please," was the first sentence she learned in English.[9]

Wald supported the right of all workers to unionize, but she was primarily involved with the immigrant Jewish laborer in the garment industry. As a group, the Eastern European Jews revolutionized the women's wear industry after 1890 by introducing the methods that made possible the mass production of quality clothing at lower prices. About 80 percent of the workers in the trade at the turn of the century were women—roughly 65,000—and three quarters of these were between the ages of sixteen and twenty-five. Many of these young immigrant women were inexperienced with work outside the home when they entered the needle trades and, therefore, were introduced into the job market as unskilled workers and "learners." These beginners, always comprising about 25 percent of the work force, were paid three to six dollars for a sixty-hour work week. Wages for skilled operators, about half the workers, were higher and at times, pieceworkers could earn as much as eighteen dollars a week. The money was considered fair, even high, when compared with other women's work, but the trade was seasonal and uncertain. It was not uncommon for women to work only six months a year. There were, too, all manner of charges, fines, and petty persecutions for lateness and for broken needles and machines. Most important, bosses and foremen regarded the laborers as inferior human beings, and that attitude encouraged sweatshop abuses. Conditions in the shops, no matter how poor, were still superior to working conditions in the tenements. Women and very young children engaged in home manufacture were untouched by even the primitive laws that regulated factory labor.[10]

To ameliorate these labor conditions, Wald functioned on various levels—as lobbyist, investigator, union organizer, and strike supporter. Most productive, perhaps, was her work as a propagandist, for she interpreted the labor movement to those who might be hostile to unions. Her tales of the working woman's valor were designed to gain public sympathy, while her descriptions of the working woman's conditions were intended to rouse public support for change.

One of the most reluctant converts to the workers' cause was Jacob Schiff, who was essentially conservative and "resented what he called the tyranny of the labor trust."[11] Soon after coming to the East Side, Wald wrote to Schiff about a strike of the Brotherhood of Cloakmakers which, she said, caused great "suffering" among the people. In an effort to appeal to the banker's biases, she concentrated upon the need to shorten the hours of work so that the immigrant laborers could attend night school.[12] Schiff's interest in his fellow Jews was reinforced by personal contact with workers at Henry Street's dining table. Cyrus Adler, the banker's biographer, was told by Wald of an occasion

> when Schiff was having a discussion with a Jewish tailor about a strike. The discussion ended by his putting his arm on the tailor's shoulder and their exchanging Hebrew quotations which . . . placed them upon a footing of equality and cordiality.

Schiff came to accept the need for collective action by labor and often helped to mediate jurisdictional disputes. He continued to question, however, the wisdom of the strike and doubted that agitation would improve the condition of life for the workers unless there were wider improvements like housing reform.[13]

Schiff was also reluctant to donate money openly to the garment strikers' cause for "it was bound to lead to misunderstanding" for him and the strikers. He did, nevertheless, on Wald's recommendation, aid needy individuals and even donated money secretly to union treasuries.[14] The friends did not always agree on labor issues. On one occasion, Schiff wrote Wald a letter of apology after an evening of argument when the banker chastized Henry Moskowitz and Wald for creating prejudice against an employer.[15] And at another time, Schiff "questioned [Wald's] . . . judgment in espousing the workingmen's side in a threatened strike, believing that a compromise on disputed hours and pay . . . was better than interrupted employment." Representatives of the garment manufacturers and contractors and the workers were called to a meeting at Henry Street in the hope of arbitrating the dispute. When this proved to be impossible, Schiff agreed that the workers had to walk out, "and throughout the strike, he aided with money and sympathy."[16]

The Settlement House was open at all times for union meetings, but Wald soon realized that a larger hall was needed. She "pledged . . . that whenever it came into our power, we would provide a meeting place for labor . . . gatherings and a forum for public debates that would not sacrifice the dignity of those who used it." In 1904, Clinton Hall was opened for the workers.[17]

Both *The House on Henry Street* and *Windows on Henry Street* as well as almost all her speeches to middle-class audiences were designed to raise the social consciousness of the group. While she appealed to both men and women, she particularly tried to show that women ought not to be alienated from the labor movement. As the coordinators of human values, it was the obligation of women to support the organization of workers. Laborers, Wald said, especially foreigners, were inarticulate, sometimes from timidity or fright and sometimes from inability to express themselves in English. This handicap plus the need for money forced the workers to accept any conditions offered by the employers. Protests by individuals usually resulted in the dismissal of the malcontents. Neither the employer, nor the state, nor the public placed any value upon the worker, and nonunion sweatshops were a means of perpetuating poverty among laborers, especially the unskilled. Continuing, Wald used her background in nursing to describe the illness and disease that were the results of that poverty. She questioned the effects of long hours of work that left little time for education and little strength to rear children. Wage earners, also, were deprived of the recreational outlet, the need for play, that all humans have. Lastly, she told her audiences, unfair labor conditions produce class antagonisms, for when the "poor are poorer . . . what is called 'class feeling' has been intensified."[18]

The worst abuses of the sweatshops were magnified when manufacture was carried on in the home. There, Wald declared, people toiled "under conditions that, even though I have seen them myself, seem now to be a bad, bad dream."[19] Tenement manufacture was conducted in two- and three-room apartments.

> It was not uncommon to see the machines working where members of the family ate and slept for twelve, fourteen and— in busy times—as many as eighteen hours in twenty-four. Occasionally the work was interrupted, for not more than an hour or two, for the birth of a child.[20]

The crimes of tenement manufacture were perpetrated, not only upon the worker, Wald claimed, but also upon the consumer. Cigarette papers were sealed by "bedridden tuberculosis patients" and children's clothing was made in homes "where there was contagious disease" such as diphtheria. The public, she said, had to protest these conditions. Reform would benefit all, not only the worker. For Wald, the abuse of labor by indifferent employers became "unendurable" and she had to "cry out against the inhumanity of it all."[21]

The trade union movement was to Wald the lever for social betterment for the worker. Unions promised "better pay, wider distribution of opportunity for work through shortened hours, and what was very vital to many of them, the collective bargaining which held the group together . . . and did not sacrifice the individual."[22] Using the young women of the garment industry as her examples, Wald detailed the struggles of the "girl workers" to organize. Immigrant women, in particular, had distinct problems because they were more liable to misfortune and exploitation than any other group and for years they had suffered their grievances and accepted conditions without complaint. Most of the young women were from Italy and Russia and were accustomed to poverty and oppression in their old countries. The Italian girls, Wald said, were particularly submissive because "their men, whether father or brother, kept them under their control."[23]

With little formal knowledge of the theories of collective bargaining, the Russian girls led by an occasional "Joan of Arc" learned to stand together to get better conditions for all. These young women, who had perhaps learned a sense of solidarity in anti-Czarist activities, became a major force in the girls' industrial world in New York City. What was unknown to the general public, Wald declared, was the degree of unselfishness and enormous social conscience of the girls. Over and over, Wald told of "their spirit of sacrifice" to achieve their vision of the better life, one that offered more than "hard, grinding, soul-stultifying labor." One girl, who was earning high wages, still joined a picket line saying, "This is not a strike for self. Only by all standing together can we get better conditions for all." Another young woman, offered five dollars a week over her usual salary, declined to scab during a strike. "You cannot buy my conscience for money," she said. Wald used these and other anecdotes to impress her audiences. She told of Fannie, who spent the money she had saved to study dentistry to support her family during a strike period and surrendered her future without complaint. There was also Clara Lemlich, another of the young women, who had to sacrifice her dreams of further education because of a strike and did so with no mention of her suffering. Or, Wald could tell of Ella who quit a good job to join a picket line saying, "How can I be satisfied when so many of my sisters are suffering?" Wald stressed the group ethic developed by these young women who passionately believed that each could do nothing, but together they could gain everything. They were willing to sacrifice themselves as individuals to save "the weaker sisters who cannot struggle unaided by them."[24] Wald urged her audiences to remember these young women and to spread the word "Do all you can to make public sentiment for fair play in work and pay."[25]

In 1906, Wald wrote of the frustrations encountered by union organizers in attempting to build strong and permanent organizations of female workers.

> Historic precedent, lack of education in administration, and the conventional tradition of women . . . , the hope of marriage, insufficient trade training, the demand for cheap and unskilled labor in many trades, and therefore the easy substitution in the ranks of the women wage earners

precluded large, permanent unions for women. An equally great obstacle was "sex antagonism . . . the disparagement and ridiculing by the men of the girls in their attempts to take their place in the industrial world."[26]

For these reasons, Wald helped to found the National Women's Trade Union League in 1903, and later became a member of the executive committee of the New York City League. She "recognized," she said, "the importance of the movement in enlisting sympathy and support for organization among the working women." The WTUL made it

> possible for women other than wage-earners to identify them-
> selves with working people, and thus give practical expression
> to their beliefs that with them and through them the realization
> of the ideals of democracy can be advanced.[27]

The league, which was patterned on a British model, was different from other Progressive reform groups in that its prime function was not the promotion of legislation. Rather, its principal objective was to "investigate the conditions of working women, to promote the best type of trade unionism in existing organizations, and to assist in organizing trade unions in all trades where women are employed."[28]

The American Federation of Labor endorsed the league, but there are questions as to the depth of the moral and financial support given by the larger union and its president Samuel Gompers. Wald tended to be more sympathetic to the AFL leader than some of her friends, including Florence Kelley, who called him an "aged Dodo," or Margaret Dreier Robins, head of the WTUL, who had frequent differences with Gompers on questions of policy. Modern historians, too, are critical of the alliance between the WTUL and the male union members. Nancy Dye claims that the association often forced league members to "subordinate their commitment to feminism for a conservative trade union philosophy that was usually incompatible with their constituents' needs as workers and as women."[29]

Nonunionist middle-class "allies" were included in the member-ship of the WTUL and were invaluable particularly in the organi-zational years for administration, fundraising, and explaining the labor point of view to other middle-class women. The relationship between the working women and their "allies" was sometimes filled with tension resulting from class differences despite good inten-tions to achieve sisterhood. Leonora O'Reilly counted many middle-class women as close friends, yet she distrusted the "allies" and twice resigned from the WTUL in protest against the elitism of what her sister unionist, Rose Schneiderman, called the "Mink Brigade."[30]

The League also attempted to educate working women who did not understand the value of unionism. They had to be taught to pay

dues and especially not to scab in time of strike. They had to learn
to assert themselves at union meetings even when faced with criticism from male members. At times, unionization took "almost
superhuman powers," for the women "didn't want to do it."[31] The
best organizers, according to the president of the national league,
Margaret Dreier Robins, were the union women themselves. The
WTUL, therefore, established a school for organizers in order to
train them.[32]

Despite its problems, Wald viewed the league as valuable and
claimed that its worth extended "far beyond the immediate purpose
of the women who work."[33] It had vital importance to the feminist
cause for it taught women to be independent. Moreover, it was the
place where women working both inside and outside the home met
to share interests and experiences. The WTUL, created on the
premise of sisterhood, tried to cut through class lines and, for a
brief time at least, forged a coalition for women's rights, especially
suffrage.

When the league was formed, Wald made Henry Street and
Clinton Hall available as meeting places and individual members of
the Settlement made contributions, both financial and personal.
Lavinia Dock served as an organizer and the Lewisohn sisters became large financial contributors to the union. As a member of the
New York board, Wald was on frequent call as a speaker at meetings of union sympathizers.[34] Wald's active role in the WTUL was
short, and her reasons for leaving are unclear. Possible explanations
for her departure include her appointment as representative of the
public to the Joint Board of Sanitary Control in 1910, her participation in the Lawrence strike in 1912, and her reluctance to antago-
nize the conservatives who funded the nurses and Henry Street.
Even after leaving active participation in the league, however, she
continued to support its work and to maintain friendship with its
officials. Her confession in *The House on Henry Street*, "To my regret I cannot claim to have rendered services of any value in the
development of the League,"[35] underestimates her contribution. Her
propagandizing for the cause of the working woman was essential
in order to get public acceptance of labor's aims.

The International Ladies Garment Workers Union has long been
recognized as a force for workers' interests. This needle trade organization resulted from various waves of unionism beginning in the
1800s, with the entrance of Eastern Europeans, mostly Jews, into
the trade. Conditions of work and poor pay motivated the formation
of a variety of short-lived unions and largely unsuccessful strikes.
The most significant strike, not only in the history of the garment
trades but in the organization of working women, took place in the

winter of 1909 to 1910 among the shirtwaist makers in New York. The New York WTUL threw all of its resources behind the "Uprising of the 20,000" as did the infant ILGWU. With workers from five-hundred shops walking out, it was the largest strike of women in the United States. Most of the girls were between sixteen and twenty-five years old and they represented thirteen or more national groups. A majority were Jewish, with Italian women making up the second largest contingent. The strike started in July 1909, with a dispute in the Rosen Brothers factory that ended in a victory for the workers after two-hundred people walked off the job. Other shops followed, including the Triangle Waist Company, one of the largest in the industry. Usually, working women were unable to hold out against the large firms, which had the resources to hire scabs, thugs to harass the strikers, and prostitutes to mingle with the pickets, but this time they held firm. A general strike on the shirtwaist trade was called by Local 25, an affiliate of the ILGWU, in late autumn of 1909. The vote was taken after a working woman, Clara Lemlich, delivered a "stirring 'philippic in Yiddish' " that concluded when she asked the audience to take the old Jewish oath, "If I turn traitor to the cause, I now pledge, may this hand wither and drop off at the wrist from the arm I now raise."[36]

A young woman writing about the strike, five years later, said: "I could not see the importance of the strike at the time. I was young, only 17, and did not think very much about things, but rather felt the effects of my suffering." When the general strike started, she walked out of the shop with the other working girls. She recalled that "during the strike, I had a rather hard time. I was arrested, though I did not do anything against the law, and sent to ... prison ... locked up in one cell with one striker and four prostitutes."[37]

Sympathy poured out for the strikers. The WTUL actively publicized it and sought to rouse mass support for the women workers. An information bureau was established at Clinton Hall and strike balls were organized to raise a bail fund. A sense of common cause developed between the striking women and their middle-class "allies." Wald and the family and friends of Henry Street threw themselves into the fight by picketing, observing police activities, propagandizing, and fundraising. Mrs. Henry Morgenthau, Sr., for example, deeded property to the Settlement so that it could furnish bail money for some of the more than seven hundred women who were arrested on a series of flimsy charges.[38]

The maltreatment of the women strikers stirred Wald, E. R. A. Seligman, Ida Tarbell, and Mary Simkhovich of Greenwich House to write to the newspapers that there was "ample evidence to warrant the statement that employers had received the cooperation and aid of the police" The workers had been "subjected to insult by the police" and in many cases had been "arrested when acting within their rights."[39]

The shirtwaist makers' strike ended with some small gains for the girls, many of whom were disappointed with the results. One wrote of expecting more for the hardships they had endured.

> We thought with the winning of the strike that all the suffering will be abolished. We thought that it was time already for a better life to come. You see we expected much more than what we could have gotten under the circumstances. We did not realize that that was our first great struggle.[40]

Two more strikes, in 1913 and 1916, again aided by the WTUL and the settlements, would be needed to gain greater results. Henry Street can be credited in both labor disputes with building support for the women. Theodore Roosevelt wrote that after "visiting bodies of girl strikers in Henry Street" in 1913, and listening to their stories of poor wages, family obligations, and of the fining practices of the employers, he became a convert to the cause.[41] He was one of many.

Six months after the end of the shirtwaist makers' walkout in 1910, the cloakmakers (mostly male) called for a general strike. The economic distress caused by the action reverberated throughout the Jewish community in New York and after two months, a citizens' group that included Jacob Schiff, Meyer London, and Louis Marshall stepped in to mediate. The resulting "Protocol of Peace" was "among the first industry-wide collective bargaining agreements in American economic history." The principles of protocolism, which established rights and customs on both sides and included a partial recognition of the union, were extended to other branches of the women's clothing trade in 1913.[42]

Article fifteen of the protocol resulted from the bad publicity the trade had received over the unsanitary conditions in the factories. A Joint Board of Sanitary Control was established with power to fix standards of ventilation, fire protection, pollution, lighting, and sanitation which the manufacturers and the unions were obliged to maintain. The board comprised two representatives each of the unions and manufacturers and three representatives of the public, one of whom was Lillian Wald. Twenty-eight "sanitary standards" of health and safety were compiled and both sides were committed to enforce them. Without legal status or police powers, the board had to rely upon the goodwill and cooperation of labor and management to discipline those who refused to improve conditions.

Sanitary certificates were issued to employers who complied with the established standards.[43]

The board enjoyed a reasonable success in its early years. "At present," one worker wrote, "when the Board of Sanitary Control is in existence, the sanitary conditions are considerably improved."[44] Wald, in an article written for the International Conference on Hygiene, explained the board's functions and told of the strides made in cutting down on fire hazards and overcrowding in the shops and of the improvements in toilet facilities and ventilation. She was especially proud of the work done by the board in educating workers on sanitary procedures.[45] There is little question that conditions of work improved in the large shops, especially between 1910 and 1916.

The board, however, never overcame some of its initial problems—problems endemic to the industry. Small manufacturers and subcontractors (about one-third of the shops by 1920) never joined the Manufacturers' Association and were, therefore, not susceptible to its pressures. If the unions attempted to exercise control, the shop owners moved to other locations, sometimes outside the city, or hired cheap nonunion help who were afraid to appeal to the board. After 1916, the industry lost its enthusiasm for the protocol and the board's influence and effectiveness declined. Frequently, too, the ILGWU accused the board of abandoning its neutral position to one favoring the manufacturers when the work of the board had to be defended. Regardless of these limitations, however, the board was a valuable institution in the long fight to rid the garment industry of its sweatshops.[46]

The WTUL participated in nearly all of the major strikes of the period and Wald endorsed these actions while trying to convey to others her belief that the use of "unladylike and unwomanly methods" were justified by the "sound moral purposes" of the strikes.[47] One labor dispute in which the WTUL did not participate because of AFL opposition involved the workers in the Lawrence textile mills, to whom Wald was especially sympathetic. The strike, led by the Industrial Workers of the World (IWW), was a clash between the American Woolen Company of Massachusetts and an "amalgam of foreign-born and unskilled workers, more than half of whom were women and children." Union leaders were imprisoned, militia and police were used as strike breakers, and every device imaginable was used to end the picketing. Since police and troops often clubbed the pickets, women volunteered to walk the line. They, too, were attacked and two pregnant women lost their babies. For publicity and to lighten the relief burden, the children of strikers were placed in foster homes in other cities. The police, in an effort to lessen the propaganda effect, forbade the further removal of children. The "children's crusade" ended on the day that two-hundred police and militia closed in on a group of women and children at the railway station. The lawmen clubbed the small group with what one observer described as "no thought of children who were in the most desperate danger of being trampled to death."[48]

When she heard firsthand reports of the situation in Lawrence, Wald expressed her dismay and immediately opened one of the Settlement buildings, 279 Henry Street, to serve as a link to the striking workers. Her actions and words drew great criticism, as Wald was accused of using the Settlement for propaganda purposes. She subsequently visited Lawrence and came away "reflecting with sadness on the manifestations there of how slight our hold on civilization [is]."[49]

Wald's letter to Jane Addams describing the conditions in the strike city elicited this response:

> I am so glad that you were able to go to Lawrence. The actions of the police and militia there have sounded perfectly preposterous. I am quite sure that a Russian official would feel that we had gone him "one better."[50]

The ardor of some social workers for unionism waned after World War I, but Wald, it would appear, continued to support trade unionism. In only one instance that can be documented did she appear to vacillate. In 1926 she chastized Lavinia Dock for sending money to help the box-makers' strike, saying, "I will transfer your check in cold cash to the . . . strike which seems a foolish communistic gesture that will lead them nowhere."[51] It is possible that Wald, knowing her friend's financial straits after retirement, was trying to curb her generosity, since Wald was a member of the citizen's committee for the strike. Perhaps it is more accurate to say that Wald was more discriminating when she gave her blessing to striking workers after 1920 since her health did not permit active participation in all causes. Nevertheless, she continued to sympathize and "add her name" to any labor action that was "a good cause," and never lost her belief in the need for unionism.[52]

Unionism was one weapon to protect the worker; labor legislation was a second, which had the added benefit of helping nonunion workers. Wald and many of her friends believed that it was impossible to protect women employed in manufacture without the aid of national and state law. Women, including those who were married and had children, were no longer transients in industry and as their numbers increased, legal protection became even more essential. Wald pointed out that "as a nation, we superstitiously hug the belief that our women are at home." While some laws that protect women in industry were enacted, the community was reluctant to face the reality

> that women no longer spin and weave and card, no longer make
> the butter and cheese [in the home], . . . but accomplish these
> same industries in the factories, in open competition with men,
> and except in the relatively few instances of trade organization,
> in competition with each other.[53]

The common thinking was that industrialization hurt women more than men. The studies of Josephine Goldmark revealed that the female death rate was higher and they suffered greater predisposition to disease. Of greater consequence, when women suffered, their children also suffered. Therefore, fewer hours of work and the elimination of night work benefitted not only women, but the future generations as well.[54]

Frances Perkins believed, as did most reform-minded women, that unions protected the worker, but were not strong enough. The problem was magnified for the woman in industry since "she has been trained to please people instead of standing on her rights." Additionally, most working young women believed that they were not permanent factors in the economy and were, as a consequence, shortsighted about unionism. Until the time when women recognized that they were in the labor force to stay, "legislation for women was [a] sound [idea]."[55] Wald echoed Perkins's sentiments and further claimed that the laws that raised the standards for working women would also benefit men. Females in industry could be the lever to lift the "weight of excessive toil from the neck of the human race." If the state would protect women, it would ultimately protect men.[56]

Wald worked with groups like the National Consumers' League, organized labor, and the American Association for Labor Legislation (AALL), of which she was a vice president, for the passage of wages and hours laws, safety ordinances, and workmen's compensation. She utilized the Henry Street nurses as investigators to report on the conditions of home manufacture and they supplied the ammunition used by Wald and Florence Kelley in their frequent appearances before the Congress and the New York State legislature.

New York State law provided for a sixty-hour work week in factories for women and children under the age of sixteen. Wald and her friends in the WTUL and the NCL had as their goal the establishment of the eight-hour day. A major problem for this and the enactment of other laws was getting public and judicial acceptance of the principle of the state's responsibility in the area of supervision and protection of labor. A turning point in the history of labor law was the Triangle Shirtwaist fire on March 25, 1911.

The fire broke out on the eighth floor and spread rapidly to the adjacent floors of the ten story Asch Building on Washington Place which housed the sweatshops of the Triangle Company. Locked doors, cluttered floors, and inadequate fire escapes left the working women at the mercy of the flames and smoke. An eyewitness reported that those who saw the panic could never forget it. "The heart-breaking cries of the burning girls! Like wounded animals they ran from one door to another, knocking, calling for help but all in vain." Crowds gathered in the street. Some of the people were parents or friends of the trapped workers and they watched with horror as many of the girls tried to escape from the windows.

> . . . four girls clasped their arms and jumped. Their heads were crushed, their arms still clasped around each other. The rest of the girls, seeing their co-workers killed on the sidewalk, were afraid to jump and they found their death in the fire.[57]

There was a public outcry over the one hundred forty-three lives lost in the fire. A public memorial meeting was held at the Metropolitan Opera House and the mourning audience heard speeches from prominent New Yorkers, including Dr. Henry Moskowitz, who represented the Joint Board of Sanitary Control. The most memorable address was given by a working woman, Rose Schneiderman. Wald recalled the speech of this future WTUL president who

> stood at the edge of the great opera-house stage and in a voice hardly raised, though it reached every person in that vast audience, arraigned society for regarding human life so cheaply. No one could have been insensitive to her cry for justice, her anguish over the youth so ruthlessly destroyed; and there must have been many in that audience for whom ever after the little, brown clad figure with the tragic voice symbolized the factory girl in the lofts high above the streets of an indifferent metropolis.[58]

Wald was one of the leaders of public opinion who, after the fire, formed a "Committee on Safety" to agitate to bring about an inquiry into all aspects of women's industrial work—in the factory or in the home. The New York State legislature created a commission to investigate not only fire prevention but all other labor problems. Members of the Factory Investigating Commission included chairman Robert Wagner, vice chairman Al Smith, Mary Dreier, and Samuel Gompers, all old friends of Wald. The commission held hearings, went on field surveys to factories, and gathered information. Its work, according to the biographers of Al Smith, made the social workers "happy as clams."[59]

Wald served on an advisory committee (Wages and Wage Legislation) to the commission and also testified before it. In her testimony, she said that her facts might not be very statistical but they were "based upon the knowledge . . . gained through residence in industrial sections" and on information gathered by the nurses who visit the sick in their homes. She told of manufacturing in tenement house apartments and of the "exploitation" of workers by "a parasitic trade." While stressing the harm done to the workers, usually women and children, she also told of the danger to the consumer when goods were made under filthy and unsanitary conditions, sometimes in houses later declared unfit for habitation. In one instance, Wald described a mother nursing an infant and at the same time working on a coat while her five-year-old, a truant from kindergarten, helped her sew. They "were in the same room with the father, who was there smoking a cigar with a friend, another man, watching his chattels do this work." It was not too common, Wald maintained, but there were many men who could work and chose instead to live off the labor of their wives and children. She recommended to the commission that all home work be eliminated since it was impossible to supervise and regulate. Moreover, "all organized labor is opposed to it, and quite rightly, because it does compete so directly with the wages in the factory." To benefit all workers, Wald suggested a minimum wage board to fix the pay for women.[60]

The commission met for four years and its recommendations on compulsory fire drills, a fifty-four-hour work week, fire hoses, prohibition of child labor in some occupations, and elimination of night work for women in factories were passed by the legislature, as was the prohibition of tenement manufacture—a total of thirty-six new labor laws in three years. The New York State Labor Department was reorganized and rules, regulations, and codes were established for each industry. The epic work of the commission was studied and imitated by many other states.[61]

The economic advancement of women is an essential ingredient of the feminist movement. While there are differences among women today as to the long-range benefits of protective legislation for women, there were no such divisions in the period before World War I. In the Progressive era, the means of achieving economic equality were through trade unionism and labor legislation; Lillian Wald worked for both causes.

Wald was interested in yet another category of working women—the prostitute. And with many of her contemporaries, she involved herself in the campaigns to eradicate "white slavery." Prostitution, the nurse discovered early in her career, was a fixed institution on the East Side. She learned of the "red light" district while searching for an apartment with Mary Brewster and expanded her education during her rounds. "Every single house," she wrote, "contained bedecked unfortunate creatures, who tried by a peculiar hissing noise to draw the attention of the men." It was a situation that was an "insult to womankind." Wald's attack on prostitution was not directed at its female practitioners. Rather she opposed the commercialization of vice and the political and police corruption that accompanied it. She had sympathy with the susceptible women, mostly poor and immigrant, whose special economic and social problems drove them to the streets.[62]

While her experiences showed that "all classes show occasional instances of girls who 'go wrong,'" low family income, congested homes, lack of privacy, malnourishment, and inadequate wholesome inexpensive recreation "weaken[ed] moral and physical resistance." Her investigations proved to her that young women in need of money were more likely to be "led astray" even though few who became prostitutes had a "direct mercenary incentive." More commonly, promises of marriage and better jobs were the inducements.[63]

In a series of speeches, Wald sought to teach the public that the immigrant women, in particular, were "in danger of moral contamination" and "exploitation." They arrived in the United States less worldly and more inexperienced than male aliens and often fell victim to the unscrupulous. At every stage—on board ship, at Ellis Island, on trains, and at so-called employment agencies—"immoral women and men came and selected their victims." Wald emphasized the need for legislation, both state and national, to provide special protection to these defenseless women.[64]

Wald echoed the feminist change in attitude toward the prostitute. Beatrice Forbes-Robertson Hale wrote that "these sisters were no longer regarded as the wicked, but as the wronged, not deserving of condemnation, but of assistance." The cry was no longer "brand her" but rather, "help her." The women rejected the double standard of morality; no longer would men be excused and women condemned for similar conduct.[65] Roy Lubove, the historian, states that to the Progressives, "vice was a man's business"—organized, managed, and patronized by them—and "the venom of the reformer was directed not against the prostitute," but against those who exploited her.[66] Such feminists as Carrie Chapman Catt railed against "those who live by the traffic in women," the pimps who found a profitable business in the unethical use of the sexual passions of other men. Solutions to this social problem could be found in suffrage for women, prohibition of alcohol, better pay for women, sex education, and an end to loveless marriages. The fight against prostitution became part of a greater fight to end all victimization of women.[67]

When John D. Rockefeller, Jr. was named to head a grand jury investigation of white slavery in New York, Wald wrote to advise him that it "would be a serious error to have the commission without women," and she cautioned him that all "clearminded, insightful" women would agree with her on the handling of the prostitute.[68] Three years later in 1913, in testimony before a legislative committee, Wald outlined some concrete proposals. She opposed the use of male plainclothes police for entrapment of the women. The practice was, to her, repugnant. Equally objectionable was the treatment of the women after arrest. Neither the public nor the prostitutes were served by court procedures that did not attempt to adjudge each case on a personal basis. She recommended "the appointment of women police who should patrol the streets, the dance-halls, and wherever girls and young women congregate." Well-trained women would be more effective than men in dealing with prostitution, she concluded.[69] Wald's suggestions as to entrapment, police use, and her criticism of the courts were applauded by Alice Stone Blackwell and other feminists. They also agreed with Wald's opposition to enforced medical examination of the prostitute, a practice that would "regulate vice" but not destroy it. Equally critical to the women was the principle, for it was "unfair to apply profligate women measures that are not applied to profligate men." Enforced medical examination "enacted the double standard of morals into law."[70]

Unquestionably the fight against prostitution was a defense of the alien woman and an example of the Progressives' belief that social evils could be contained or removed by legislation. Certainly the reformers displayed great naivete since they, with only a few exceptions, never admitted that some women became prostitutes by choice, not out of ignorance or even out of pecuniary need, but because the rewards—short hours and good wages—seemed to outweigh the disadvantages of such a life. Nevertheless, the vice reformers, particularly the feminists, did attempt to reeducate the public. If the traffic in women was a social evil, the prostitute was not the sole and not even the principal evil doer.

EIGHT
Full Citizenship—At Last

The most radical proposal introduced at the convention held at Seneca Falls, New York in 1848 was woman suffrage. The early feminist movement was essentially the struggle of a small group of white, Protestant, well-educated, middle-class women who, relieved of much work in their homes by the products of industrialization, sought full participation in political life. Despite massive efforts, the drive for enfranchisement had made little progress outside of the western states by the end of the century. The leadership of the women's movement was old and the organization had become narrowly based and fragmented. Total success, at times, seemed as remote as it had been in the antebellum period. The formation of the National American Woman Suffrage Association (NAWSA) in 1890 gave new impetus to the suffrage drive, which was further strengthened by cooperation with groups like the Women's Christian Temperance Union (WCTU), the Grange, and the Federation of Women's Clubs. Fresh leadership, new organizations that attracted a broader base of support, and increased emphasis upon a federal amendment made the enfranchisement of women a realizable goal by 1910.

The significance of adding New York State to the list of suffrage states was apparent to all. The WTUL's *Life and Labor* called it the "keystone of the suffrage arch,"[1] and it was claimed that if the Empire State could be won, "all the states would come tumbling down like a pack of cards."[2] It was clear that a victory in this eastern and influential state would accelerate passage of the federal amendment. Both opponents and proponents, therefore, regarded a New

York campaign, which had to enlist masses of immigrants and industrial workers, as decisive.

Annually, after 1854, voting measures were presented to the New York legislature and annually, each was ignored or rejected. A fresh start was begun in 1906 when Harriot Stanton Blatch, newly arrived from England where she had witnessed a more militant women's movement, formed the Equality League of Self Supporting Women (later called the Women's Political Union). The organization was unique in that it attempted to bring to the suffrage movement the strength and numbers of working women. Within a few years, the league enlisted 19,000 members, including Charlotte Perkins Gilman, Florence Kelley, Lavinia Dock, and Rose Schneiderman. When in 1911, the WTUL voted to support suffrage as a labor measure, the women's movement became a mass endeavor for the first time in history.[3]

At about the same time, Carrie Chapman Catt, former president of the NAWSA, came to New York to take charge of the Empire State campaign. The suffrage movement was fluid with a dozen or more groups dividing power. While Catt did not fault this condition, believing that it was good for everyone to have a job and a title, she recognized the need for strong leadership and coordinated planning. To accomplish this, she consolidated various organizations into the Woman Suffrage Party, which led a united effort for the New York State suffrage amendment through the two referenda campaigns—the first unsuccessful in 1915, and the second in 1917—needed for women to gain the vote.[4]

The fight began in October 1909 with a "Women's City Convention" held at Carnegie Hall. A month earlier, Catt met with other leaders to formulate plans and one of their ideas was to provoke the New York legislature to consider a suffrage amendment by electing a woman member "who could, within the sacred fold, by trading votes, . . . get the amendment submitted." Catt wrote to Lillian Wald, "We want *You*" to be that woman. Even though Wald would represent only one assembly district, if elected, she would be the candidate of all the women of the city.[5] While she considered the plan to be "very reasonable, very practical," Wald responded, she had to refuse the opportunity, for her work at the Settlement and lack of time would prevent her from devoting all her energies to this "good cause."[6] Catt, though disappointed, accepted the decision and went on to tell Wald about the proposed meeting. It would be organized by assembly districts with an A.D. leader for each area in an attempt to emulate the political parties. It was hoped that this would "prove the basis for future work" to carry women's suffrage to New York State. Catt feared that there would be no suffragists in some A.D.s and she requested that Wald serve as a chairperson to enlist some "good workers" like herself.[7] Wald was named honorary vice chairman of the convention and the Henry Street Settlement was represented by Lavinia Dock, who was on the House committee and served as a senatorial district chairman (in charge of at least three A.D.s—Helen McDowell, Yssabella Waters, and Beula Weldon). A platform was formulated that included a call for the utilization of women in public office as well as other feminist goals. The most important action of the convention, however, was devising tactics to pressure the New York State legislature to pass a constitutional amendment for women's suffrage.[8]

The women paraded, lobbied, canvassed, and cajoled the legislature until 1913, when "the sentiment in favor of letting the voters pass on the question . . . became too strong to be resisted." The men in Albany voted for the suffrage measure for the required second time and the issue was submitted to the voters in a referendum election in November 1915. Carrie Chapman Catt and the Empire State Campaign Committee prepared plans to convert the electorate which included dividing the state into twelve districts with further subdivisions developed along the lines of Tammany Hall's structure. The goal was to canvass block-by-block in order to reach and influence each voter. The campaign was impressive and included street dances, outdoor rallies, concerts, theater days, block parties, and parades.[9]

R. L. Duffus, Wald's biographer, wrote that she "could no more keep out of the suffrage movement than a fish could keep out of water."[10] Her experiences and interests as a nurse, social worker, reformer, and labor advocate showed her the need for women's full participation in political life. She was, she said, "hot on the suffrage question" and threw herself and the resources of the Settlement into the fight.[11]

Wald played a minor role in the formal women's groups. She held the title of honorary vice chairman of the New York State Woman Suffrage Party through 1917, and was a member of the executive committee, but she usually asked a member of the Henry Street household to represent her at meetings. Wald served the cause of suffrage in both referenda campaigns in the manner in which, she believed, she had her greatest strength. She pressured politicians, published articles, and gave speeches. "What you say," a woman wrote Wald, "has so much weight with a certain class of people who are not influenced by other suffragists."[12] The publicity that Wald gave to the women's fight had value in another respect since so many people used her as a model of what women could do if they had the power. In an article in the *Woman Voter*, Dr. Adolphus Knopf disputed the arguments of the "Antis" by pointing to "the qualities of mind and heart" he encountered in the women he met in social reform movements, such as Lillian Wald. She was, he believed, the best argument to be found for giving the vote to women.[13] Ironically, even the antisuffragists used Wald as an example because she showed what women managed to do without the vote.[14]

Wald was never a militant suffragist. She used "no weapons" other than "reason" in her appeals, for she believed that "normal people . . . tire of being told that violence is logic and hysterics reason."[15] An article in the *Henry Street Settlement Journal* reflected her view that the cause had "too many good arguments to resort to policies which disgust the sane individual and repel the sympathies."[16] Despite her aversion to militancy, however, Wald did sympathize with the actions of some radical suffragists. She wrote to friends trying to marshall American support for the Pankhursts in England, explaining that "they ask for only such representation as men had."[17] Most of all, she remained loyal to Lavinia Dock and was anxious always to help her even when the two old friends disagreed as to tactics.

Dock was active in the Congressional Union (later renamed the National Woman's Party) formed by Alice Paul and Lucy Burns, both of whom had studied in England, where they learned the confrontational methods of the Pankhursts. Dock easily adopted the aggressive strategy of the union since it reflected her own views. All of her life, Dock subordinated every interest, even the professionalization of nursing, to the fight to enfranchise women. Early in her career at the Settlement, she went to the polls and insisted upon the right to vote, hoping to be arrested for her effort. According to Wald, the police captain was a great admirer of Dock and on "election night, he came to see me to apologize." He knew that Dock wanted him to imprison her, but "he just couldn't do it. The idea was more than he could swallow" and Dock was denied her suffrage propaganda incident.[18] In her work with the National Woman's Party (NWP), Dock was one of the first pickets of the White House to be jailed and served a total of forty-three days including twenty-five days in Occoquan prison where, she claimed, conditions were so bad that she had "hard work choking down enough food to keep the life in me."[19] Wald feared for her sixty-year-old friend's health and wrote to President Wilson and Joseph Tumulty, the President's secretary, to check on prison conditions and to protest the sentencing of pickets. To Dock, Wald wrote of her affection, even though she was "not converted to the wisdom" of the militant's propaganda. "I tell you from the bottom of my heart that I hope you will not feel that you have to go to jail again. I cannot bear the thought of it. I know that the method seems right and wise to you and that there is no use discussing it."[20]

For Wald, the use of violence was unnecessary for the extension of suffrage was inevitable—the whole force of evolution was behind it. She believed in democracy and as a Democrat recognized that women represented the last large group legally excluded from citizenship. "In a country that is committed to that principle of government, there should be no intellectual question as to who has the right to be represented and who has not. Everybody has the right," she said.[21] Furthermore, it was absurd to deny the vote to such as Florence Kelley, Jane Addams, and "the multitude of women who were carrying the world's burdens on their shoulders and yet were thought to be incapable of casting a ballot wisely."[22]

New York State presented more than the usual problems to the suffragists. In addition to the traditional opposition to the extension of the vote, the women had to counter prejudice to immigrants—their own and others. They had also to gain the support of ethnic and religious minorities and from the slum dwellers in New York City. This challenge was the despair of the traditional suffragist and most hoped that the upstate counties would win great enough majorities to offset the city vote, where it was expected that the tenement dwellers, immigrants, and sweatshop workers would vote against suffrage. In previous referenda throughout the nation, women had witnessed foreign-born males cast ballots against equal political rights. Defeats occurred, as in the first California vote, it was believed, because of the "ignorant, the vicious and the foreign born," the city slum dweller, the Catholic, Jewish, Italian, and German vote.[23]

The *Woman Voter* published part of a study of the social effects of immigration. The article, by Professor Edward Ross, detailed the state of subjection of Slavic and Italian women, claiming that "Eastern European peasants are brutal in the assertion of marital rights." The woman suffrage movement in the United States, said Ross, would meet opposition from "millions of immigrants bred in the coarse peasant philosophy of sex." It would take a struggle to maintain "in the future the Christian conception of womanhood."[24] Most suffragists protested that these foreign men, with no training, education, or background to understand the workings of democracy, had the vote and could deny it to women who deserved it. In 1896, Elizabeth Cady Stanton sent a letter to be read at a hearing of the House Committee on the Judiciary.

> Allow me, honorable gentlemen, to paint you a picture. . . . The central object is a ballot box guarded by three inspectors of foreign birth. On the right is a multitude of coarse, ignorant beings, designated in our Constitution as male citizens—many of

them fresh from the steerage of incoming steamers. . . . Policemen are respectfully guiding them all to the ballot box. . . . Each in turn depositing his vote, for what purpose he neither knows nor cares.

Some years later, Anna Howard Shaw elaborated on this antiforeigner theme.

No other government has subjected its women to the humiliating position to which the women of this nation have been subjected by men. . . . In Germany, German women are governed by German men; in France, French women are governed by Frenchmen; and in Great Britain, British women are governed by British men; but in this country, American women are governed by every kind of a man under the light of the sun.[25]

Locally, the *National Voter*, the voice of the New York City Suffrage Party, carried article after article relating the problems of the capable women who were kept from the ballot box by the coarse and ignorant foreigner.[26] Even Carrie Chapman Catt added her voice. In a letter to the *New York Times*, she questioned the aptitude of foreign men to vote with no test of any kind. Was the ability to cast a ballot "inate in the male and foreign to the nature of the female?" she asked.[27]

Clearly, the immigrant and the feminist were separated by a wide cultural barrier. Suffragists often espoused views that violated the traditions and church teachings of the newcomers, especially those who arrived in vast numbers from Italy, Austria-Hungary, and Russia. Traditionally, also, as historian Olivia Coolidge observed, the "American suffragists had held aloof from the working class leaders, especially those from the emerging trade union movement." Susan B. Anthony and Elizabeth Cady Stanton had made some efforts to draw in the working woman, but their successors, with a few exceptions, had little understanding of the industrial poor.[28]

The New York suffragists would have preferred to convince the familiar middle-class, native-born groups, but to win in the Empire State, this attitude was impossible. They had to reach "friends of all nations."[29] From the start, the feminists enlisted the help of the settlement workers who dealt and lived with the aliens and sweatshop workers. Settlement women understood immigrants and could perhaps convince them to use their votes for reform. The Henry Street nurses had particular influence in terms of Americanization and political education. In addition to providing medical care, they "shared a special kind of intimacy with the whole neighborhood."[30] Harry Roskolenko in his chronicle of the East Side, *The Time That Was Then*, told of the six yearly visits made to his home by a Henry

Street nurse to deliver a new baby, to care for the mother and infant, to clean the apartment, and "impart wisdom."[31] While originally the nurses worked only on the East Side, by 1910 they were providing services throughout the city. In that year, forty-seven nurses made fifty thousand calls and by the time of the second referendum in 1917, there were one hundred Henry Streeters making almost a quarter of a million home visits.[32] According to William O'Neill, the nurses demonstrated to the immigrant voter that there were "liberated women who interested themselves in womanly concerns."[33]

Josephine Goldmark, in a broadcast address, called Lillian Wald "the great interpreter of one social class to another, of the newcomer and the alien to the native-born, of people of different racial backgrounds to one another, of the under-privileged to the over-privileged."[34] And it was in the role of interpreter that Wald performed her greatest service in the fight for women's suffrage. Like many women in the WTUL, Wald believed that the vote was essential for the working woman. Work prepared her for citizenship and she could use the ballot to gain protective legislation. In turn, the suffragists needed the numbers of the wage earners to build a winning coalition. The two mutually distrustful groups needed someone like Wald to mediate their differences. Leonora O'Reilly sometimes called on the settlement leader to "add a bit o'cheer" to lessen tensions and to remind everyone that cooperation was necessary for a successful women's movement.[35] Wald's prime function was to explain the need for suffrage to the immigrants so that they would support the referendum and to explain the immigrants to American-born citizens so that they would not fear the vote of the newcomers. To each group, she used arguments designed to minimize fears and for both groups she conveyed ideas that would appeal to male voters.

Lawyer Everett P. Wheeler was executive chairman of the Man-Suffrage Association Opposed to Political Suffrage for Women and a leader of the "Antis." While he used all of the traditional arguments to gain converts, he emphasized the disruption of the family and a resulting sexual revolution because of women voting.[36] Wald, who knew Wheeler, responded to a letter he wrote to the *Times*:

> I do believe that the home and the mother are the sources of society. One of the reasons why I am a suffragist is because I want to dignify them in every way, and have the influences and traditions of the home brought into government.[37]

In her speeches and writings, Wald tended to disregard a warning from Catt not to "promise what women will do with the vote,"[38] and, like many other women, claimed that females in politics would contribute an interest in humanitarian reform. Both sexes, Wald reassured her audiences, would work together to the interests of better government. Often she made reference to those nations with political equality to show that women almost always develop "those inclinations which are traditional" and vote to support home and children. Women in politics, both immigrant and native born, would work to preserve that which is valuable and important to them.

Since most Americans viewed all recent aliens as a less than desirable mass, Wald sought to show the virtues of her neighbors on the East Side. In her book, *The House on Henry Street*, and in a series of speeches before the first referendum in 1915, she described the intelligence of her new friends. The immigrants were ardent patriots who made contributions to the country that offered escape from oppression. Moreover, the East Siders were wise and independent voters. Wald suggested that "the fear of the immigrant . . . vote is confined to the people who do not know them or have had the most limited experience with them." Statistics indicated that her neighbors showed great discrimination in their voting habits. The Jewish vote in Manhattan and the Bronx (the areas of greatest concentration) was an "overwhelming vote for Anti-Tammany candidates and the selection of individuals, irrespective of party." The East Sider could "hardly be called an ignorant immigrant voter." Wald drew attention to the high literacy rate of the children of the foreign born as an illustration of the value placed upon education by the immigrants. Also, since the Naturalization Act of 1906 required people to speak English and to sign their petitions, "persons naturalized since 1906 are required to have a higher degree of literacy than is enjoyed by some of our native citizens."[39]

Foreign women, in particular, were praised. Since it was believed by some that they were overburdened and unfit for the vote,[40] Wald took pains to answer the critics. She testified to the "earnest concern" of the immigrant women and to "their effort for the things that make life happier and safer for children and men and women." They had direct knowledge of the effect of laws upon family life and they knew from bitter experience about labor conditions. "And these women *care*. It would be extraordinary if they did not care," she said. The vote was important to these European-born women and proof of this concern could be found in the Henry Street neighborhood. "Almost any night, if you come to the East Side, you would see women, working class women and mothers as well, standing on soap boxes, giving earnest expression to their convictions upon the value of the extension of the franchise to them." One in particular, a "motherly looking woman . . . makes her appeal . . . to a respectful group of laboring men." This "mother in Israel," who works in a factory six days a week, "intelligently and interestingly . . . develops her plea, and her appeal to men's reason brings sober nods of approval." Russian men and women, Wald added, had "sacrificed much to get to this land of political equality" and were anxious to take a full part in American life. "I doubt that a single man or woman could be found among them opposed to granting the franchise to women."[41]

To back up her claims, Wald worked to insure the Jewish vote on behalf of suffrage. In a letter to the *Jewish Daily Mail*, she appealed to males to recognize the value of their wives and daughters who worked hard and shared "the duties of life." Women who voted would remain good mothers and good wives. In fact, "it might be easily proved that women are better mothers . . . and wives in the country where they have shared in the responsibilities of the franchise." Wald concluded:

> We no longer ask men . . . to vote for women because of their rights; we ask men to vote for women because it is just and because women, having had education and training, and having shared in the advantage of a partial democracy, should be called on to perform their full duties.[42]

The work done for suffrage by the Settlement women, especially Lavinia Dock in the 1915 campaign, is best measured by the reports "From the Assembly Districts" in the *Woman Voter*. Though the political lines changed through the years, the residents of the Henry Street Settlement were largely responsible for voters in the second through the eighth assembly districts. Visits to Jewish trade union meetings, street gatherings, suffrage forums at the Settlement, and propaganda geared to the immigrants were part of the campaign, as were visits from neighborhood heroes like unionist Joseph Barondess and socialist leader Meyer London, both of whom spoke at suffrage rallies.[43] Results of these efforts showed as early as March 1911, when Dock reported that the foreign born on the East Side were interested in enfranchising women. All of the Yiddish language newspapers devoted space to the question, especially the influential *Vorwarts*. Dock concluded that "the suffrage sentiment of this extreme down-town section is very strong," a fact that was borne out in informal polls taken in Jewish and Italian neighborhoods in the second assembly district in 1913 and the third A.D. in 1915.[44]

In the months before the 1915 vote, many began to question the conventional thinking as to the sources of suffrage strength. Carrie Chapman Catt expressed disappointment over the upstate sentiment[45] and the *New York Times* reported that "the women suffragists . . . have not found the rural districts fertile soil for their propaganda as did suffragists in other states." Many campaigning women were met by indifference and even hostility, which led to early predictions that the upstate counties would produce unfavorable majorities.[46] By contrast, Wald wrote in *House on Henry Street*, published in 1915, "The conviction that the extension of democracy should include women has found free expression in our part of the city."[47]

Election day brought defeat to the suffragists in all but five counties of New York State, with a vote of 748,332 against to 553,348 in favor of the amendment.[48] Harriot Stanton Blatch's immediate interpretation of the results was to blame the immigrant vote. She complained that

> No women in the world are so humiliated in asking for the vote as the American woman. The English, the French, the German women all appeal to the men of their own nationality. The American woman appeals to men of twenty-six nationalities, not including the Indian.

Blatch had asked for a polling place on the East Side and was assigned as a poll watcher on Eldridge Street, where she "saw young men who had been in this country but a short time" voting on the suffrage question. She did not question their right to citizenship "but I call it tyranny and license for them to have power to pass upon me and upon the native born women of America, and a disgrace that the men of our country will force us to submit to it. We have been hypocrites too long."[49]

Whatever the validity of these sentiments in the past, they were open to challenge in New York where the city vote for suffrage was less adverse than that of the state as a whole. Wald was quick to make this point in a widely published letter to the editor of the *Times*. She wrote that perhaps Mrs. Blatch was so busy with the campaign that she did not have the time to notice the East Side vote. "Analysis . . . from the first to the twelfth Assembly Districts, shows a comparatively favorable acceptance of the extension of democracy" and with only one exception, "no other part of the city did as well."[50]

Abram Lipsky wrote another response to Mrs. Blatch in the *American Hebrew*. He compared the results in six assembly districts in which the native-born voter constituted 40 percent or more of the total vote with six districts having 10 percent or less native voters. The results indicated little variance between the performance of the native-born and immigrant voters.

M = Manhattan B = Brooklyn Q = Queens	A.D.	Percentage of voters who were native born or of native parents	Percentage of vote for suffrage
M	27	51.5	44.3
B	17	45.6	44.6
M	15	45.3	42.3
M	25	44.1	47.7
Q	4	41.3	44.6
M	19	40.0	48.3
M	30	2.4	36.5
M	6	2.4	50.8
M	8	2.5	49.3
M	10	5.9	44.3
M	4	7.0	47.5
M	26	7.1	50.5

Using figures based on the 1910 census, Lipsky proceeded to break down the vote of 1915 on ethnic lines.

Borough	A.D.	Ethnic composition	Percentage of vote for suffrage
M	30	Data not available	n.a.
M	6	39% Russian, 39% Austrian, 2.4% native born	50.8
M	8	65% Russian, 2.5% native born	49.3
M	10	34% Russian, 19% Austrian, 5.9% native born	44.3
M	4	51% Russian, 7% native born	47.5
M	26	57% Russian, 7.1% native born	50.5

Lipsky, in other statistical tables, showed that other nationalities did not endorse suffrage as did those of the East Side and other areas of Jewish concentration. He concluded "that the strongest support of woman suffrage came from the native born Americans and from the foreigners, chiefly Russian and Austrian, who inhabit the districts east of the Bowery," and some parts of Harlem and the Bronx. The strongest opposition from foreign-born groups came from those of German, Italian, and Irish birth.

> Mrs. Blatch, therefore, was only half right in her choice of a foreign district in which to watch. She went to a district that had next to the lowest percentage of pure Americans, but it happened to be one that furnished nearly the strongest support of her cause. . . . The Russians and Austrians whom she most suspected stood, for good or ill, shoulder to shoulder with the men of her own race in this particular campaign.[51]

It is interesting that Wald and the Settlement women had predicted these trends in their constituency early in the 1915 campaign.

The fight to win the 1917 referendum began immediately after the first defeat. Catt, in a letter to all chairpersons of the Woman's Suffrage Party, declared that "a cause with a half million votes . . . will never be treated with contempt again," and she called a meeting to present her "winning plan" for New York State.[52] The second referendum differed from the first. In 1915, the woman suffrage issue competed for attention on the ballot with a referendum on a new state constitution and many women believed that this was done by design by the politicians in order to confuse the issues and defeat the suffrage measure. In 1917, the enfranchisement issue would be on the ballot alone, although by the spring of the year, other considerations had intruded. The World War intervened and represented both a threat and an opportunity for the women. Would the voters condemn the movement because of Congresswoman Jeanette Rankin's vote against American entrance into the war, Jane Addams's presidency of the Woman's Peace Party, and Lillian Wald's leadership of the American Union Against Militarism? Or would the citizens of the state respond to the many women who were becoming involved in war work and patriotic causes? By 1917, also, the suffrage movement had gained enough status so that it "was no longer a supplicant at the doors of party conventions" and both political parties were committed, at least in theory, to extending the vote to women. President Wilson, who had resisted the demands of the suffragists in his first term, became an advocate of the federal amendment. Suffrage emerged as one of the Democratic war aims and even Tammany Hall, by the year of the second referendum, was really neutral on the issue.[53]

Wald agreed to serve on the new statewide suffrage committee. The chairwoman, Harriet Laidlow, wrote to her saying, "Your name will mean so much to us," and she gave Wald the title of vice-chairman for Manhattan. She was expected to give "assistance and . . . advice" while the real work of the post would go to Edith Borg of the Settlement.[54] The East Siders duplicated their massive effort of 1915, more rallies, canvassing, literature, petitioning, clubs, and work through various Jewish groups like the Workingmen's Circle. Borg tried hard, but Wald's correspondence indicates that she had to step in frequently because of what the Woman's Suffrage Party termed Borg's "impracticality."[55] Whatever the internal problems, Catt could in honesty claim that "no such campaign was ever conducted in the United States for any cause as that in New York."[56]

Wald's pacifism did create one serious policy difference with the Woman's Suffrage Party when the majority of the executive committee offered the services of the organization during the war crisis. While Wald agreed to uphold the decision with the understanding that it only committed the women to relieving "suffering or distress in any form," she regretted "the resolution because it seemed . . . to be one more expression that might increase the tension and perhaps the war spirit."[57] Statewide, Wald's stand probably was not applauded, but no doubt it met a more favorable reaction on the East Side where the workers, many of whom were socialists, tended to be antimilitarist and pacifist.[58]

Throughout the referendum campaign, the specter of an adverse immigrant vote continued to haunt the traditional suffragists and most hoped that the upstate vote would improve enough to provide a winning margin. To the dismay of many, voters outside of New York City again voted against the amendment. The *New York Times* headlined its story "Suffrage Fight Won in the Cities," for it was the urban population that provided the victory. In Manhattan, for example, the vote was 129,412 (59%) in favor and 89,124 (41%) against the extension of the franchise. Most revealing, a study of the assembly districts that formed the constituency of the Henry Street Settlement shows that the favorable votes in half of these districts were significantly higher than the 59 percent average of the whole borough:

Henry Street Settlement Area Suffrage Referendum Votes by Assembly District[59]

Assembly District	Affirmative Votes		Negative Votes		Total Votes
	Number	Percent	Number	Percent	
2	4482	63	2603	37	7085
3	5669	53	5032	47	10701
4	4348	73	1583	27	5931
5	5301	51	4993	49	10294
8	5003	67	2454	33	7457
10	5899	60	3991	40	9890
Total Votes	30702	60	20656	40	51358

Over the years, many explanations have been proposed for the victory in New York in 1917. It has been said that the enfranchisement of women was an idea whose time had come, that even the political bosses recognized that they had to change their policy. How then, can the defeat of the suffrage forces in Ohio in the same year be explained? The United States was involved in World War I for only six months when the referendum was held and it seems unlikely that the vote was given to the women as a reward for national services. In New York City (and therefore for the state as a whole), the reason the victory was won was the formation of a coalition of Eastern European immigrants, industrial workers, and middle-class women, who manufactured public opinion in favor of woman suffrage. A large measure of the credit for creating the climate that made possible this successful effort must be given to such settlement houses as the one on Henry Street and such leaders as Lillian Wald.

After years of work, Wald wrote to Jane Addams, "We are nearly bursting over our citizenship. . . . I had no idea that I could thrill over the right to vote."[60] Important as the victory was to individuals, it was even more critical to the cause. The *Woman Citizen* proclaimed that

> The carrying of New York State is the greatest single victory that the suffrage cause . . . has yet won. It breaks the backbone of the opposition; it forces the blindest reactionary to see the handwriting on the wall; it insures the speedy passage through Congress of the nation-wide suffrage amendment.[61]

With "the thrill of new citizenship" still upon her, Wald embarked on a new program. She wrote a friend, "We are going to be terribly busy from now on trying to educate the voter. I thought when the vote was won that I would have a minute or two a day, but it seems not to be working that way."[62] Wald's time was spent in initiating citizenship classes at the Settlement for the new voters. While she and other suffragists had argued throughout the campaign that women had knowledge of political and civic affairs, they now claimed that the newly enfranchised had to make "themselves fit for citizenship" through study and observation. "What will we profit by the franchise," she said, "if we do not make this a safer and better city?" Voting implied not only a privilege but duties, and duties implied a familiarity with the mechanics of politics. Wald hoped that women would use their campaign energies to inform themselves so that they could play an important role in government.[63]

Wald had always eschewed permanent identification with any political party and remained issue- and candidate-oriented. Since she was so successful in influencing platforms and electing reform-minded politicians, she believed that this was a path to be followed by all women. She urged the new voters to remain an independent determining minority rather than enter and be absorbed by any party organization. Men were often ruled by political machine bosses and Wald was loath to see women follow the same path. The new voters were in the position where they could demand definite social programs from both parties and they could demand that these programs be enforced. If they did not align themselves with either party, women could pick the good and criticize the evil in both organizations in order to profit the community as a whole.[64]

Wald's reasoning was representative of that of the women of the NAWSA, who after the passage of the Nineteenth Amendment reorganized into the League of Women Voters (LWV), a nonpartisan group that concentrates on fact-finding and lobbying. The league needs no defense of its work, which is superb, but it was not—except in 1920—and is not a political organization; it is an interest group. The LWV could be as effective if it were made up of disfranchised women. Wald would have served members of her sex more effectively if she had urged the new voters to enter political parties, to gain a constituency, to wield influence by choosing candidates, and to develop reputations for achievement and ability. To claim power, women had to reach the places where final decisions for the political process were made. Wald and the other women who pleaded for nonpartisan activities retarded the political progress that the new voters might have made in the next two generations. Indeed, many modern students of the suffrage crusade are critical of the time and effort devoted to the vote considering how few lasting changes resulted from that reform. Even the suffragists themselves felt the need to justify their actions when, after a number of years, they could not claim that all their ideals had been realized.[65]

Wald never maintained that suffrage would "be a panacea for all the ills of social and political life," nor did she believe that the reform would result in the millennium.[66] Nevertheless, she can be accused of "over-selling" suffrage. To win converts, Wald did not hesitate to deny her feminism if her audience contained "Antis" to whom feminism assumed a pejorative meaning. She also gave her listeners reason to believe that all women were genuinely interested in social reform because of their background and training. She was probably too much the realist to believe her own propaganda, but suffrage was important to her, and she, no doubt, felt justified in using whatever tactics were necessary to achieve success. It is likely that Wald would have understood the attitude of Helen Hall who, in an interview more than a half century after the passage of the nineteenth amendment, expressed amazement that anyone would question the significance of gaining the ballot for women.[67]

NINE

The War—Nothing the Same Again

World War I altered the nature of both social reform and feminism since belief in society's ability to remove social, economic, and sexual injustice was weakened in the face of the disruption of international peace. The outbreak of the war, in large measure, caused the reformers to divert their time and energy from domestic improvement to international affairs. Though some, like Wald, toiled for change after the war, they never regained their pre-war momentum, and their efforts were always diluted by work in the various peace movements and by the need to defend themselves from attack by super-patriot groups.

Pacifism had a long history in the United States. In the period prior to 1914, however, it was usually a movement initiated, organized, and led by men. Women often supplied membership and workers within the established peace societies and many of the women's groups like the WCTU and the Daughters of the American Revolution (DAR) endorsed pacifist goals, but the women did not provide a unique philosophy. By contrast, the female peace groups that emerged as a result of World War I represented "in both ideology and tactics . . . a new note in American pacifism."[1]

Women like Jane Addams and Lillian Wald recognized that war would divert the nation's attention from social reform to military spending. Further, the concept of war was itself "an anachronism . . . , a throwback in the scientific sense," for they had daily evidence of the ability of different peoples to live together in harmony. Settlement workers lived in cosmopolitan neighborhoods and saw Jews and Gentiles, Russians and Germans, Austrians and

Italians living together in harmony. If individuals could enjoy good relations, nations could as well, they reasoned.[2] People who lived in settlements, said Wald, were internationalist in outlook because they knew that the fundamental problems of all peoples were the same.[3]

The unique feature of the peace movements formed by the women after 1914 was their blend of feminism and pacifism. The woman's movement worked for sexual equality in every area of domestic activity; it now called for a voice in international decisions as well. At first, the revolt against war was small and limited to the social workers, but, as Sondra Herman observed, "Jane Addams and Lillian Wald soon expanded it by making it a women's revolt. Never was American feminism more militant than in its pacifist crusade."[4] War destroyed homes and devastated families, and women, who were so much affected by armed conflict, had the right to participate in the decisions of war and peace. The questions were too important to be left in the hands of professional diplomats using the traditional methods of diplomacy. If women had international power, they would be less inclined to be stirred by martial oratory. Tied to the peace goals, therefore, was the demand for universal suffrage.[5]

Of course, not all feminists were pacifists. While all the peace workers remained suffragists, many suffragists, including Carrie Chapman Catt after 1917, came to regard the war as a tool in gaining the vote. Between the end of 1915 and April 1917, war work became increasingly attractive as a means of gaining political as well as economic advantages. When the United States entered the world conflict, the pacifists became an embarrassment in some cases to the suffrage movement. Lavinia Dock was typical of many women who began as workers for peace and then, when the United States was involved as a belligerent, called for "a fight to the finish."[6]

Women reacted within days after the invasion of Belgium in August 1914. A committee, which included Wald and Mrs. Fanny Garrison Villard, organized a protest against the fighting. About thirteen hundred women representing a broad spectrum of organizations and dressed in black marched down Fifth Avenue in a parade the *New York Herald* described as "impressive." In its "wide variety and in its universal humanity, this was a parade the like of which has never been seen in New York." Mrs. Villard was quoted as saying that the procession

> serves to make women realize it is a crime to send sons and husbands out to be slaughtered. Women must be trained to realize what the enormity of war is. It is time that they cease to

accept what men, in the exuberance of their patriotism or enthusiasm say regarding things.[7]

According to the biographer of Emily Balch, these women "were the first in 1914 . . . to *think* internationally." They "attempted to do what had never been done before by women acting together as women: to enter into international political activity."[8]

Late in 1914, a group that included Wald, Oswald Garrison Villard of the *Nation*, Jane Addams, Paul Kellogg, Max Eastman, Crystal Eastman, Reverend John Haynes Holmes, Florence Kelley, and Rabbi Stephen Wise organized a series of meetings at Henry Street that led to the establishment of the American Union Against Militarism (AUAM) (at first called the Anti-Preparedness Committee). Wald, who stood in the ideological middle of the group, was elected president of the union which, she said, represented every shade of opinion that could be united against war. By the end of 1915, the AUAM had grown to six thousand members and was a powerful influence against militarism and for peace. It was an extension of the Progressive reform impulse and members of the union stressed the "social cost of war," because they believed that any international conflict threatened social progress. Members of the union, therefore, lobbied against conscription and military preparedness and for peaceful solution of international disputes. The high point for the AUAM was its successful work to avert a Mexican-American war in 1916.[9]

Wald spoke on various platforms hoping to convert her audiences to the pacifist cause. The final abolition of war depended, she maintained, upon the work of men *and* women. Never before in history were women "so organized or self conscious as now"; they had the training and power to turn the world against militarism, death, and destruction. "It is fitting that the world should ring with their outcry against this blasphemy upon the things that they hold most sacred." Women, more than men, are the victims of war, she asserted. Males who love their homes want to fight and kill to protect their families by destroying the homes, wives, and children of other men. "Unfettered by custom," women are "less stimulated than men by the call to force." The "hollowness of the appeals by which men have been stirred to battle" is clearer to women. They can work together for each other by having their voices "rise . . . above the sounds of battle" on behalf of "those against whom war has ever really been waged—women and children."

It is of especial importance, Wald concluded, that after the war, civilians rather than military men dominate the peace terms, for "the soldier's attitude to woman has not changed, certainly not in several generations." The military had never acknowledged the change in the female role, nor abandoned the "traditional orthodoxy as to 'woman's proper place.' " It takes a long time to "change habits of thought and what some are pleased to term secondary sex characteristics, namely—the mental and physical attributes, not directly resulting from sex functions, but from the conditions of life imposed by them." New habits of thought were essential for women to be given the opportunity to contribute to the peace. "The old tradition of woman's place in society as the home-maker and housekeeper and nothing else" must be eliminated so that women "may establish their right to participate in the councils of the state in the future, that diplomacy and statecraft may include the human interests that women have always held as precious."[10]

The Woman's Peace Party (WPP) emerged from this feminist-pacifist sentiment. Its members were, Addams wrote, women who were "ardent for peace and believed that women had a special obligation to withstand war as a human institution."[11] The impetus for the formation of the WPP was the speaking tour of Emmeline Pethick-Lawrence, a British suffragette, and Rosika Schwimmer, a Hungarian feminist. Both women came to the United States in hopes of arousing antiwar sentiment and gaining support for the idea of a negotiated peace settlement. They found sympathetic audiences throughout the country. When in New York City, Pethick-Lawrence met Carrie Chapman Catt, who initiated the idea of a conference of women's groups, and Crystal Eastman, who urged the Briton to see Jane Addams about a peace party for women. Addams accepted the suggestions and invitations were sent out under her name for a "meeting to consider the organization of a National Peace Commission of Women."[12]

Three thousand women from almost every important female organization met in Washington and adopted a peace platform that in many ways anticipated Woodrow Wilson's Fourteen Points. There were suggestions for the limitation of arms and for a concert of nations to substitute for balance of power in international affairs. The most unusual part of the platform was the demand that women be given a share in the decisions of war and peace. "The mother half of humanity" insisted upon equal rights and power.[13]

Wald was not a founding member of the Woman's Peace Party.[14] She also missed participating in its single most important action—the International Congress of Women that convened at the Hague in April 1915. No greater evidence of the international character of the "women's network" may be offered than the Hague Conference, which grew out of the International Woman Suffrage Association. The equal vote group was unable to meet because of the war and to compensate for this, Dr. Aletta Jacobs of Amsterdam suggested a meeting to show that women could maintain their sense of solidarity despite war. Along with women from neutral nations, women of the belligerent countries would be invited to display their rebellion against a war that was not of their making.[15]

Addams, who had been elected president of the WPP, received an invitation from Jacobs to attend as head of an American contingent. Because she wanted "a strong delegation," Addams was most anxious that Wald join the party going to the Hague.[16] The Henry Streeter refused, noting that:

> All my inclinations lead me to accompany you, and to add one more protest against war. I think the call and response on the part of the women in this country is dramatic and has great publicity value. I do not believe that my going or remaining at home would add to or detract from that.

Wald considered her responsibilities at home too great to abandon.[17] Addams wrote twice more in attempts to pressure Wald to reconsider her decision and Addams's companion, Mary Rozet Smith, also tried to urge Wald to go by describing Addams's disappointment because of her refusal. "She is awfully wishful of your going," Smith wrote, in a last effort to get Wald to join the American delegates.[18]

The Henry Streeter's behavior is not easy to understand. It is possible that her refusal to attend the Hague congress resulted from her unwillingness to be identified with a failing effort, particularly one that was open to ridicule. This seems unlikely, however, in light of her future affiliation with the women's peace efforts. More likely, Wald declined because she was busy with the 1915 suffrage referendum in New York State and was eager to see that campaign through to a successful conclusion. Also, it was a period of great activity for the American Union Against Militarism and Wald was frequently called on to speak and work for that group which was waging a campaign against preparedness. Her ties to President Wilson were strong in 1915, and she may have believed that she was more effective as a peace worker at home where she had a measure of influence.

Much has been written about the Hague Conference with its 1,500 representatives of eleven nations. The camaraderie of the women and their seriousness of purpose impressed observers, even those ready to laugh at the efforts of the "peacettes." The delegates named their group the Women's International Committee for Permanent Peace, set their headquarters in Amsterdam, and adopted two major resolutions. The first reiterated the peace principles of the WPP including the right of women to participate in diplomatic negotiations and to have equal rights. The second resolution adopted by the congress called for a conference of neutral nations "which shall without delay offer continuous mediation" to end the war, with suggestions of terms of peace coming from the belligerent powers. The congress appointed a women's committee to visit the leading European statesmen to engender interest in and possible support for the plan.[19]

At home, Wald undertook to answer the critics of the Hague proposals. One who was particularly harsh in his judgments was Theodore Roosevelt, who called the platform "silly and base," while comparing the women to the Copperheads during the Civil War.[20] To counteract such negative comments, Wald continued to stress her belief in women's role as the conservers of life. Traditionally, they banded together to protect what was important to them, and now women were organizing to protest war and to offer reasonable substitutes for settling international disputes.[21] In the summer of 1915, Wald wrote to President Wilson requesting an audience for Jane Addams so that she might explain the work done by the women at the Hague.[22] Meanwhile, the American Union Against Militarism adopted the concept of the conference of neutral nations, and the history of both the WPP and the union for almost two years was one of unrelenting pressure upon Wilson to endorse the conference plan.[23]

Wilson met with the women pacifists so many times that his advisor, Colonel Edward House, in his diary described the subject of their visits as "the same old story."[24] In reality House, even when mocking the women, seemed sympathetic when compared to Secretary of State Robert Lansing, who was openly hostile to the concept of mediation. Wilson offered words of conciliation to the women and despite their frustration at his inaction, they believed him to be a man of peace, sincerely concerned with avoiding entrance into the war. Both Wald and Addams, unlike many suffragists, supported the president for reelection in 1916 and publicly accepted his reservations as to their proposals and his unwillingness to commit himself as evidence of executive "strategy." Privately they had their doubts about Wilson, but his peace note of December 18, 1916 to the warring nations and his "peace without victory" speech to the Senate the following month restored their hope that the president was ready to assume the role of wartime mediator. After the war, with the wisdom of hindsight, Addams reported that by early 1916, she noticed the "glaring differences between the President's statement of foreign policy and the actual bent of the Administration."[25]

The pacifists tried but could claim no success in stemming what they saw as Wilson's drift toward militarism. The proponents of "preparedness" seemed to have converted the president who, in 1916, supported an enlarged army and expanded shipbuilding program, even as both the WPP and the AUAM fought against these evidences of America's movement toward war. Early in 1916, Wald testified before the Senate Committee on Military Affairs to protest the "dangerous program of military and naval expansion to divert the public mind from the preparation for that world peace which it might be our country's privilege to initiate at the end of the war."[26] To combat the propaganda of the militarists, the pacifists called an antipreparedness meeting at Carnegie Hall, where they hoped to alert Americans to the "great peril to America" of an arms building race. Wald, one of the speakers, tried to define what she believed to be the major issue. It was not a question only of pacifism, she reported, rather she feared for the salvation of democracy if the United States adopted the European armament system.[27]

Wilson still represented the greatest hope to the women, and in May 1916, Wald headed a delegation to pressure him to withdraw his support of the preparedness program. The president informed the group, "I am just as much opposed to militarism as any man living," but he denied that the new legislation to increase the size of the army and navy was unreasonable. A nation that was helpless militarily could not go to a peace conference "on a basis intelligible" to the belligerents. "In the last analysis," Wilson said, "the peace of society is obtained by force." During the interview, Wald questioned the president's logic and raised the possibility of a stampede by the militarists that Wilson could not withstand.[28] She summed up the meeting to friends by saying, "We enjoyed our interview with the President" and believe he is "sincerely opposed to militarism," but "we are unconvinced" by his philosophy.[29] Wald never publicized her doubts. To the press, she mentioned only Wilson's recognition of the dangers of militarism.[30]

The elation felt by the pacifists in January 1917 over Wilson's "peace without victory" speech did not last long. The events of the next two months moved the United States to a declaration of war. The Wald-Wilson correspondence is testimony to her efforts up to and even after April 2, 1917 to divert the president from a war course. She assaulted the president with her presence and by letter on the issues of conscription, submarine warfare, armed neutrality, a league of nations, and civil rights for conscientious objectors. She reminded him of his natural allies and of his need for the "nameless men and women who have been so proud and so happy to believe in you, to push from behind where you were leading on before."[31]

America's entrance into World War I did not alter Wald's pacifist sentiments. She wrote her friend Yssabella Waters:

> I know the whole world is suffering from the war but I feel it
> down to my very toes. I feel it in every fiber of my body. Ever
> since I have been conscious of my part in life, I have felt conse-
> crated to the saving of human life, the promotion of happiness
> and the expansion of good will among people, and every expres-
> sion of hatred and the dissolution of friendly relations between
> people fairly paralyzes me.[32]

During the war, Wald served on the Red Cross Advisory Committee
and on various other groups involved with health matters. Where
early in the war she had protested the move to send nurses to Europe through the Red Cross, she now witnessed 20 percent of the
nation's nurses in the military. The only bright spot was that her
old comrade Annie Goodrich was appointed Dean of the Army
School of Nursing.[33]

America's participation in the war ended the solidarity of the
Henry Street group. Some in the AUAM, like Rabbi Stephen Wise,
came to support the war; others remained pacifist but disagreed
over help for conscientious objectors and the image presented to the
public by its more confrontational members. Wald could not keep
control over the widely divergent group and in the summer of 1917
resigned from the AUAM, fearing that its increasingly radical activities and tactics would decrease her influence on government after
the war. The Civil Liberties Bureau of the union, led by Crystal
Eastman and Roger Baldwin, evolved into the American Civil Liberties Union while other members of the group later formed the Foreign Policy Association. Wald maintained contact with both groups
and with the leadership of each.[34] Ironically, Wald's caution about
her image did not produce the results she hoped for. In the post-
World War I climate of conservatism, all pacifists were tainted.

With the collapse of the AUAM, the Woman's Peace Party became
the center of Wald's pacifist activity and she was chosen an honorary vice-president of the New York City chapter, which was the
most militant of the party. Wald did not actively participate in the
workings of this local branch but was involved with the national
WPP. Before the Hague meeting adjourned, the participants of the
first International Congress of Women agreed to hold a second conference at the end of the war which would meet at the same time as
the peace treaty deliberations, since diplomats were "seldom representative of modern social thought" and were generally unrespon-
sive "to changing ideas."[35] Wald was named to the "Committee of
Five," which was a planning group for American delegates to this
second international meeting set to convene in Zurich on May 12,
1919. Financing a representation of thirty-five women from the
United States was a problem and both Wald and Addams searched
for "victims" willing to donate money.[36]

Wald's trip to Europe in the spring of 1919 served other purposes as well. She represented the United States Children's Bureau at the International Health Conference at Cannes and took the opportunity to publicize public health nursing and the need for trained women to play a large part in health matters in the postwar world. Wald, Addams, and other women friends also toured the French battlefields en route to Switzerland and the trip reinforced their views of the devastating effects of war and their desire for a new international order.[37]

One hundred and twenty-six delegates representing fourteen nations met in Zurich. Florence Kelley commented that while the meeting had its share of "weak sisters," no one was obstructive and never had she seen "so generous a spirit in any group of human beings."[38] The biographer of the Woman's Peace Party, Marie Degen, claimed that the "congress completely transcended nationalist cleavages and refused to recognize any interruption of the spiritual solidarity of women." It was a universal sisterhood. The congress adopted the permanent name, Woman's International League for Peace and Freedom (WILPF). In their program, the delegates demanded the "establishment of full equal suffrage and full equality for women with men politically, socially and economically." Most important, the WILPF was the first group to protest the harshness of the terms relating to Germany in the Treaty of Versailles, while at the same time strongly supporting the concept of the League of Nations.[39]

When she returned to the United States, Wald tried to promote the concepts of the Zürich conference, but she met with little success even among the people who had supported her programs in the past. She wrote to James G. McDonald of the Foreign Policy Association that she did not possess the "means of influencing the President" any longer. "I think the situation has grown beyond the personal equation and that our faith is now in the lap of the gods."[40] Even her old friend Paul Warburg refused her appeal to support the Treaty. While he favored the league, he said, the treaty was "an immoral document" designed "to protect our selfish interests."[41] Wald continued her efforts in the 1920 election when she campaigned for presidential candidate James Cox and the ratification of the Versailles agreement. She appealed especially to women to show the "power and true purpose" of their new vote. They were being given a great opportunity, she said, "to show what woman's suffrage means and to save the country from the horrors of war and bankruptcy."[42]

During the 1920s and 1930s, Wald continued her work for peace through disarmament. She remained a vice chairman of the New York branch of the WILPF and was a major spokeswoman for that group. She tempered her argument that women were less warlike than men and more concerned for peace; both sexes were alike, she maintained, and they were eager to prevent war. She continued to claim, however, that women were less likely than men to be aroused to mass action and deeds that they would not perform as individuals. The newly enfranchised women were free to express themselves and they ought to send a message that they want peace and security. But, she said, women's desire for security should not be translated into war preparation, for protection could be secured without military reserves. In a speech entitled "Disarmament," Wald concluded that

> women throughout the world . . . [were] expressing themselves as never before. We do not feel that this is in opposition to the aspirations of men, but that we are with the vast numbers, united in a noble fellowship for a noble cause.[43]

Near the close of her active career, Wald took part in a disarmament and peace demonstration. In 1931, a women's peace caravan traveled to Washington to present President Herbert Hoover with petitions. Wald was particularly pleased with the quick response of the nurses—almost six thousand signatures came from the small group. Despite the efforts of the women, Wald did not feel that the president was receptive to them.[44] Earlier she had written to Ramsay MacDonald in England, "Strictly entre nous, we are very much irritated at the apparent lack of outspoken vigor on the part of Mr. Hoover. Personally, I am not surprised." And to Alice Lewisohn Crowley, she commented, "I spoke a piece to the President . . . , and he had a grouch on him thick as a London Fog."[45]

Events in Germany and Japan in the early 1930s bewildered Wald, who had come to believe that the world was more intelligent than in the years before the last war and, consequently, more difficult to arouse. She likened the Nazis to the Ku Klux Klan and wrote to the LWV and the WILPF leadership to determine if there was "not something that the women's organizations ought to do in protest against the German situation?" She also petitioned President Roosevelt, hoping to influence him as she had done Wilson in his first term.[46] In 1934, Wald wrote a letter to Mrs. John D. Rockefeller, Jr. that is particularly revealing of her feelings about the rise of Nazism.

> You know how I felt about the war propaganda, the efforts to stir to hatred the peoples of the earth, but in some ways the Hitler effort seems more disastrous because it jeers at all the good and spiritual. . . . Though I think the Hitler anti-

Semitism is more brutal than anything else they do, it is fundamentally not more dangerous than their other outrages; it is not more dangerous than their suppression of Catholic freedom and liberal thought and their suppression of the rights of women.

Wald urged her wealthy friend to assail Nazism by showing that Hitler's anti-Semitism was really anti-Christian thought. She knew of Mrs. Rockefeller's interest in the YWCA and hoped that the organization could promote this idea.[47]

Two years before her death in 1940, Wald wrote to Freda Kirchwey of the *Nation* magazine, "I am a pacifist and have been all my life and I do not see any reason for changing my opinion. . . . My principles as to peace and war are unchanged."[48] Wald may never have learned of the outbreak of World War II in Europe. Her friends, knowing her convictions and how ill she was in her last year of life, tried to keep newspapers from her.[49]

It is easy to maintain that the record of the women pacifists was one of continuous failure. Their attempts to end World War I by mediation, to prevent the preparedness program in the United States, to keep America out of the war, and to ratify the Treaty of Versailles came to nothing. Their ultimate failure was the outbreak of World War II. The women were no doubt naive, or at least seem so in the light of the comment from Jane Addams that if only the public were informed, it would respond to talks of peace.[50] Yet from the viewpoint of the women's movement, the peace workers did accomplish a great deal, for they showed that the common interests of women could cut across national lines. Above all, they showed that women were capable of performing on the international stage.

The frustrations and failures of the immediate pre-World War I years did not prepare Wald for the problems she would encounter after 1918. She had lost many battles in her years of public life, but she was always admired and loved even by her opponents. Wald's self-described "militant pacifism" was to many both radical and unpopular. For the first time, Wald held a position that was not susceptible to compromise and pragmatic solution because she had a vision of international relations that was unacceptable to most of her fellow citizens. For these convictions and others, Wald "became intimate" with what historian Staughton Lynd described as "that deeper sense of separation from which the radical suffers."[51]

A pacifist was, to a large extent, *persona non grata* in many circles during the war. On the whole, most peace workers accepted this as did Jane Addams as "practical politics."[52] Even before America's entrance into the conflict, the *New York Times* tended to lump pacifists, Germans, and pro-Germans together in its headlines and referred to the AUAM as a "radical pacifist organization," suggesting that it was maintained by German contributions.[53] Given this sentiment, it followed that Wald's peace work led the "patriots" to suspect her of subversive activity. Distrust of Wald was reinforced by her close association with the aliens' cause in a time, 1919 to 1920, when the immigrant was under attack, and by her support of unionism and frequent endorsement of Socialist candidates. She became even more of a target when the East Side, with which she was identified, applauded the news of the Russian Revolution. Lastly, Wald as a feminist sought to change the social structure and to advocates of the status quo, those who demanded women's equal participation in political, economic, social, and international affairs appeared revolutionary.

The attacks upon Wald brought her personal pain. She was a person who needed love and was accustomed to it. Criticism, however, had even more serious repercussions because the Henry Street Settlement and the Visiting Nurse Service depended upon individual contributions for survival. After the war, the needs of both of these services grew. Fundraising, under the best of circumstances, was difficult, but now that Wald was labeled a "radical," she found "the dreadful responsibility of getting money" more tiring and time consuming than ever before.[54]

Wald was grateful to the many old supporters who remained loyal. She wrote Ruth Draper, the actress, "Your really generous check gave us all a thrill. . . . It is very difficult to get money now,— on the other hand, the need is very great."[55] But Wald's letters to old friends contain fewer references to those who donated funds than to the burdens and anxieties of conducting million-dollar campaigns. "I get so depressed at getting this . . . across," she complained. "I am going to have a terrible struggle about more money. The rich people are most panicky these days with regard to anybody who stands out for liberalism."[56] J. Horace Harding was one of the first to withdraw his usual contribution because of Wald's "activities and association" with pacifism. Moreover, he did not care for some of her associates and believed their activities were "disloyal and bordering the line of treason." Since he was now "so out of sympathy" with Wald, her views, and her associates, Harding was going to give his aid to works with which she was not connected.[57] Harding was not alone in his attitudes. Another of the largest contributors on Wald's list, Mrs. Stephen V. Harkness, withdrew her support for Henry Street because she considered its founder to be "socialistically inclined."[58]

Wald tried to defend her views and activities by telling such critics as Harding that President Wilson had assured her that her pacifism had neither embarrassed the country nor weakened the government.[59] Her detractors were rarely convinced by these arguments. She attempted to remain philosophical; nevertheless, the extent of her personal pain at this time is clear. In the summer of 1919, she wrote to Lavinia Dock that

> my political attitude is making some of our generous friends uneasy. . . . Poor things, I am sorry for them—they are so scared. It is foolish since, after all, counting things in the large and wide, I am at least one insurance against unreasonable revolution in New York.[60]

Many of the "patriot" groups most critical of Wald and her female friends grew out of the suffrage fight. The New York victory seemed to some to illustrate the connection between socialism and the women's movement, since the vote was won in the cities. When women like Addams, Wald, and Kelley also associated themselves with the peace movement, the link to subversion became even clearer to people like Everett Wheeler, a leading "Anti." In 1917, he and other antifeminists organized the American Constitutional League to "uphold and defend the American Constitution against all foreign and domestic enemies." This group, in conjunction with the National Association Opposed to Woman Suffrage (which had many of the same members), issued a pamphlet entitled "How Woman Suffrage was Imposed on New York State." The publication sought to prove that in New York City, the franchise victory was the result of the socialist vote. It quoted the party slogan that "Every Socialist is a suffragist" and the words of prominent party members like Morris Hillquit and Benjamin Schlesinger, president of The International Ladies Garment Workers Union, who claimed that working women would vote socialist when they were given the franchise.[61]

The first official statement against the women was delivered in January 1919, when Archibald Stevenson of the Military Intelligence Division read into the record of the United States Senate Committee investigating German propaganda, headed by Senator Lee Overman, the names of sixty-two men and women who had been leaders in the pacifist movements, and may have been "actively engaged in opposing the military law of the country." This "Who's Who in pacifism and radicalism" included Addams, Wald, historian Charles Beard, Villard, and Balch.[62] Immediately, Wald wired Addams to learn of any actions the Chicagoan planned to take. Wald claimed that she "did not mind personally" but believed that the "irresponsible and inaccurate" action was "a national disgrace."[63]

Friends of the "Who's Who" women rallied to their support and this plus the fact that, early in 1919, Wald organized nursing care in New York City during the influenza epidemic helped restore, for a brief time, her damaged reputation. She reported to her uncle, Sam Schwarz, that being named an "undesirable citizen" may have had certain advantages. At least, the indignity to her helped some of the others on the list.[64] Her biographer Duffus, however, described Wald as "depressed and overwhelmed" by the actions of the Overman committee.[65] Throughout 1919, Wald actively defended herself and others from critics. She especially deplored the "scandalous attacks on aliens," and tried to rouse support against the un-American "policy of exile and deportation" of immigrants, without "open trial and testimony of evidence." Always the pragmatic diplomat, she wrote to wealthy businessmen of the need for immigrant labor in industry. Self-preservation dictated, if nothing else did, an end to the assault on aliens and immigrants.[66]

The Stevenson charges on radicalism motivated still another investigation. In March of 1919, the New York State legislature named Senator Clayton Lusk to head a committee "to investigate the scope, tendencies and ramifications of . . . seditious activities" in American society. Emulating the activities of Attorney General A. Mitchell Palmer for the federal government, Senator Lusk initiated raids against organizations suspected of "domestic radicalism." The committee's findings were published in a four-volume report that stated, in part, that "at least one hundred trade unions" were controlled by revolutionaries and that the social welfare movement was Bolshevik-inspired.[67] The Lusk committee investigation resulted in the abrogation of the civil rights of many organizations and individuals. The *Woman Citizen* was among the critics of the committee's activities, which included the expulsion of five socialist members of the New York State legislature. The action moved Wald to write former governor Charles E. Hughes that "the best of us are bewildered these days, and it is no strain upon the imagination to perceive what an un-American persecution may mean to the ordinary boys and girls."[68] She also protested to Governor Al Smith against other "suppressive measures" passed by the "reactionary Legislature." When Smith vetoed the Lusk Laws, which included making the Socialist party illegal and requiring a loyalty oath from teachers, Wald commended her old neighbor for his "statesmanship, judgement and sanity."[69] She was less successful in influencing Smith's successor, Nathan Miller, who subsequently signed the legislation.

"The month of January, 1920," historian Robert K. Murray observes, "marked the height of the Great Red Scare." After that, "the crest of hysteria passed" and "public fear was never again as intense."[70] In that month, Wald reported to the Lewisohn sisters that things were getting better and that it looked as if she and they would soon "be put upon the desirable list."[71] She proved to be overly optimistic, for within two years, women reformers were again under attack.

In 1922, the *Woman's Protest*, an antisuffrage publication, became the *Woman Patriot*, a Washington biweekly edited by Mary Kilbreth, dedicated to the "defense of the family and the state" and to the fight "against feminism and socialism." The enemy included women like Jane Addams, Lillian Wald, Julia Lathrop, Margaret Dreier Robbins, and Florence Kelley, who, together, it was claimed, created organizations designed to destroy the home and ultimately the country. The *Woman Patriot* was not alone in attacking the women. It was supported by such groups as the National Civic Foundation, but Kilbreth's publication played the most visible role.[72]

Wald was not included in the list of "women dictators" by the super-patriots, nor was she ever abused as much as Florence Kelley and other female friends. She was, however, identified with the nursing profession which was targeted by the publication, and she was mentioned in the widely publicized "spider-web" chart. This drawing gave the names of about fifty persons and connected them by lines to groups like the WTUL, the WILPF, and the Children's Bureau, which were allegedly directed or inspired by the Bolsheviks. The overlapping lines of the spider-web were designed to illustrate the existence of an interlocking directorate of women involved in world conspiracy. The *Woman Patriot* printed what has been called this "curious mixture of truth and fiction" and permitted it to be reprinted in other right-wing publications.[73]

Wald's key role in the establishment of the Children's Bureau also came under attack, for the bureau was singled out as an agency to be abolished since it deprived parents of the full guardianship of their children. When the Child Labor Amendment to the federal Constitution was introduced after the Supreme Court invalidated state and federal law and was supported by the bureau, the WTUL, and the NCL, the *Woman Patriot* went into action. Assisted by other rightist groups, the publication initiated a campaign to show that the amendment was the work of communists, intimating that it may even have been written by Leon Trotsky. Florence Kelley was the prime villain and, as a result, was the most slandered by the patriots. The facts of her marriage to the "foreigner" Lazare Wischnewetsky were resurrected. She was the instigator, but, it was claimed in a right-wing pamphlet, "every Bolshevik, every extreme Communist and every Socialist in the United States is back" of the Child Labor Amendment.[74]

The attack on the women was intensified when extension of the Sheppard-Towner Maternity and Infancy Act was under discussion by Congress in 1926. The legislation provided matching federal funds for state allocations earmarked to improve the health of mothers and their children. The *Woman Patriot* viewed Sheppard-Towner as still another part of the Communist conspiracy. Labeling it the "Engels-Kelley Child Welfare Scheme" or the "Kollontay [sic]-Lathrop Maternity System Program," the publication smeared all of its supporters including Wald and her nurses, who were the "profiteers" in the Maternity Act and, therefore, backed it in self-interest.[75] Senator Thomas F. Bayard of Delaware read into the *Congressional Record* the articles from the *Woman Patriot* that declared that the nation was being tricked by Bolshevik measures under the guise of women's legislation. The same "underground" of Communists that established the Children's Bureau was now at work to further deceive and defraud the public by its control of children, youth, and women. Florence Kelley, Senator Bayard maintained, was the leader of the "revolution by legislation," but she was aided by colleagues like Addams, Wald, and Catt who mustered the votes. Wald's trip to the Soviet Union in 1924 was probably part of the plot, Bayard thought, for he noticed that the "full force of communist strength in America was openly proclaimed to 'compel' the state legislatures" to comply with Sheppard-Towner after the nurse's return to this country.[76]

The years of combatting the attacks of the super-patriots took their toll. Actions and philosophies that had been applauded in an earlier period were now considered subversive and the heroines of the women's movement were now adjudged by some to be enemies of the state. The women reformers of the Progressive era who broke away from the sexual stereotypes found that their time and energy had to be directed to rebuttal of slander and defense of old programs rather than to greater progress. By the end of the 1920s, Wald reported to her friend Ramsay MacDonald, "The stones flung at us for many years are at present turning to caresses." Though there were residues of baiting throughout the next decade, she would in her last years be honored by people whose "clapping hands" at one time "held a brick-bat"[77] and whose compliments, it seemed to her, now contained "enough treacle . . . to make a molasses cake."[78] Many factors combined to slow the feminist impulse after the suffrage victory, but no analysis is complete that omits the attack upon the women by the super-patriots who created an environment hostile to any further substantive change in the role of women. The ten years of the witch hunts should have and could have been spent in consolidating the women's movement and setting new goals for sexual equality. The feminists were not permitted this opportunity.

TEN

What Happened to the Feminist Movement after 1920?

*T*he fate of feminism after the passage of the suffrage amendment is of profound interest to contemporary historians. Some claim the women's movement dwindled and died, while others question whether it declined at all, believing that the feminist thrust was merely slowed by the events of postwar society. An examination of the facts of Wald's life offers some clues to the answers to these questions. Wald worked as hard as she was able for women's rights after 1920. Her goal of female equality remained constant; successes, however, were less frequent than before the war. She continued to endorse candidates who she believed recognized an enlarged women's role, but she did not regain a friend in the White House until 1933. By then, the world had changed for Wald and her contemporaries. The Red Scare period of the 1920s made it necessary for her to transfer some of her energies from reform to self-defense and fundraising, and the economic depression of the next decade caused a further reordering of her priorities.

Although younger women, such as Mary Dewson and Frances Perkins, followed in the footsteps of the Walds and the Kelleys, their work had less mass appeal after the war. Youth took advantage of the benefits won by the older generation, but it may be that easier access to education and the professions hampered the development of a feminist consciousness. Self-fulfillment became the goal and women who achieved a measure of success as individuals forgot or became, as Anna Howard Shaw predicted, "uninterested in the fight for women's equality as a class."[1]

Wald often spoke of the "revolutionary" changes "in the outward life of women since their occupations . . . moved from the homes into the office, the factory and the workshop." There was nothing, she believed, that was "denied to woman, either young or old if she had but the desire and the will to fulfill those desires." The new era after suffrage was won offered great challenges, since there was "freer admission . . . to professional and public life." Yet, Wald found that fewer women were willing to accept these challenges. Perhaps, she said, the seeming indifference was the result of thinking that equality would come as a matter of course. Strenuous effort was no longer necessary.[2]

The "new woman" of the 1920s was in large measure a foreign creature to Wald and her friends. The residents of the Henry Street Settlement wrote a birthday "ode" to their Head Worker in 1923, which illustrated their emotions.

> Such awful hats, such awkward ways,
> They talk so loud with nasal wheeze
> We watch with wonder as they peer about
> Who can they be? Who can they be?
> There's not a thing could ever phase [*sic*]
> These modern eccentricities,
> They smoke each cig unto the end,
> And then a butt is thrown,
> On fragrant incense that we used to burn,
> Wherewith the gods we might invoke,
> We love the fragrance, but we do not yearn
> To learn to smoke, Sisters
> To learn to smoke.[3]

Many of the new generation were uninterested in, even hostile to those things that Wald believed to be most important. Novelist Sinclair Lewis wrote *Ann Vickers* about a liberal, feminist social worker who realized herself as a woman only after she learned to love a man. Vickers even discovered the meaning of feminism through love. Throughout the novel, Lewis satirized liberal "uplifters," the value of settlements, and "famous name" suffragists. He alluded to lesbianism among the women and gave to Vickers five lovers, one abortion, and one illegitimate child.[4] Wald confided to friends that she was furious at the author and the image he presented of the woman reformer. Since Lewis was a Nobel Prize winner, he was likely to be believed.[5]

It was especially hard for Wald to comprehend the absence of idealism in the young. She took a trip to Mexico with Jane Addams and Mary Smith and, as was her habit, wrote to her Henry Street family of her adventures. One can sense Wald's amused wonder at her encounter with "a blond bobbed, rouged, gum-chewing college girl," who was "en route to teach in a Methodist mission school" which was selected, not out of a desire to serve but "because she had 'majored in Spanish'."[6] New attitudes were even embraced by Settlement workers and in this case, Wald was not amused. At one time, the Henry Street women felt the need to send a tongue-in-cheek formal dinner invitation to their busy Head Worker "to give ... [them] an opportunity of making your acquaintance."[7] By way of contrast, in 1929, Wald had to remind the residents of the importance of the weekly meeting so that they might be informed on pending legislation and other matters. Personal interests seemed more important to some of her younger colleagues.[8]

As a politician and a pragmatist, Wald knew the value of reaching the public. Through the twenties, therefore, she sought to understand the younger generation and to enlist its support. In public interviews, she did not ignore the "apathy" of the youngsters and their reluctance to "give of themselves" to matters of public interest, but more often, she told of her admiration of the new generation. Wald especially applauded their candor and willingness to speak out where their parents might remain silent.[9] There was, she wrote the settlement worker Helena Dudley, great promise in the young ones.[10] And in *Windows on Henry Street*, Wald noted that, "during the 'jazz' period, we did not realize ... that our much criticized young people often gave better account of themselves than did their elders. In those hysterical years, the emphasis on sex" was often criticized. She, however, supported the frankness of the young and believed it to be better than the "hypocrisy and surreptitious experiment that so generally characterized sex behavior in the pre-War years."[11] When compared to many of her Progressive era colleagues, Wald managed to be more in step with the new times. By the late 1920s, if photographs are accurate, she even succumbed to the fashion of bobbed hair, a practice she had "discriminations about" earlier in the decade.[12]

Wald even tried to understand the thinking of the postsuffrage women on the issue of marriage and/or career. *Equal Rights* and the *Women's Journal* as well as the popular publications devoted much space to an examination of women's traditional role in the home. The feminists of Wald's generation discovered that many of their daughters chose not to decide between marriage and career, but rather to have both. By 1925, Wald modified somewhat her earlier thinking. Her secretary wrote for her:

> She sees no reason why talents, particularly creative contributions ... , should be lost to the world because of a woman's marriage. She has no doubt that being a mother and a good

one has strengthened the ability as well as the technique of
many an unusual woman.
Miss Wald sees the difficulties, however, of having two
careers. . . . Nevertheless, she has known remarkable women
who were able to manage both.[13]

Wald's views would hardly satisfy women who were neither
"unusual" nor "remarkable" and yet wished to combine two careers,
but essentially Wald was like many other women during this period
of transition—searching for a new position for females. It is open to
debate whether any solution to the question of women's role would
have been found if the Red-Baiting period had not curtailed the
time that could be devoted to it. Further steps to full equality were
more difficult to gain in the 1920s, and then some had to be postponed for a generation because of the depression of the 1930s.

Genevieve Parkhurst, in a perceptive article in *Harper's* written
in 1935, attributed the difficulties of feminists to the economic
problems of the Great Depression. After 1929, "economizing" frequently was translated into discharging married women regardless
of abilities or obligations. Discriminations in work and pay were always abundant, but during the depression, they were even more
widespread—even gaining government sanction—and fewer women
were able to establish themselves economically.[14] Sadly, the old feminists like Wald stood too silent as women lost many of the rights
they had struggled for in earlier years. While the National Woman's
Party and the League of Women Voters did protest, for the most
part, discriminations in work and pay were accepted if it meant
greater employment for men. The debate over women's role came to
an end as the public accepted as fact that unmarried females belonged in jobs traditionally described as "women's work," and married women belonged in the home so as not to provide competition
on the labor market.[15]

Women were successful in securing a few legislative victories after World War I and these achievements motivated historian Stanley Lemons to write that "the major current of American feminism,
'social feminism,' was slowed in the 1920's, but it neither failed nor
was destroyed."[16] Charlotte Perkins Gilman, in 1927, enumerated
"Woman's Achievements Since the Franchise" and included many of
the projects with which Wald was associated, including legislation
to make women eligible to serve on juries.[17] A second legislative
gain pertained to citizenship. Prior to the 1920s, married American women, even the native born, assumed the nationality of their
husbands. Thus females lost their citizenship upon marriage to
aliens while males, on the other hand, did not lose their rights

when married to foreigners. The Cable Act, passed as a result of a women's lobby, sought to remedy this inequity by giving women the right of individual citizenship and naturalization. The act of 1922, however, included provisions that continued discrimination against females, both American born and alien, particularly after the passage of the Immigrant Quota Law of 1924. Wald supported the Cable Act because the old law "expatriated [women] by marriage." Later, she sought improvements in the act to benefit such women as her friend Alice Lewisohn Crowley, who married an alien prior to 1922 and who lived overseas, so that these people would no longer lose their citizenship and would be able to reenter the United States without waiting for their nationality quota. In 1930 and 1931, the women were successful in amending the original Cable Act and thereby gaining a measure of parity in this area of citizenship and immigration rights.[18]

Wald gave her greatest energies to the effort to pass the Sheppard-Towner Maternity bill in 1921. This "measure for women, won by women" was the single example in the 1920s of the United States government's assumption of some responsibility for social welfare. Originally introduced in 1918 by Congresswoman Jeanette Rankin, it provided for federal funds and matching state monies to be used to promote maternal and infant health care. The Children's Bureau administered all operations on the national level, and in the states, advisory committees were established with women comprising at least half of the membership. All women were urged to support Sheppard-Towner to save the lives of thousands of mothers who would die in childbirth and the lives of babies under one year who would die because of the lack of trained care. The campaign for the legislation brought back memories of the prewar period. The Children's Bureau gathered statistics on infant mortality and disease and reform outlets like the *Survey* published the data. America's backward position among the nations of the world was stressed to the public and to the members of Congress, many of whom opposed the measure because it gave control to the bureau, which they claimed was staffed by "office holding spinsters."[19]

Proponents of Sheppard-Towner included almost all organized women's groups led by the Women's Joint Congressional Committee. Experienced lobbyists like Florence Kelley testified before a Senate hearing and Wald's views were expressed by Elizabeth Dines, a Henry Street nurse.[20] For Wald, the legislation was important for three reasons. It was a women's measure, it further recognized the responsibility of the state in welfare areas, and it gave additional powers to the public health nurses by charging them with instructing parents in maternal and infant hygiene. Julia Lathrop, chief of the bureau, wrote to Wald that the "public health nurse is essential to any plan of health welfare work, public or volunteer and here *you* are in a very strong position."[21] Given the increased responsibilities of the nurses, opposition to Sheppard-Towner came from a familiar source—physicians. For example, the *Illinois Medical Journal* reported that the legislation was sponsored by "endocrine perverts" and "derailed menopausics."[22] Wald answered the critics of the legislation—both medical and others—as she worked to have the maternity bill passed in Congress and later to have New York State enact an enabling measure. She emphasized the need for pre- and postpartum care and education. Both *fathers* and mothers, she said, want and need help in assuming the responsibility of caring for children. Simple education and attention by nurses, who would go into the homes, would save lives.[23]

The Sheppard-Towner Maternity and Infancy Protection Act was passed by Congress in 1921. Congressional appropriations to implement the legislation ran to 1927 and then were extended to 1929. The measure's success in promoting the welfare of mothers and babies did not prevent opposition to its renewal when funds were exhausted. Senator Bayard's charge that Sheppard-Towner was a feminist-socialist-communist conspiracy to nationalize American children was read into the *Congressional Record* and provided propaganda for the enemies of extension, who hoped not only to prevent reenactment of the maternity bill, but also to destroy the Children's Bureau by removing some of its power. The women again tried to rouse public support and national organizations like the League of Women Voters and the WTUL rushed to help with the effort. It became evident, however, that President Hoover would not fight for the renewal of Sheppard-Towner and that Congress, timid because of the Red-Baiting, was unwilling to pass a controversial measure in an election year (1930).[24] Wald sadly reported, "All those who know the plight of . . . mothers and their babies regret that the measure has lapsed."[25]

When the women's groups formed a unified front on matters like the Cable Act and Sheppard-Towner, they achieved a degree of success. When they divided on an issue, they accomplished little. A case in point is the Equal Rights Amendment (ERA), which has been a subject of controversy for over sixty years. The roots of the rift stretched back to the suffrage campaign when the Congressional Union, which became the National Woman's Party, differed in tactics and policy from the National American Woman's Suffrage Association. The militancy advocated by Alice Paul and her followers was repudiated by Catt and the other leaders of the NAWSA. Nevertheless, the women's movement held together for years and Catt contended that women were human beings with brains and convictions; they should not be expected to act as a unit.[26] The feminist movement had never been an ideological monolith. The goal of sexual equality was held by all, but different women envisioned different means to this goal. Late in her life, even Alice Paul admitted that the movement as "a sort of mosaic." Each woman "puts in one little stone, and then you get a great mosaic at the end."[27] Unfortunately, the attitude of mutual tolerance was strained in the 1920s on the issue of the ERA.

A new Woman's Party was formed in 1921, during a meeting held after the ceremonies to celebrate the installation of statues of Lucretia Mott, Elizabeth Cady Stanton, and Susan B. Anthony in the Capitol. Disagreements on plans for the ceremony led Harriot Stanton Blatch to describe Paul as "dictatorial" after she dismissed all the women, including Wald and Addams, from an arrangements committee.[28] Nevertheless, the Henry Streeter attended the convention as a delegate, as did Addams, who represented the WILPF, and Lavinia Dock, who represented the nurses. Another delegate, Freda Kirchwey of the *Nation*, recorded her impressions of the meeting. She pictured the leadership of the new NWP as a "veritable tank" that "rolled over the assembly, crushing protestants of all sorts." Issues like the participation of black women, birth control and disarmament, marriage and divorce laws were pushed aside. It seemed to Kirchwey and others that everything was to be subordinated so that a federal Equal Rights Amendment proposal could be introduced.[29]

All feminists wanted to remove sexual discrimination and improve the status of women. They could all support the general objectives of the proposed amendment—equality before the law regardless of sex—and it was undoubtedly tempting to all life-long feminists to endorse the ERA. Women like Florence Kelley had devoted years to fighting for equal opportunity in schools and professions, equal pay for equal work, and changes in marriage and divorce law, but they feared what the amendment would do to the protective labor legislation for women, which had been so hard-won and defended in the courts. The classic *Muller* v. *Oregon* decision of 1908 that upheld protective legislation for women on the ground that the future mothers of the nation required the special consideration of the state was being modified by the courts of the 1920s. Kelley would have preferred postponement of the ERA for the immediate future, and called the amendment position on labor legislation for women, "topsy turvy feminism."[30]

The introduction of the ERA in the Sixty-eighth Congress at the close of 1923 set off a debate that would continue for decades. Arguments were carried on the pages of the women's publications and in popular magazines as well. Opponents of the amendment regarded it as an additional handicap to the working woman who was unorganized or whose union was too weak to bargain equally. Union women believed in equal rights for women and men in industry and they hoped to remove economic handicaps from men, but they were unwilling to surrender the industrial progress they had already made. If the ERA passed, they said, women would lose and men would gain nothing. When, in the future, industrial women were stronger, they would not need special legislation. Until then, females needed the laws that guaranteed them decent hours and conditions of work.

The National Woman's Party claimed that an amendment was necessary to remove all legal disabilities from women. Piecemeal methods would not work. Protective legislation for women, while designed to help, really hampered because women were separated into a special caste with children and labeled "incompetent." Laws regulating wages, hours, and conditions of labor should cover both sexes and these laws would be passed for both as soon as sexual distinctions were removed from the law.[31]

The ERA was an issue until the end of Wald's life. While *Equal Rights*, the NWP publication, claimed that "one of the greatest assets of the . . . campaign was the genuine spirit of sex solidarity that had developed among women,"[32] for Wald, the amendment divided the women's network that had been welded together over the prewar decades. The women who worked together to professionalize nursing, for unionism and labor reform, for suffrage, peace, the Cable Act, and Sheppard-Towner found themselves on opposing sides on the question of the ERA. Differences had always existed, but they were now exacerbated and seemed more important. Zona Gale, the playwright and Wald's old friend, favored the amendment, as did Crystal Eastman of the WPP. The nurses were divided, with many of the "old girls" actively supporting the ERA. Wald was asked to speak to her friend to modify her views when Annie Goodrich, Dean of the Yale University School of Nursing, spoke as a representative of the professional woman in favor of the ERA.[33] Lavinia Dock chaired the Nurse's Council of the NWP and was a frequent contributor to *Equal Rights*. She felt keenly her separation "from old associates in the woman movement, and hard to differ from trade union friends, when one is still heart and soul in sympathy with labor," but she believed that women were adults and should not be linked with children in legislation.[34] Dock's letters to Wald frequently attempted to persuade her old comrade "that for women adults—protective sex laws are only a deception leading to all sorts of possible exclusions and segregations."[35]

Wald's conduct in relation to the Equal Rights Amendment is difficult to analyze. Her belief in the need for protective legislation was firm. Until women's unions were stronger, laws were needed to improve the standards of work. These laws would, she believed, raise the conditions of work for men as well, for women and men rise and fall together in the labor market. Given these sentiments, it is logical to assume that Wald would be among the strong opponents of the ERA, yet there is no record in her papers or writings on the measure until 1938. Congressional hearings on the amendment were held in 1924, 1925, 1929, 1931, 1932, 1933, and 1938, at which Florence Kelley, Rose Schneiderman, and representatives of the LWV and the WTUL testified against the amendment and hundreds of letters were included in the record. Yet the Henry Streeter did not speak up. There is no mention of Wald until 1938, when she wrote to Senator George Norris protesting the amendment.

> . . . I think I have always been . . . consistent. Ever since the Women's Party has suggested that theoretically women should be on equal terms with men, and have discarded the advantages that come to them for physiological reasons, I have been opposed to this phase of their law.
> For nearly 40 years I have promoted all the protective measures that women require in order to fulfill their duties as women and as mothers. I would be glad to have men have as much protection, but we certainly do require, until the millenium [sic] comes, such protection for them and so I am very much opposed to the equal rights amendment.[36]

At the same time, Wald wrote to Katherine Faville, head of the Visiting Nurse Service, urging her and the other nurses to oppose the amendment because it "would do great harm to many women."[37]

Several explanations of Wald's long silence are possible. The first, that her health precluded active participation in the anti-ERA movement, must be discarded after an examination of Wald's activities, since she remained at least partially involved in many other areas in those years. A second possible reason has greater validity. By the time of the 1938 congressional hearings, Florence Kelley, the most prestigious of the ERA foes, was no longer alive to carry on the fight and Wald, always loyal to her friends, believed that she had to lend her name to the opposition. To Faville, she explained, "I worked so hard and so did Mrs. Kelley and all our group at that time, to get protection for women and girls, and now fanatics—that's what I think they are—would destroy all we did!"[38]

If however, Wald felt that keenly the need to defeat the ERA, why didn't she speak out earlier? Given her practical mind, the most likely reason is that Wald never took the measure too seriously. . Many present-day historians place great importance upon the ERA as a factor in the death of feminism. William O'Neill claims that the leaders of both sides of the measure overreacted, and while the women were not far apart in ideology and membership, their intemperate language drove a lasting wedge between those for and those against the ERA.[39] Considering the quantity of material printed, the emphasis placed upon the amendment is understandable. It may be misleading, nevertheless, to use this as a measure of judgment, for the ERA does not appear to have permanently divided the women. They worked together in the same period for Sheppard-Towner and the Cable Act, to protect married women from being discharged from their jobs, for female jurors, and many other measures. Perhaps historian Clarke Chamber's assessment of the ERA fight offers the most valid explanation. He wrote, the amendment "squabble was of no particular significance—the proposed Amendment never had a chance of serious consideration."[40] It is likely that the pragmatic Wald realized this and saved herself for more productive campaigns. If the feminist movement declined after 1920, the causes are to be found in the economic conditions and social climate of the nation, not in the behavior of the feminists.

Wald should be faulted for her timing in entering the ERA debate. Kelley and the others who fought the amendment in the 1920s did so at a time when the administration and the courts were openly unsympathetic to the aims of working people. The year, 1923, for example, witnessed both the introduction of the ERA into Congress and the Supreme Court decision in *Adkins* v. *Children's Hospital*, which declared the minimum wage to be unconstitutional. But by the time Wald intervened, her friends were in power and New Deal legislation removed many of the arguments against the amendment. It would have benefitted women had Wald rethought her position. The ERA would have been defeated anyway, but she did not serve the feminist cause by criticizing it.

Any consideration of Wald's work after 1920 must include a knowledge of her health. If she personified the feminists of the Progressive era, a partial answer to the question of what happened after suffrage is that the women who provided leadership grew older, more tired, and had health problems which slowed their work. Time took its toll. As a young woman, Wald prided herself on superhuman energy and endurance but in the 1920s, she suffered a series of debilitating illnesses that curtailed her public performances and forced her to spend more and more time at her Connecticut home— away from her center of power, Henry Street. By 1933, she reluctantly retired from an active role in the Settlement and the Visiting Nurse Service.

The death of old comrades and loved ones was another blow. She mourned the losses of her mother, brother, Helen Dudley, Elizabeth Farrell, and Rebecca Shatz of the Settlement, Mr. and Mrs. Jacob

Schiff, Felix and Paul Warburg, Addams, and Kelley. It seemed that every year brought new grief. A note to Lavinia Dock gives evidence of Wald's frame of mind in 1932. "Dear Elizabeth Farrell could not overcome the pernicious anaemia and the bad heart. The line grows very thin when Florence Kelley and Elizabeth Farrell go within a few months of each other, and it is hard to face."[41]

As early as 1922, Wald confessed to being "pessimistic about my-self—I do not seem to accomplish anything, despite my perpetual motions."[42] She was "desperately tired," and the following spring, a trip to Mexico, which was supposed to restore her strength, resulted in an intestinal and bronchial infection.[43] Two years later, she had a hysterectomy which further drained her energy. Wald's letters to her friends during this period are filled with details of her medical condition. At no time was the importance of the women's network more evident than when they were ill, for they relied upon each other for comfort and help. Her friends gave Wald their support and urged her to *"really, truly honest to God,—Rest."*[44] They understood how disappointing it was for her to discover that "she had so little strength" and could not "tackle the universe."[45] When she felt well, Wald plunged back into action claiming that she felt "as young and ardent" as she "did more than thirty years ago."[46] Nevertheless, even she had to admit sometimes that she was growing older. "I woke up with a cold and a carbuncle, sixty years old and everybody knew it. Terrible!" she complained to Addams in 1927.[47]

The Great Depression came early to Henry Street. By the end of 1928, Wald reported that unemployment was growing, and that the situation "absorbs the greatest part of my time." The prosperity of the 1920s was unprecedented for a few, but it did not percolate down to the poor on the East Side, she said.[48] The records of the social workers and the Visiting Nurses were barometers of economic conditions and both groups now found the demands upon them greater than ever before. As their case loads increased because other agencies hit by the depression referred clients to Henry Street, the nurses and social workers also had to contend with salary cuts. In 1932, Wald wrote, "The worker who goes into the home to give financial relief or to watch over the health of the family must daily gird herself as though for battle." She wondered what kept the nurses going and how long they could continue with heavier work loads combined with the uncertainty brought on by decreased income.[49]

The depression created few personal financial problems for Wald, who lost little money in the crash, but all of the organizations with which she was associated were in trouble. She doubled her efforts in working for the unemployed and the children, and at the same time, she had to devote increased time to fundraising. Many former subscribers could no longer give as much money and some discontinued their donations. At one point, Wald and Felix Warburg threatened to curtail the services of the Visiting Nurses, who made 70,000 more calls in the first six months of 1932 than in a comparable period two years earlier, unless the city provided some money.[50] Wald's letters to her friends were filled with despair. She wrote to one,

> I don't know what we'll do unless we get more money, the situation is tragic. We have a bare one-third of our money, and we will just have to keep on asking people who gave small sums to give larger and talking, talking it all the time. It's the worst winter I have had, and I began, you know, in the terrible time of '93.[51]

And to another friend she said, "I think this is a good time for the social workers; the only people who seem to be employed,—Alas!"[52] The problem of raising money haunted Wald "by day and night." She became, in her last years, the high-powered executive for whom fundraising, which she had always hated, was an end unto itself.

Under the pressure of financing the Settlement and the need to watch the misery of the depression, Wald, who normally viewed the world with optimism, grew increasingly depressed. She told her friends that she was filled with "despondency," "discouragement," and "disappointment."[53] In 1931, she was forced to curtail her work "owing to low blood count,—and depression—and *weltschmerz*." Her efforts to slow down and become a "slacker" came to nothing, for "the jangle of the telephone nearly drove me wild," she wrote. "Not just the jangle, but because I knew it meant more problems for which I could offer no help." She could not escape, Wald wrote, "the depression that overcomes me."[54]

At the end of 1932, Wald was hospitalized for a complex illness caused by a congenital abnormality at the juncture of the stomach and the esophagus that created internal bleeding and anemia. Her recovery was slow, though she continued to hope "to be 100% in action soon."[55] This never came to pass, because in 1933, Wald suffered a heart attack and stroke, which resulted in a temporary facial paralysis, and loss of hair and speech. For a woman of Wald's vanity, these disfigurements were the source of great pain, which she cloaked with humor. She cautioned her secretary not to "refer unless necessary to my not being well. They might order crepe."[56] Wald wrote one friend that she was "ugly as sin,"[57] and described herself to Dr. Alice Hamilton as having lost "all hair including eyebrows, eyelashes, et cetera."[58] She could still say, however, "I will have lots of jokes to tell you about this illness."[59]

Wald never lost her interest in public affairs. She left the hospital to vote for Franklin Roosevelt in 1932, and strongly supported the New Deal. Writing to Frances Perkins to congratulate her and the president on the passage of the Social Security bill, Wald added, "I wish that Sister Kelley had been saved to know that. Her life would have been more happily ended."[60] Wald mourned for herself as well, because now that "her friends were in power," she was "not functioning one hundred per cent."[61]

Wald retired to her country home in Westport, Connecticut, never to return after 1932 to Henry Street, "to see . . . [her] beloved friends."[62] She learned to accept her physical disabilities, but insisted that there "was nothing wrong . . . from the neck up" and claimed that she was still "very young, part of me."[63] Her health continued to deteriorate and in 1937 she had another heart attack and stroke that further restricted her. She wrote of her condition that, "My chief trouble is that my tongue gets twisted when I talk and when you haven't legs nor a tongue you feel somewhat handicapped."[64] Herbert Lehman observed Wald in those years and remembered: "She failed quite noticeably in the last years of her life. Her memory wasn't very good. She wasn't able to do much work. She always remained a woman of great charm. She was really a great character."[65]

In 1933, Wald stepped down as Head Worker at Henry Street in favor of Helen Hall. The older woman was complimentary of Hall's ability and asked those with personal loyalties to her to help their new leader; nevertheless, it was difficult for Wald—despite her desire for a peaceable change of leadership—to surrender the power she had enjoyed for forty years. She confessed that "of course one is anxious about a beloved child that has taken life and more than life."[66] When difficulties arose in the Settlement in 1936, it brought Wald full circle. She had started her career as a nurse, dedicated to the autonomy of her profession, and at the end of her life she supported the nurses when they clashed with Hall on the same issue. The Visiting Nurses believed that they could not accept a lay person directing their activities, and Wald understood their arguments. While it might be difficult for Hall to comprehend, she wrote to her successor, the "nurses must speak for themselves."[67] The Henry Street Settlement was separated from the Visiting Nurse Service before Wald died on September 1, 1940. Two months later, twenty-five hundred people attended a Lillian Wald memorial service to pay tribute to the pioneer nurse, settlement worker, reformer, and feminist.[68]

A letter written by Paul Kellogg to Wald before her death can serve as a summary of her work. "Your youth and strength and hope and leadership bore fruit not only in practical accomplishments which will stand for all time, but in deepening and spreading your social insight and understanding as yeast in American life."[69] The women's revolution, like all movements for change, required propagandists to popularize the cause. Wald served this need for suffrage, trade unions for women, professionalization of nursing, the women's peace movement, and almost every other campaign to effect sexual equality. Many of her colleagues were better educated than Wald was. Without the learning (and possibly the intellect) of Kelley, Addams, or Balch, she never attempted to develop a philosophical rationale for her feminism. Instead, she relied upon her personal assets—understanding of people, public prestige, political wisdom—to persuade, lobby, and cajole for reforms that pragmatically she understood were only half-way measures. Only time and constant work would bring the "millennium" she envisioned.

Wald was instinctively a feminist. As a young woman, she violated the stereotype of a woman's place by becoming a nurse. In later life, she emerged as a model of what women could do in the public sphere. Critics can with some reason fault her for devoting too much time to fundraising and currying the favor of the powerful, for involving herself in too many causes, and for being tied to the Victorian ideology of her childhood prescribing marriage and motherhood for most women. Wald, however, understood the sources of her strength. Her power lay in the popularity and reputation she had gained through the Henry Street Settlement and the Visiting Nurse Service and these bases had to be maintained, so that her "wise council and public prestige" could be used to benefit the movements for social reform and equality for women.[70]

Wald and the other women of the Progressive era differed often in ideology and methods, but they were unusually tolerant in their acceptance of these differences. They—Addams, Kelley, Dock, Schneiderman, Goldman, Paul, Wald, and the others—had in common a feminist consciousness that responded to the challenge of the socialist journal, the *New York Call*, that the women "make sisterhood a fact."[71]

Notes

VNS   Archives of the Visiting Nurse Service of New
                York
WTUL   Women's Trade Union League

Introduction

1. Lillian D. Wald to Carolyn Van Bearcome, 25 January 1932, NYPL, Wald MSS. The Wald Biographical Material file includes a list of 255 groups to which Wald belonged in 1933, NYPL, Wald MSS.

2. Beatrice Forbes-Robertson Hale, *What Women Want: An Interpretation of the Feminist Movement* (New York: Fred A. Stokes, 1914), p. 3.

3. William O'Neill, *Everyone Was Brave: A History of Feminism in America* (Chicago: Quadrangle Books, 1969) made the distinction between the feminists that has been accepted by other historians such as J. Stanley Lemons, *The Woman Citizen: Social Feminism in the 1920's* (Urbana: University of Illinois Press, 1973) and William H. Chafe, *The American Woman: Her Changing Social, Economic and Political Roles, 1920–1970* (New York: Oxford University Press, 1972).

4. Lillian D. Wald, *The House on Henry Street* (New York: Henry Holt, 1915), p. 260.

5. "The Reminiscences of George Alger," COHC, pp. 243–59.

6. Wald to Mrs. John Wood Stewart, 6 September 1922, NYPL, Wald MSS.

7. Wald to Mrs. Hitchcock, 22 September 1910, NYPL, Wald MSS.

8. Wald, *Windows on Henry Street* (Boston: Little, Brown, 1934), p. 319.

9. John Elliott, Radio Speech, 10 April [?], NYPL, Wald MSS.

10. Wald to John Schiff, 8 February 1932, NYPL, Wald MSS.

11. Wald, *House on Henry Street*, p. 114.

12. Wald, *Windows*, pp. 3–4.

13. Elliott, Radio Speech, 10 April [?], NYPL, Wald MSS.

14. Wald to Mr. Loeb, 18 May 1916, NYPL, Wald MSS.

15. Allen Freeman Davis, *Spearheads for Reform: The Social Settlements and the Progressive Movement, 1890–1914* (New York: Oxford University Press, 1967), p. xii.

Chapter One

1. *New York Times,* 2 September 1940, p. 15.

2. Wald to Louis Marshall, 13 August 1903, NYPL, Wald MSS.

3. Wald to Helen Hall and Paul Kellogg, 11 November 1935; Wald to Marguerite Wales, 24 August 1936, NYPL, Wald MSS. Helen Hall, interview, 20 May 1975.

4. Wald to Lavinia Dock, 15 April 1931, NYPL, Wald MSS.

5. Wald to Mrs. L. C. McGlashan, 28 August 1925; Wald to Felix Warburg, 18 December 1932, NYPL, Wald MSS. Robert H. Bremmer, "Lillian

D. Wald," in *NAW,* 3: 526; Robert L. Duffus, *Lillian Wald: Neighbor and Crusader* (New York: Macmillan, 1938), pp. 3–4.

6. Bremmer, "Lillian Wald," p. 526; Duffus, *Lillian Wald,* pp. 1–4.

7. Robert Riegal, *American Feminists* (Lawrence, Kans.: University Press, 1968), p. 189; Sonya Rudikoff, "Women and Success," *Commentary* 58 (October 1974), p. 53.

8. Duffus, *Lillian Wald,* pp. 2–5; Beryl Williams, *Lillian Wald: Angel of Henry Street* (New York: Julian Messner, 1948), pp. 14–19.

9. *New York Times,* 2 September 1940, p. 15.

10. Duffus, *Lillian Wald,* pp. 2–12; Williams, *Lillian Wald,* pp. 13–25.

11. Wald to Dock, 8 January 1925; Wald to Samuel Schwarz, 15 February 1918; Wald to Florence Schwarz, 11 July 1914, 21 April 1915, NYPL, Wald MSS.

12. Wald to Karl Hesley, 17 April 1933, NYPL, Wald MSS.

13. Wald to Samuel Schwarz, 31 December 1919, NYPL, Wald MSS. Wald expressed the same thought in Wald to Y. G. Waters, 14 November 1919, NYPL, Wald MSS.

14. Wald to Anne O'Hare McCormick, 17 June 1931; Wald to Anna Woerishoffer, 10 December 1923; Wald to Eugene Kinckle, 9 July 1932, NYPL, Wald MSS.

15. Stuart Rosenberg, *The Jews of Rochester, 1843–1925* (New York: Columbia University Press, 1954), pp. 13–130; Blake McKelvey, "The Jews of Rochester: A Contribution to Their History During the Nineteenth Century," *PAJHS* 40 (September 1950), pp. 59–67; Wald to *The World,* 8 March 1919, NYPL, Wald MSS; Nathan Glazer, *American Judaism* (Chicago: University of Chicago Press, 1957), pp. 22–59; Blake McKelvey, *Rochester on the Genesee: The Growth of a City* (Syracuse: University Press, 1973), p. 58; Stephen Wise, *Challenging Years: The Autobiography of Stephen Wise* (New York: G. P. Putnam's Sons, 1949), p. 34.

16. Temple membership records for the late nineteenth century have been destroyed, but Berith Kodesh cemetery papers indicate that the Walds were members.

17. Wald to Asa Gallup, 8 April 1915; Gallup to Wald, 10 April 1915, NYPL, Wald MSS.

18. Wald to Mrs. William Jasspon, 20 May 1931, 1 June 1931; Wald to Mrs. William Hull, 22 May 1931, 1 June 1931, NYPL, Wald MSS.

19. Wald to Israel Zangwill, 13 November 1923; Zangwill to Wald, 19 November 1923, NYPL, Wald MSS; Moses Rischin, *The Promised City: New York Jews, 1870–1914* (Cambridge: Harvard University Press, 1967), p. 205. In *The Maimie Papers,* ed. Ruth Rosen and Sue Davidson (Old Westbury, N. Y., 1977), p. 307, Maimie, an admirer of Wald, expressed amazement that she was a Jew.

20. Wald to Madison Peters, 13 February 1918, NYPL, Wald MSS.

21. Wald to Mr. and Mrs. Musseys, 5 October 1931, NYPL, Wald MSS.

22. Dock to Wald, 24 April 1927, NYPL, Wald MSS. It would appear that the feminist Dock was guilty of lapses, too. Wald's secretary asked Dock why she had referred to the deity as him. "I should expect you to speak of the Lord herself." Eleanor Linton to Dock, 18 July 1933, NYPL, Wald MSS.

23. Rosenberg, *Jews of Rochester,* pp. 5–157; McKelvey, "Jews of Rochester," pp. 61–68; McKelvey, *Rochester,* p. 101.

24. Zosa Szajkowski, "The Attitude of American Jews to East European Jewish Immigration (1881–1893)," *PAJHS* 40 (March 1951), pp. 222–32; Rosenberg, *Jews of Rochester,* pp. 51–157; McKelvey, "Jews of Rochester," pp. 66–67; Oscar Handlin, "American Views of the Jew at the Opening of the Twentieth Century," *PAJHS* 40 (June 1951), pp. 323–44.

25. Emma Goldman, *Living My Life,* 2 vols. (1931; reprints, New York: Knopf, 1970), 1: 16.

26. Duffus, Notes on the Biography of Lillian Wald, n.d., in Wald Biographical Material, NYPL, Wald MSS; Duffus, *Lillian Wald,* pp. 24–25.

27. Wald to Harriet Barry, n.d. [1932], NYPL, Wald MSS; Duffus, *Lillian Wald,* pp. 1–15; Williams, *Lillian Wald,* pp. 19–25; Wald, *House on Henry Street,* p. 71; Wald to Duffus, 23 February 1937, NYPL, Wald MSS.

28. Wald's correspondence is filled with letters to her sister. After her second marriage, to Frank Cordley, Julia moved to Washington, D.C. and Wald was a frequent visitor in her home. For examples of Wald's letters to her nieces and nephews see Wald to Tom Barry, 10 January 1902, 7 December 1917, NYPL, Wald MSS; Wald to Lillian Wald Holmes, 15 May 1917, 27 December 1917, CU, Wald MSS.

29. Wald to Naomi Deutsch, 20 October 1927, NYPL, Wald MSS.

30. Duffus, *Lillian Wald,* pp. 1–15; Williams, *Lillian Wald,* pp. 18–30; Wald, *House on Henry Street,* p. 71.

31. Wald to John Foster Carr, 30 June 1920, NYPL, Wald MSS.

32. Gordon Haight, *George Eliot: A Biography* (New York: Oxford University Press, 1968), p. 5; Barbara Hardy, "Mill on the Floss," in *Critical Essays on George Eliot,* ed. Barbara Hardy (New York: Barnes and Noble, 1970), pp. 42–58.

33. George Eliot, *The Mill on the Floss,* 2 vols. (New York: Merrill and Baker, n.d.), 2: 362–63.

34. Allan E. Reznick, "Lillian D. Wald: The Years at Henry Street" (Ph. D. diss., University of Wisconsin, 1974), pp. 14–15. Reznick was able to obtain the 1882 prospectus of Miss Cruttenden's school.

35. Wald to George P. Ludlum, 27 May 1889, NYPL, Wald MSS.

36. Duffus, *Lillian Wald,* pp. 16–17; *New York Herald Tribune,* "Lillian Wald, Obituary," 3 September 1940, NYPL, Wald MSS; Thomas Woody, *A History of Women's Education in the United States,* 2 vols. (New York: Octagon Books, 1966), 2: 148, 179–82.

37. Wald as quoted in her obituary in the *New York Times,* 2 September 1940, p. 15.

38. Alger, COHC, p. 264. The description of Wald is taken from her passport of 17 January 1910, NYPL, Wald MSS.

39. Duffus, *Lillian Wald,* p. 16.

40. Wald to Madison Peters, 13 February 1918, NYPL, Wald MSS.

41. Alger, COHC, p. 265. Alger enjoyed carrying on an innocent flirtation with Wald over the years and she seemed to have been amused by the attentions of a younger man. Alger to Wald, 5 December 1914, 8 December 1914, 26 December 1914; Wald to Alger, 21 December 1914, NYPL, Wald MSS comprise a record of the incident with the unflattering photograph.

42. Wald to Rita Morgenthau, 3 December 1930, NYPL, Wald MSS.
43. Wald to Arthur Brisbane, 28 November 1932, NYPL, Wald MSS.
44. Wald to Owen Lovejoy, 1 March 1932, NYPL, Wald MSS.
45. Wald to Mr. Reznick, 18 April 1934, NYPL, Wald MSS.
46. Henry Street Residents to Wald, 1919, NYPL, Wald MSS.
47. Duffus, *Lillian Wald,* pp. 17–18; Williams, *Lillian Wald,* pp. 30–34.
48. Wald, Speech at the New York State Suffrage Convention, Rochester, New York, 15 October 1914, NYPL, Wald MSS.
49. Blake McKelvey, "Women's Rights in Rochester—A Century of Progress," *Rochester History* 10 (July 1948), pp. 1–24; Susan B. Anthony, Elizabeth Cady Stanton, and Ida Husted Harper, eds., *History of Woman Suffrage,* 6 vols. (1881–1922; reprint, New York: Source Book Press, 1970), 2: 627–715, 3: 395–443, 4: 1–31, 839–73; Rosenberg, *Jews of Rochester,* p. 112.
50. Vida Scudder, *On Journey* (New York: E. P. Dutton, 1937), pp. 77, 106.
51. David Reisman, "Two Generations," in *The Woman in America,* ed. Robert Jay Lifton (Boston: Houghton Mifflin, 1965), p. 76.
52. Wald to the new staff members of the Visiting Nurse Service, 12 December 1938, NYPL, Wald MSS.
53. Duffus, *Lillian Wald,* pp. 17–19.
54. Wald to the *New York American,* 20 June 1923, NYPL, Wald MSS.
55. Duffus, *Lillian Wald,* p. 19.
56. "The Reminiscences of Isabel Maitland Stewart," COHC, pp. 18–23.
57. Wald, Speech to Junior Auxiliary, "The Volunteer in Social Work," New York City, 19 October 1922, NYPL, Wald MSS.
58. Wald to George P. Ludlum, 27 May 1889, NYPL, Wald MSS.

Chapter Two

1. JoAnn Ashley, *Hospitals, Paternalism, and the Role of the Nurse* (New York: Teachers College Press, 1976), p. 19.
2. For almost forty years, Wald spoke and wrote about her work. Her speeches followed the same form and usually gave a brief history of nursing, an explanation of the work being done, and an appeal to talented young women to enter the field. For examples see Wald, "Rough Notes for Talk on Nursing," 1912; Speech at Johns Hopkins Hospital, 1 May 1918; Speech, "New Aspects of Old Social Responsibilities," Vassar College, 12 October 1915; Speech, "New Aspects of an Old Profession," Wellesley College, 1912; Speech, "History and Development of Nursing in Social Welfare Work," Columbia University, 1911, NYPL, Wald MSS. Where sections of the speeches are quoted below, they will be cited as Wald, Speeches on Nursing, rather than by the title of the individual address.
3. Wald, *Windows,* p. 76.
4. Wald, Speeches on Nursing, NYPL, Wald MSS.
5. Lavinia L. Dock, "Nurses' Debt to the Feminist Movement," *Equal Rights,* 17 August 1929, p. 221.

6. Michael Davis to Wald, 3 April 1916, NYPL, Wald MSS.

7. Charles Dickens, *Martin Chuzzlewit* (New York: Books Inc., n.d.), p. 471.

8. Florence Nightingale to *Macmillan's Magazine*, n.d. [1867]; Nightingale to Mr. Rawlinson, 8 October 1860, 16 February 1861; Nightingale to Mrs. C. C. Mathews, 7 November 1868 in *Letters of Florence Nightingale*, ed. Lois Monteiro (Boston: Boston University Nursing Archives, 1974).

9. Isabel Stewart and Anne Austen, *A History of Nursing* (New York: G. P. Putnam's Sons, 1962), p. 111. In "Florence Nightingale's Feminist Complaint: Women, Religion, and Suggestions for Thought," *Signs: Journal of Women in Culture and Society,* 6 (Spring 1981), pp. 395–412, Elaine Showalter writes of Nightingale's courageous fight to lead an independent life. Her critical attitude toward the women's rights movements often masked her support of women's emancipation from the duty of obedience.

10. Adelaide M. Nutting and Lavinia L. Dock, *A History of Nursing: The Evolution of Nursing Systems from Earliest Times to the Present,* 4 vols. (New York: G. P. Putnam's Sons, 1907–12), 2: 172–206.

11. The Society of the New York Hospital, *The School of Nursing of the New York Hospital: Fiftieth Anniversary, 1877–1927* (New York: Society of the New York Hospital, 1927), pp. 9, 51.

12. Wald, *House on Henry Street,* p. 26.

13. Nutting and Dock, *History of Nursing,* 3: 215.

14. Annie Goodrich, "To Explain Happiness," *AJN* 50 (October 1950), p. 598.

15. Wald, Speeches on Nursing, NYPL, Wald MSS.

16. Estelle Hall Speakman, "Womanliness in Nursing," *AJN* 3 (1902), p. 182.

17. Dock, "Nurses' Debt to the Feminist Movement," p. 221.

18. Stewart, COHC, pp. 31–35. Ashley, *Hospitals,* does not agree with Stewart and claims that most nurses were too timid and reluctant to fight as hard as they should have.

19. Dock as quoted in Stewart, COHC, p. 455. Wald used almost the same words in the manuscript of an article she wrote for *Good Housekeeping* (1932), NYPL, Wald MSS.

20. Dock, "Nurses' Debt to the Feminist Movement," p. 221; Stewart, COHC, pp. 119, 141–42; Wald to Helen Hall, 19 May 1936, NYPL, Wald MSS.

21. Wald to Mrs. Simon Flexner, 14 December 1931, NYPL, Wald MSS.

22. Wald, Speeches on Nursing, NYPL, Wald MSS.

23. Stewart, COHC, p. 139.

24. Dock to Wald, 12 December 1898, NYPL, Wald MSS.

25. Dock to Wald, 24 September 1904, CU, Wald MSS; Dock to Wald, 1 August 1933; Wald to Dock, 23 May 1918, 8 January 1925, NYPL, Wald MSS.

26. Dock to D. Baldy, 28 February 1909, NYPL, Wald MSS.

27. Dock to Wald, n.d. [ca. 1900], NYPL, Wald MSS.

28. Stewart, COHC, pp. 139–40.

29. Nutting, Speech for Barnard's Quarter Century Celebration, Barnard College, New York City, 29 April 1915, NYPL, Wald MSS.

30. Lillian Wald, "Adelaide Nutting," *AJN* 25 (June 1925), p. 450.

31. Teresa Christy, "M. Adelaide Nutting," *Nursing Outlook* 17 (January 1969), pp. 20–24; Wald to Nutting, 16 January 1912; Nutting to Mary S. Gardner, 11 October 1916, SL, Gardner MSS; Nutting to Wald, 8 November 1914, 5 February 1915, 28 October 1920, NYPL, Wald MSS.

32. Wald to Mrs. Munson, 16 May 1930, NYPL, Wald MSS.

33. Wald, "Comrade Annie W. G.," *The Henry Street Nurse* (May-June 1923); Goodrich to Wald, 29 May 1929, NYPL, Wald MSS.

34. Wald, Speeches on Nursing, NYPL, Wald MSS.

35. Dock to Wald [1918], NYPL, Wald MSS.

36. Nutting to Wald, 13 May 1929, NYPL, Wald MSS.

37. Wald to Dock [1920]; Wald to Marguerite Wales, 24 April 1936, NYPL, Wald MSS.

38. Wald to Edith White, 6 Janury 1923, NYPL, Wald MSS; Yssabella Waters, *Visiting Nursing in the United States* (New York: Charities Publication Committee, 1909), p. 13.

39. Wald, *Windows*, pp. 70–110; Wald, *House on Henry Street*, pp. 26–27; Lillian Wald, "District Nursing," *University Studies* 1 (October 1905–January 1906), pp. 136–37; Lillian Wald, "Development of Public Health Nursing in the United States," *The Trained Nurse and Hospital Review* (June 1928), pp. 689–92; Wald, Speeches on Nursing; Dr. C. E. A. Winslow, "Public Health Nurse," *Johns Hopkins Alumnae Magazine* (July 1934), NYPL, Wald MSS

40. Wald to Nutting, 13 May 1911; Nutting to Wald, 23 May 1911, TC, Nutting MSS.

41. Dr. C. E. A. Winslow, "The Influence of Lillian Wald Reaches Round the Earth," *Better Times* (1934), NYPL, Wald MSS.

42. Stewart, COHC, p. 149.

43. Wald to Agnes Leach, 10 March 1930, NYPL, Wald MSS.

44. Nutting to Wald, 8 November 1914, 28 October 1920, NYPL, Wald MSS.

45. Paul U. Kellogg, "A Pioneer Woman of the City Frontier," *New York Times Magazine*, 13 March 1927, p. 23.

46. Wald to Elizabeth Farrell, 14 September 1932, NYPL, Wald MSS.

47. Dock to Wald, 3 March 1918, NYPL, Wald MSS.

48. Stewart, COHC, pp. 24, 66. Ashley, *Hospitals*, pp. 76–80 emphasizes this point as does Susan Reverby, "The Search for the Hospital Yardstick: Nursing and the Rationalization of Hospital Work," in *Health Care in America: Essays in Social History*, ed. Susan Reverby and David Rosner (Philadelphia: Temple University Press, 1979), pp. 206–25.

49. Wald, *Windows*, p. 75.

50. Dock to Wald, 30 June [?], CU, Wald MSS.

51. Wald, Speeches on Nursing; Wald to editor of the *Evening Post*, 11 June 1918, NYPL, Wald MSS; Wald, *Windows*, pp. 72–73.

52. Dock to Wald, 4 March [?], CU, Wald MSS.

53. Wald, "Sickness at Home," 1907–1908, NYPL, Wald MSS.

54. Dock, "What We May Expect from the Law," *AJN* (October 1900), reprinted in *AJN* 50 (October 1950), p. 599.

55. Wald to Governor William Sulzer, 2 April 1913, CU, Wald MSS.

56. Wald to Herbert Croly, 27 November 1918; Wald to the editor of the *New York Tribune,* 6 February 1920; Wald to Dr. Livingston Ferrand, 20 March 1931, NYPL, Wald MSS.

57. Wald to L. S. Rowe, 20 October 1921, NYPL, Wald MSS.

58. Wald to Jane Delano, 24 April 1918, CU, Wald MSS.

59. Wald to Smith, 9 March 1920, NYPL, Wald MSS; Wald to Smith, 9 December 1927, 12 December 1927, 15 February 1926, 17 December 1927; Smith to Wald, 27 December 1923, 18 February 1926, 16 July 1926, 28 July 1926, 29 July 1926, 22 December 1927, FDRL, George Graves MSS.

60. Sarah Roosevelt to Marvin McIntyre, n.d., FDRL, FDR MSS.

61. Wald to Caroline O'Day, 25 February 1935; Wald to James Farley, 25 February 1935, NYPL, Wald MSS; Farley to Wald, 25 February 1935; Wald to Eleanor Roosevelt, 25 February 1935; Eleanor Roosevelt to Wald, 2 March 1935, FDRL, Eleanor Roosevelt MSS.

62. Wald to John Kingsbury, 13 December 1935, NYPL, Wald MSS.

Chapter Three

1. Duffus, *Lillian Wald,* pp. 22–25.

2. Wald to the editor of the *New York Times,* 28 February 1928, NYPL, Wald MSS.

3. Yssabella Waters to Wald, 9 September 1902, CU, Wald MSS; Wald, *House on Henry Street,* pp. 1–3.

4. S. J. Woolf, "Miss Wald Has Seen an Ideal Blossom," *New York Times,* 1 December 1929, p. 11. The same story is related in Wald, *House on Henry Street,* pp. 3–6; Nutting and Dock, *History of Nursing,* 3: 216–17; Wald, "A Brief Outline," March 1937, NYPL, Wald MSS.

5. Duffus, *Lillian Wald,* pp. 34–35; Wald, Speech to Judeans, 13 December 1931, NYPL, Wald MSS.

6. Wald, *House on Henry Street,* p. 8.

7. Wald, "Public Health in the Last Thirty Years," De Lamar Lecture, John Hopkins University, 2 March 1925, NYPL, Wald MSS.

8. Louis Harap, *The Image of the Jew in American Literature* (Philadelphia: The Jewish Publication Society of America, 1974), pp. 479–84.

9. Wald to Robert Moses, 19 February 1934; Wald to Fiorello La-Guardia, 1 March 1934; Wald, Speech, "Lower East Side Reminiscences," 23 January 1927; Wald, Speech, "Charles B. Stover, Memorial," 30 April 1929; Wald, Speech, "In Memory of Charles Stover," 4 May 1930; Wald, article for *Unity* magazine, 10 September 1928, NYPL, Wald MSS; Wald, *House on Henry Street,* pp. 279–82; Leonora O'Reilly, "Diary, 1896-May, 1898," SL, O'Reilly MSS; Charles Shively, "Leonora O'Reilly," in *NAW* 22: 651–53.

10. Wald, *House on Henry Street,* p. 10.

11. Vida Scudder, *On Journey* (New York, 1937), pp. 109–11, 136–43, 160.

12. Ramsay J. MacDonald, "American Social Settlements," *The Commons* 2 (February 1898), p. 4.

13. Rita W. Morgenthau, Radio Speech, 15 October 1953; Wald, "A Brief Outline," March 1937, NYPL, Wald MSS; Duffus, *Lillian Wald,* pp. 35–36.

14. Cyrus Adler, *Jacob H. Schiff: His Life and Letters* 2 vols. (New York: Doubleday, Doran, 1928), 1: 389–92; Wald to Carl C. Dickey, 24 December 1924, NYPL, Wald MSS.

15. "The Reminiscences of Bruno Lasker," COHC, 170–71.

16. Clarke A. Chambers, *Seedtime of Reform: American Social Service and Social Action, 1918–1933* (Minneapolis: University of Minnesota Press, 1963), p. 214.

17. Schiff quoted in Stephen Wise, *Challenging Years: The Autobiography of Stephen Wise* (New York, 1949) p. 101.

18. Adler, *Jacob Schiff,* 2: 341–57; Alger, COHC, pp. 259–60.

19. Adler, *Jacob Schiff,* 1: 358. Schiff left Wald $50,000 in his will, Executors of Schiff's Will to Wald, 23 September 1921, NYPL, Wald MSS. In addition, the family gave her $40,000 for her personal use during her lifetime and Mrs. Schiff willed her $50,000 in 1933. Wald used the bulk of these monies for the nurses and the Settlement.

20. Wald to Schiff, 14 July 1893, 24 July 1893, 25 July 1893, 29 July 1893, 4 July 1893, 29 August 1893, 2 October 1893, 3 November 1893, 28 November 1893, 4 January 1894, 22 January 1894, 4 March 1894, 2 February 1894, 1 October 1894, 11 October 1894, 11 November 1894, 8 December 1894, 1 November 1894, 11 February 1895, 26 March 1895, 10 April 1895, NYPL, Wald MSS. Other letters may be found in the Wald papers of the VNS. Wald's need for assurance and advice is well illustrated by the number of letters she wrote to Schiff in her first two years on the East Side.

21. Schiff to Wald, 7 March 1898 in Adler, *Jacob Schiff,* 1: 356.

22. Dock to Wald, 28 September 1920, NYPL, Wald MSS.

23. Riis to Wald, 9 November 1896, NYPL, Wald MSS; Adler, *Jacob Schiff,* 1: 385–88, 2: 228–31, 290.

24. Wald to Nutting, 16 October 1915, TC, Nutting MSS.

25. Wald to Schiff, 11 February 1895, NYPL, Wald MSS.

26. Schiff to Wald, May 1913 in Adler, *Jacob Schiff,* 1: 384–85; Schiff to Wald, 31 December 1912, NYPL, Wald MSS.

27. Paul Warburg to Wald, 2 July 1912, NYPL, Wald MSS.

28. Wald to Felix Warburg, 29 May 1917; Wald to Paul Warburg, 27 December 1917, NYPL, Wald MSS.

29. Wald to John Schiff, 8 January 1933, NYPL, Wald MSS.

30. Schiff to Wald, June 1902 in Adler, *Jacob Schiff,* 1: 384.

31. *Report of the Henry Street Settlement, 1893–1913,* published by the Henry Street Settlement (New York, 1913); *Report of the Henry Street Settlement, 1893–1918,* published by the Henry Street Settlement (New York, 1918). NYPL.

32. Wald to James Loeb, 17 May 1912, NYPL, Wald MSS.

33. Allan Nevins, *Herbert H. Lehman and His Era* (New York: Scribner's, 1963), pp. 77, 31; "The Reminiscences of Herbert Lehman," COHC, pp. 34, 146–51, 187–90.

34. Wald to Lehman, 27 March 1928, 17 April 1928, NYPL, Wald MSS.

35. Wald to Louis Abrons, 21 April 1925, NYPL, Wald MSS; Benjamin Schoenfein, interview, 10 June 1975; Betty Friedman, interview, 20 June 1975; Clara Rabinowitz, interview, 6 May 1979; Laurie Johnston, "Some Brokers Have Achieved Landmark Status," *New York Times*, 30 November 1980, pp. 1R, 6R.

36. Allen Freeman Davis, *American Heroine: The Life and Legend of Jane Addams* (New York: Oxford University Press, 1973), p. 70.

37. Wald, *House on Henry Street*, p. 11.

38. Wald, *Windows*, pp. 229–30.

39. Wald, *House on Henry Street*, p. 17; Wald, *Windows*, pp. 55–56; Wald, interview with Mrs. Georgiana Beaver Judson, in the Bridgeport *Sunday Post*, 4 June 1939, p. 5, NYPL, Wald MSS.

40. Wald to Mrs. Josephine Bowen, 17 December 1932, NYPL, Wald MSS.

41. Alice Henry, "Life and Letters of Josephine Shaw Lowell," *Life and Labor* (July 1914): 196–200.

42. Schiff to Brewster, 17 November 1894 in Adler, *Jacob Schiff*, 1: 383; Wald, *House on Henry Street*, p. 81; Duffus, *Lillian Wald*, pp. 56–57.

43. Frances Hackett, "The Permanent War," *New Republic*, 8 January 1916, p. 255.

44. Duffus, *Lillian Wald*, p. 25.

45. Lasker, COHC, pp. 178–79.

46. Wald to Calvin Coolidge, 12 December 1923; Wald to Mrs. L. Meyer, 21 November 1932; Wald, Speech, "Americanism," 1 March 1919; Wald, Speech, "The Interpretive Value of the Settlements," 12 April 1909, NYPL, Wald MSS.

47. Wald to Schiff, 29 July 1893, 4 January 1894; Dock to Wald, 1905, NYPL, Wald MSS; Elizabeth Hasanovitz, *One of Them: Chapters from a Passionate Autobiography* (Boston: Houghton Mifflin, 1918), pp. 85–86.

48. Rose Cohen, *Out of the Shadow* (New York: George Doran, 1918), p. 276.

49. Samuel Joseph, "Jewish Mass Immigration to the United States," in *Trends and Issues in Jewish Social Welfare in the United States, 1899–1952*, ed. Michael Freund and Robert Morris (Philadelphia: The Jewish Publication Society of America, 1966), pp. 15–23; Wald to Solomon Lowenstein, 19 February 1931, NYPL, Wald MSS.

50. Schoenfein, interview, 10 June 1975; Rabinowitz, interview, 6 May 1979; Hasanovitz, *One of Them*, p. 73.

51. Cohen, *Out of the Shadow*, pp. 230–32, 248–53.

52. Wald, De Lamar Lecture (2 March 1925), NYPL, Wald MSS.

53. Wald to Karl Hesley, 5 December 1932, NYPL, Wald MSS.

Chapter Four

1. Wald, *Windows*, p. 10.

2. Dock to Wald, 5 March 1927, NYPL, Wald MSS.

3. Wald to Herrman, 8 July 1924, NYPL, Wald MSS.

4. Allan Nevins, *Herbert Lehman and His Era* (New York: Scribner's 1963), p. 78.

5. "The Reminiscences of Frances Perkins," COHC, p. 169.

6. Wald, *House on Henry Street*, pp. 163–68.

7. Theodore Roosevelt to Wald, 5 January 1909; Lehman to Wald, 24 December 1910, NYPL, Wald MSS; Lillian Wald, "Need for a Federal Children's Bureau," *Supplement to the ANNALS* 33 (March 1909), pp. 23–28; James A. Tobey, *The Children's Bureau: Its History, Activities and Organization* (Baltimore: Johns Hopkins University Press, 1925), pp. 1–5.

8. Wald to James Loeb, 17 May 1912, NYPL, Wald MSS.

9. Wald, Speech at a dinner for Dr. Felix Adler, 3 February 1922, NYPL, Wald MSS.

10. *Woman Voter,* May 1912, p. 20.

11. Nancy Weiss in Susan Tiffin, *In Whose Best Interest? Child Welfare Reform in the Progressive Era* (Westport, Conn.: Greenwood Press, 1982), p. 237.

12. Lovejoy to Wald, 8 October 1924; Wald to Lovejoy, 15 October 1924; Wald to Smith, 7 January 1924, NYPL, Wald MSS.

13. Kelley to Wald, 17 February 1927, 4 April 1927, NYPL, Wald MSS.

14. Wald to Sen. Robert Wagner, 11 February 1928; Wald, "Memo for Sen. Wagner," 11 February 1928, CU, Wald MSS; Wald to Sen. Wagner, 14 March 1932; Wald to Sen. Royal Copeland, 15 March 1932; Wald to Women's City Club, 11 January 1933; Wald to Agnes Leach, 11 January 1933; Wald to Alger, 11 January 1933; Wald to Perkins, 29 June 1933; Wald to Gen. Hugh Johnson, 17 July 1933; Wald to Gov. Lehman, 17 December 1934; Wald to the editors of the *New York Post,* the *Daily News,* and the *World Telegram,* 29 January 1935, NYPL, Wald MSS offer only a sample of Wald's activities in favor of the elimination of child labor during this period.

15. Wald, Speech, "History of the Children's Bureau," to the National Conference of Social Work, 18 May 1932, NYPL, Wald MSS.

16. Allen Freeman Davis, *Spearheads for Reform: The Social Settlements and the Progressive Movement, 1890–1914* (New York: Oxford University Press, 1967), p. 84.

17. Wald, *House on Henry Street,* pp. 161–63.

18. Wald, *Windows,* p. 49.

19. Wald, *House on Henry Street,* p. 162.

20. Lasker to Wald, 29 April 1926, 30 November 1927; Wald to Lasker, 30 April 1926, 2 December 1927, CU, Wald MSS.

21. Wald to John Collier, 13 May 1931; Wald to Roger Baldwin, 13 March 1931; Wald to A. A. Berle, Jr., 19 March 1931; Wald to Mrs. Meredith Hare, 7 May 1931, NYPL, Wald MSS.

22. Ruth Logan Roberts, Speech at Citizen's Committee of New York City Award Meeting, 5 March 1937, NYPL, Wald MSS.

23. John Johnson, Wald Memorial Service, 1 December 1940, NYPL, Wald MSS.

24. Lehman, COHC, p. 150.

25. Nurse quoted in Louise M. Fitzpatrick, *The National Organization for Public Health Nursing, 1912–1952: Development of a Practice Field* (New York: National League for Nursing, 1975), p. 35.

26. Alger, COHC, pp. 248–50.

27. Helena H. Smith, "Lillian Wald: Rampant But Respectable," *New Yorker,* 14 December 1929, p. 32; Lasker, COHC, pp. 186–87.

28. Warburg as quoted in Alger, COHC, pp. 258–59.

29. Perkins, COHC, pp. 324–27.

30. Floyd Dell, *Women as World Builders: Studies in Modern Feminism* (Chicago: Forbes, 1913) p. 34.

31. Alger, COHC, pp. 251–56.

32. Smith, "Lillian Wald," pp. 33–36.

33. Wald, Speech, New York State Suffrage Convention, Rochester, New York, 15 October 1914, NYPL, Wald MSS.

34. Duffus, Notes on the Biography of Lillian Wald, in Wald Biographical Material, NYPL, Wald MSS.

35. Wald, "Women in the Campaign," *New York Evening Post,* 3 November 1913, NYPL, Wald MSS.

36. Louis Ougust and Jane Hitchcock, in *Henry Street Settlement Journal* 2 (November 1906), p. 1.

37. Wald, *Windows,* pp. 59–60.

38. Alice Lewisohn Crowley, *The Neighborhood Playhouse* (New York: Theater Arts Books, 1959), p. 36.

39. Wald to Hylan, 22 December 1917, NYPL, Wald MSS.

40. Wald, Speech, Women's City Club of New York City, 7 December 1917, NYPL, Wald MSS.

41. Wald to Hughes, 3 March 1909, NYPL, Wald MSS; Robert F. Wesser, *Charles Evans Hughes: Politics and Reform in New York, 1905–1910* (Ithaca: Cornell University Press, 1967), pp. 302–39.

42. Wald, *House on Henry Street,* pp. 290–94.

43. *Equal Rights,* 18 August 1928, p. 219; Allen F. Davis, "Crystal Eastman," in *NAW,* 1: 543–45.

44. Wald, Obituary, "T. R., The Social Worker," *Survey,* January 1919 (n.p., n.d.); Wald to H. Hagedorn, 22 May 1920,, NYPL, Wald MSS.

45. Moskowitz to Wald, 2 August 1912, NYPL, Wald MSS.

46. Jane Addams, "The Progressive Dilemma: The New Party," *American Magazine* 75 (November 1912): 14.

47. Jane Addams, *The Second Twenty Years at Hull House, September, 1909 to September, 1929* (New York: Macmillan 1930), p. 33.

48. Dreier to Wald, [1912], NYPL, Wald MSS. Other friends, like Addams, Leo Arnstein, and Henry Moskowitz, also sought to coax Wald into the Progressive party.

49. Wise to Wald, 24 August 1912, NYPL, Wald MSS.

50. Addams to Wald, 15 August 1912, NYPL, Wald MSS; Addams, *Second Twenty Years,* pp. 35–37.

51. Wise to Wald, 24 August 1912, NYPL, Wald MSS.

52. Morgenthau to Wald, 8 August 1912, NYPL, Wald MSS.

53. Wald to Harriman, 10 August 1912, 12 August 1912; Wald to Morgenthau, 12 August 1912, NYPL, Wald MSS.

54. Roosevelt to Wald, 9 July 1914, NYPL, Wald MSS.

55. Wald to Goldmark, 12 May 1914, 19 August 1914; Wald to Mrs. E. H. Harriman, 8 August 1914; Wald to Herbert Parsons, 28 May 1914; John P. Mitchel to Wald, 26 October 1914, NYPL, Wald MSS.

56. Wald (through her secretary) to Mrs. C. C. Rumsey, 20 January 1919, NYPL, Wald MSS.

57. Perkins, COHC, pp. 435–44.

58. Wald to Mary MacDowell, 27 September 1928, NYPL, Wald MSS.

59. Wald and Elliott to _____ , [this was a form letter to U.S. welfare workers. The recipient's name was filled in individually.] 29 September 1928, NYPL, Wald MSS. *Equal Rights,* the organ of the National Woman's Party, applauded Smith's appointment of women but endorsed Hoover because Smith favored special protection for women, and the *Life and Labor Bulletin,* published by the National WTUL, was critical of Smith because of his position on the Child Labor Amendment. One friend who did back Wald's stand was Lavinia Dock, who did not believe that Hoover was "honest" on the question of women's rights, Dock to Wald, 23 October 1928, 16 September 1928, NYPL, Wald MSS.

60. Wald to Addams, 18 September 1928, NYPL, Wald MSS.

61. Wald to Oswald Garrison Villard, 22 October 1928, NYPL, Wald MSS.

62. Addams to Wald, 20 September 1928; Breckinridge to Wald, 2 October 1928; Wald to Taylor, 25 October 1928; Wald to Julian Mack, 4 October 1928, NYPL, Wald MSS.

63. Kellogg to Wald, 1 October 1928, NYPL, Wald MSS.

64. Wald to Villard, 22 October 1928, NYPL, Wald MSS.

65. Wald to Mary R. Smith, 14 September 1928, NYPL, Wald MSS.

66. Wald to Ramsay MacDonald, 7 November 1928; Wald to Dr. G. E. Sehlbrede, 8 September 1928, 14 September 1928, NYPL, Wald MSS.

67. Wald to Lehman, 14 March 1931, NYPL, Wald MSS.

68. Wald to Elizabeth Farrell, 14 September 1932; Wald to Harriett Barry, 14 September 1932; Wald to Katherine Biggs McKinney, 19 September 1932; Wald to Charles C. Burlingham, 21 September 1932; Wald to Irene Lewisohn, 21 September 1932; Wald to Sam Schwarz, 23 September 1932; Wald to Walter Lippman, 29 September 1932; Wald to Arthur Sulzberger, 29 September 1932; Wald to the *New York Times,* 29 September 1932; Wald to the *Brooklyn Eagle,* 29 September 1932; Wald to Lehman, 26 July 1932, 5 October 1932; Wald to Dock, 12 November 1932, NYPL, Wald MSS.

69. Wald to Mrs. William A. McLaren, 7 July 1932; Wald to Mr. and Mrs. Warren Eberle, 29 October 1932; Wald to Dock, 24 October 1932, NYPL, Wald MSS.

70. Wald to Alice Crowley, 27 July 1932; Wald to McLaren, 27 July 1932; Wald to Sophonisba Breckinridge, 11 August 1932; Wald to E. Roosevelt, 18 August 1932; Wald to Mrs. James Roosevelt, 11 October 1932, NYPL, Wald MSS.

71. While this letter was written during the 1936 election, the statement expressed Wald's feelings in 1932 as well. Wald to Felix Warburg, 24 July 1936, NYPL, Wald MSS.

72. Wald to Lehman, 6 October 1928, NYPL, Wald MSS.

73. Wald to Ishbel MacDonald, 14 December 1932; Wald to Ramsay Mac-Donald, 30 January 1933, NYPL, Wald MSS.

74. Amy G. Maher to Dewson, 22 March 1932, SL, Dewson MSS.

75. A. A. Berle in interview in the *New York Times,* 23 November 1933. Wald makes the same point in *Windows,* pp. 319–20.

76. Wald to Agnes Leach, 30 December 1932; Wald to E. Roosevelt, 20 March 1933; Wald to Perkins, 9 March 1933; Wald to Lehman, 17 December 1934, NYPL, Wald MSS; Wald to E. Roosevelt, 25 November 1935; E. Roosevelt to Wald, 3 December 1935, FDRL, Eleanor Roosevelt MSS; Frances Perkins, *The Roosevelt I Knew* (New York: Viking Press, 1946), p. 78.

77. Wald to A. A. Berle, 26 July 1937, FDRL, Berle MSS.

78. Wald, "Why I Am For Roosevelt," [1936], NYPL, Wald MSS.

79. Susan Ware, *Beyond Suffrage: Women in the New Deal* (Cambridge: Harvard University Press, 1981), pp. 16–17.

80. Arthur Schlesinger, Jr., *The Politics of Upheaval* (Boston: Houghton Mifflin, 1966), pp. 438–40. Wald was pained by Smith's conversion from liberalism in the 1930s and wrote to Berle that she "felt that I had attended a funeral and I don't think there will be a resurrection here," Wald to Berle, 5 February 1936, FDRL, Berle MSS.

Chapter Five

1. Wald to Henry Moskowitz, 3 January 1933, NYPL, Wald MSS.

2. Dreier to Wald, 1925, NYPL, Wald MSS.

3. Wald to Nina Warburg, 16 March 1923, NYPL, Wald MSS.

4. Wald to Nathan, 18 October 1932, NYPL, Wald MSS.

5. Wald to Mrs. Schiff, 16 October 1932, NYPL, Wald MSS.

6. Wald to Page Cooper, 11 January 1926, NYPL, Wald MSS.

7. Wald to Dock, 1 October 1926, NYPL, Wald MSS.

8. Wald to James Loeb, 6 January 1910, NYPL, Wald MSS.

9. Waters to Wald, n.d., CU, Wald MSS.

10. Clara Rabinowitz, interview, 6 May 1979.

11. Alice Lewisohn Crowley, *The Neighborhood Playhouse* (New York: Theater Arts Books, 1959), pp. 5–8.

12. *Henry Street Settlement Journal* 25 (10 March 1928), p. 1.

13. Carole Klein, *Aline* (New York: Harper & Row, 1979), pp. 57–67. Aline Bernstein's fame as a scenic designer is now eclipsed by her relationship with the novelist Thomas Wolfe.

14. Helen Hillard to Wald, 30 June 1905, CU, Wald MSS.

15. "At Last," 10 March 1909, CU, Wald MSS.

16. Ellen Condliffe Lagemann, *A Generation of Women: Education in the Lives of Progressive Reformers* (Cambridge: Harvard University Press, 1979), p. 100.

17. Perkins, COHC, pp. 200–201.

18. Addams to Wald, 4 June 1917; Wald to Smith, 29 May 1918, NYPL, Wald MSS are only two of the many letters with the same general theme. Alice Hamilton to Agnes Hamilton, 26 November 1896 in Barbara Sicherman, *Alice Hamilton: A Life in Letters* (Cambridge: Harvard University Press, 1984), p. 127, claims that Addams believed that Henry Street had the "true settlement atmosphere."

19. O'Sullivan to Wald, 3 March 1919, NYPL, Wald MSS.

20. Wald to Allen, 14 November 1922, LC, Allen MSS.

21. Wald to Hamilton, 13 March 1919, NYPL, Wald MSS.

22. Wald to Kate Ladd, 24 August 1932, NYPL, Wald MSS.

23. Wald to Mary O'Sullivan, 4 March 1931, NYPL, Wald MSS.

24. Wald to Walker, 5 November 1930, NYPL, Wald MSS.

25. Wald to Hoover, 14 June 1930, NYPL, Wald MSS.

26. Wald to Paul Cravath, 14 November 1930, NYPL, Wald MSS.

27. Lenroot as quoted in Jill Conway, "Grace Abbott," in *NAW,* 1:4.

28. Wald to Perkins, 23 November 1932, NYPL, Wald MSS.

29. Wald to "no salutation," 23 November 1932, NYPL, Wald MSS.

30. Wald to FDR, 18 December 1932, NYPL, Wald MSS.

31. Wald to Breckinridge, 30 December 1932, NYPL, Wald MSS.

32. Wald, Speech to the Women's League for Peace and Freedom, 12 January 1931; Wald, "Jane Addams," *Unity,* 17 June 1935; Wald, Speech at Town Hall, New York City, 1929; Wald to Nobel Prize Committee, 16 January 1923; Wald to Viscount Takahashi and family, 17 March 1923, NYPL, Wald MSS; Lillian Wald, "An Afterword" in *Forty Years at Hull House* by Jane Addams (New York: Macmillan, 1935).

33. James Weber Linn to Wald, 25 January 1936, NYPL, Wald MSS.

34. Addams to Wald, 8 November 1920; Wald to Addams, 10 November 1920, NYPL, Wald MSS.

35. Rita Morgenthau, Radio Speech, 15 October 1953, NYPL, Wald MSS.

36. Alger, COHC, pp. 269–72.

37. Kelley to Wald, 11 January 1909, CU, Wald MSS.

38. Kelley quoted in Clarke A. Chambers, *Seedtime of Reform: American Social Service and Social Action, 1918–1933* (Minneapolis: University of Minnesota Press, 1963), p. 47.

39. Wald, Speech before the Memorial Meeting of the NAACP, Washington, D.C., 20 May 1932, NYPL, Wald MSS; Wald, *Windows,* pp. 42–44, 329–30.

40. Florence Kelley, "My Philadelphia," *Survey,* 1 October 1926, pp. 7–11, 50–57; "When Co-education Was Young," *Survey,* 1 February, 1927, pp. 557–61, 600–602; "My Novitiate," *Survey,* 1 April 1927, pp. 31–35; "I Go to Work," *Survey,* 1 June 1927, pp. 271–74, 301. Kelley wrote this series of articles that detailed her life when she was under attack by "patriot" groups in the Red Scare period of the 1920s.

41. Wald, *Windows,* p. 43.

42. Kelley to Dewson, 17 February 1924, SL, Dewson MSS.

43. Kelley to Nicholas or John Kelley, n.d., CU, Kelley Family MSS.

44. Kelley to Caroline Kelley, 16 July 1901, 1 May 1904; Mary Smith to Kelley, 25 August [?], CU Kelley Family MSS; Wald to Kelley, 11 April 1901; Sister Henrietta [?] to Kelley, 31 January 1917, NYPL, Kelley Family MSS.

45. Maud Nathan, *The Story of an Epoch Making Movement* (Garden City, N.Y.: Doubleday, Page, 1926), pp. 54–56. Wald and Addams were opposed to Kelley taking the post with the NCL, and she made the decision without "family blessing." See Kelley to Wald, 24 January, 1899, 23 March 1899; Addams to Wald, 13 February 1899, NYPL, Wald MSS.

46. Wald, *House on Henry Street*, pp. 243–47; Wald *Windows*, pp. 258–61; Addams to Wald, 31 December 1910, 25 January 1919; Wald to Breshkovsky, 27 February 1919; Blackwell to Wald, 15 March 1913, 7 September 1915, 26 April 1919, 21 January 1929, CU, Wald MSS represent only a few of the letters exchanged. References to Breshkovsky can also be found in Emma Goldman, *Living My Life*, 2 vols (1931, reprint, New York: Knopf, 1970) Vol 1: 1, 359–64, 2: 661–63 and in various editions of *Life and Labor* and *Woman Citizen*.

47. Wald to Dreier, 14 July 1933, NYPL, Wald MSS.

48. Goldman, *Living My Life*, 1: 160; Alix Kates Shulman, ed., *Red Emma Speaks: Selected Writings and Speeches by Emma Goldman* (New York: Vintage Books, 1972), pp. 176–85.

49. Wald to Goldman, 16 December 1910; Goldman to Wald, 12 November 1904, November [1904], 29 November 1910, 15 December 1910[?], NYPL, Wald MSS; newspaper clipping (masthead removed), 14 November 1920; Addams to Wald, 17 September 1901, CU, Wald MSS.

50. Wald to editor of *Justice*, 13 January 1911, CU, Wald MSS; Wald to R. W. Gilder, 24 June 1909, 14 July 1909, NYPL, Wald MSS.

51. Emma G. Smith [Goldman] to Wald, November [1904], 12 November 1904, NYPL, Wald MSS.

52. H. Weinberger to Wald, 12 May 1928, CU, Wald MSS.

53. Goldman to Wald, 15 December [1910], NYPL, Wald MSS.

54. James R. McGovern, "Anna Howard Shaw: New Approaches to Feminism," *Journal of Social History* 3 (Winter 1969–70): 133–53.

55. Gordon Haight quoted in Allen Freeman Davis, *American Heroine: The Life and Legend of Jane Addams* (New York: Oxford University Press, 1973), p. 46.

56. Doris Faber, *The Life of Lorena Hickok, E. R.'s Friend* (New York: William Morrow, 1980).

57. Blanche Wiesen Cook, "Female Support Networks and Political Activism: Lillian Wald, Crystal Eastman, Emma Goldman," *Chrysalis* 3 (Autumn 1977): 48.

58. Gerda Lerner, "Where Biographers Fear to Tread," *Women's Review of Books* 4 (September 1987): 11–12.

59. Balch to Wald, 26 September 1924, NYPL, Wald MSS.

60. Wald to Waters, 30 April 1917, 4 October 1917, NYPL, Wald MSS.

61. Wald to Kelley, 4 April 1921, NYPL, Wald MSS.

62. Wald to Dock, 22 June 1932, NYPL, Wald MSS.

63. Wald to Abbott, 25 May 1932, NYPL, Wald MSS.

64. Arthur to Wald, n.d., CU, Wald MSS.

65. Wald was only one of many women who could inspire devotion. Lavinia Dock addressed Alice Paul as "My Beloved Diety," in Dock to Paul, 9 May 1945 as cited in Leila J. Rupp, "The Women's Community in the National Woman's Party, 1945 to the 1960s," *Signs* 10 (Summer, 1985): 732.

66. Wald to Glenn Koenig, [1920], NYPL, Wald MSS.

67. Carroll Smith-Rosenberg, *Disorderly Conduct* (New York: Oxford University Press, 1985), pp. 245–69, writes of the interest in lesbianism and its study by Sigmund Freud, Havelock Ellis, and Richard Krafft-Ebing. It is unlikely that Wald was unaware of attitudes toward homosexuals.

68. Ibid., 53–76.

69. Davis, *American Heroine*, p. 306.

70. Alger, COHC, p. 250.

71. Helen Hall, interview, 20 May 1975.

72. Vida Scudder, *On Journey* (New York: E. P. Dutton, 1937), pp. 213–14.

73. Kittredge to Wald, n.d., CU, Wald MSS.

74. Goldman quoted in Cook, "Female Support Networks," p. 57.

Chapter Six

1. Wald to Kennedy, 5 September 1912, VNS.

2. Wald, "Are Women Happier Than They Used to Be?" for the *Forum,* but not sent, October 1928, NYPL, Wald MSS.

3. Wald, Speech, "New Aspects of Old Social Responsibilities," Vassar College, 12 October 1915; Wald, Speech, "What Business Are Women About," at Annual Meeting of New York Nurses' Association, 20 October 1915; Wald, Speech at Columbia University, 29 October 1915; Gertrude Barnum, "Memorandum" provided the outlines for the 1915 speeches on women and feminism; Wald, Speech, "Women and Politics," 13 September 1920; Wald, Speech, "Social Work and Training of Volunteer Social Workers," National Conference of Social Work, 6 March 1923, NYPL, Wald MSS.

4. Wald, Speech, "What Business Are Women About"; Wald, Speech, "New Aspects," NYPL, Wald MSS.

5. Wald, Speech at Manhattan Trade School, 15 April 1924, NYPL, Wald MSS.

6. Wald, "Are Women Happier?" NYPL, Wald MSS.

7. Wald to Nina Warburg, 14 November 1930; Wald to Eva Von Baur of the *Evening Sun,* 3 August 1915; Wald, interview in the *New York Times,* 11 July 1910, p. 11, NYPL, Wald MSS.

8. Emma Addams to Wald, 23 July 1915; Wald to McDowell, 26 July 1915; Wald quoted in the *Chicago Herald,* 29 July 1915; McDowell to Wald, 4 August 1915, TC, Nutting MSS.

9. Nutting to Wald, 8 October 1914, NYPL, Wald MSS.

10. Wald, *House on Henry Street,* pp. 268–69.

11. Wald, Speech, "New Aspects"; Wald, Speech, "Social Possibilities of Club Work," n.d.; Wald, Speech, "What Business Are Women About"; Wald,

Speech, "Social Work and Training"; Wald to Edithe C. Strauss, 2 December 1919, NYPL, Wald MSS.

12. Wald, Speech, "Social Possibilities," NYPL, Wald MSS.

13. Wald, Speech, "Disarmament," 11 November 1931, NYPL, Wald MSS.

14. Wald to Mr. and Mrs. Sylvan Bier, 20 October 1931, NYPL, Wald MSS.

15. Mary Agnes Hamilton, *Margaret Bondfield* (New York: Thomas Seltzer, 1925), pp. 184–85.

16. Wald to John Kingsbury, 25 April 1923, NYPL, Wald MSS.

17. Wald to Robert Foerster, 14 February 1913, NYPL, Wald MSS.

18. Wald, Testimony before the New York State Commission on Widowed Mothers' Pensions, *Report on the Relief for Widowed Mothers* (Albany, 1914), p. 32.

19. Wald, interview, [1928], NYPL, Wald MSS.

20. Wald, *Windows*, pp. 147–49; Wald, "Best Way to Help the Immigrant," 1907, NYPL, Wald MSS.

21. It is worth noting that both Margaret Sanger and Emma Goldman used their experiences as nurses and midwives on the East Side as the motivation for their interest in birth control.

22. Goldman, *Living My Life,* 2: 553–57, 569–70; Goldman, "Marriage and Love," in Shulman, *Red Emma Speaks,* 158–67.

23. Linda Gordon, *Woman's Body, Woman's Right: A Social History of Birth Control in America* (New York: Penguin Books, 1977), pp. 159–85; Carl N. Degler, *At Odds: Women and the Family in America from the Revolution to the Present* (New York: Oxford University Press, 1980), pp. 195–209; David M. Kennedy, *Birth Control in America: The Career of Margaret Sanger* (New Haven: Yale University Press, 1970), 173–87.

24. Wald to Knopf, 22 September 1916, CU, Wald MSS.

25. Wald to Juliet Barrett Rublee, 29 October 1920, NYPL, Wald MSS.

26. Sanger to Wald, 20 April 1921, 11 October 1921; Wald to Sanger, 14 October 1921, CU, Wald MSS.

27. Dock to Wald, 15 October 1921, NYPL, Wald MSS.

28. Wald to Sanger, 25 February 1929, 2 October 1931; Sanger to Wald, 9 March 1929, 1 October 1931, 5 October 1931, CU, Wald MSS.

29. Wald to Chedwick, 23 June 1932, NYPL, Wald MSS.

30. Marguerite Wales, "Memo for Miss Wald," 22 June 1932; Wales, "Bulletin to Supervisors, Re: Birth Control Policy," 10 January 1934, VNS.

31. Degler, *At Odds,* pp. 231–32.

32. Richard Drinnon, *Rebel in Paradise: A Biography of Emma Goldman* (New York: Bantam Books, 1973), p. 206.

33. Wald to Lehman, 17 Decmeber 1934, NYPL, Wald MSS.

34. Wald to Karl Hesley, 5 December 1932, NYPL, Wald MSS.

35. Wald, *Windows,* p. 333.

36. Inez Haynes Irwin, "These Modern Women: The Making of a Militant," *Nation,* 1 December 1926, p. 555.

37. Scudder, *On Journey,* 212–13.

38. Wald to Rosamond Walling, 19 August 1932, NYPL, Wald MSS.

39. Wald to Hsui Lan, 29 September 1930, NYPL, Wald MSS.

40. Kellogg to Wald, n.d., CU, Wald MSS.

41. Degler, *At Odds,* pp. vi-vii, 144–65, 436–37.

42. Dock to Wald, 24 September [1904], CU, Wald MSS shows Dock's attitude about women retiring to the home.

43. Dock to Wald, 30 September 1931, 30 August 1931; Dock to Eleanor Linton [Wald's secretary], 2 July 1933, NYPL, Wald MSS.

44. Wald to Dock, 2 October 1931, NYPL, Wald MSS.

45. Addams, *Second Twenty Years,* pp. 196–98.

Chapter Seven

1. Wald, Speech at Manhattan Trade School, 24 April 1924, NYPL, Wald MSS.

2. Hamilton quoted in Allen Freeman Davis, *Spearheads for Reform: The Social Settlements and the Progressive Movement, 1890–1914* (New York: Oxford University Press, 1967), p. 103.

3. Wald, Speech, "Some Social Values of the Settlement," 2 December 1908, NYPL, Wald MSS.

4. [George Alger?], "Florence Kelley," February 1932, NYPL, Wald MSS.

5. Wald, article for the *Princetonian,* 17 January 1922, NYPL, Wald MSS.

6. Wald, *House on Henry Street,* pp. 201–4.

7. Wald, "Summary of Our Federal Activities," NYPL, Wald MSS; Davis, *Spearheads for Reform,* pp. 133–35.

8. Leonora O'Reilly, "Dairy, 1896-May, 1898," SL, O'Reilly MSS.

9. Rose Cohen, *Out of the Shadow,* (New York: George Doran, 1918), p. 85.

10. Lewis Levitzki Lorwin [Louis Levine], *The Women's Garment Workers: A History of the International Ladies Garment Workers Union* (New York: B. W. Huebsch, 1924), pp. 144–47; Mabel Hurd Willett, *The Employment of Women in the Clothing Trade* (New York: Columbia University Press, 1902), p. 73.

11. Cyrus Adler, *Jacob H. Schiff: His Life and Letters,* 2 vols. (New York: Doubleday, Doran, 1928), 1: 291.

12. Wald to Schiff, 1 November 1894, 11 November 1894, NYPL, Wald MSS.

13. Adler, *Jacob Schiff,* 1: 389, 292–93.

14. Wald, *Windows,* p. 117.

15. Schiff to Wald, 27 November 1910, CU, Wald MSS.

16. Wald, *House on Henry Street,* pp. 282–83.

17. Ibid., 220–28.

18. The section on labor is a distillation of Wald's ideas expressed in Wald, "Miss Wald's Remarks on the Resolutions Offered by the Committee of Fifteen," 16 October 1919; Wald, Speech, "Carroll Club—Re: Trade Unionism," n.d.; Wald, "Memorandum for Miss Amy Maher," n.d.; Wald, Speech, "Crowded Districts of Large Cities," [1894/1895]; Wald, Speech, "Interpreting the Immigrant," Council of Jewish Women, Baltimore, Maryland,

26 February 1911; Wald, Speech, "Utilizing the Immigrant," Free Synagogue, New York City, 22 December 1907; Wald, Speech at Manhattan Trade School, NYPL, Wald MSS; Wald, "House on Henry Street, pp. 156–57, 200–13; Wald, *Windows,* pp. 23–26, 326–27.

19. Wald, Speech at Manhattan Trade School, NYPL, Wald MSS.

20. Wald, article for the *Princetonian,* NYPL, Wald MSS.

21. Wald, Speech, "Crowded Districts," NYPL, Wald MSS.

22. Wald, Speech, "Carroll Club," NYPL, Wald MSS.

23. Wald, Speech, "Immigrant Women in New York," to Brooklyn Consumers' League, 11 January 1911, NYPL, Wald MSS.

24. Ibid.; Wald, Speech, "Interpreting the Immigrant;" Wald, "Russian Jewish Immigrant," *American Hebrew,* 14 April 1911, NYPL, Wald MSS; Wald, *House on Henry Street,* pp. 204–10.

25. Wald, Speech, "Crowded Districts"; Wald, article for the *Princetonian;* Wald, Speech, "Carroll Club," NYPL, Wald MSS.

26. Wald, "Organization among Working Women," *ANNALS 27 (May 1906): 638–45.*

27. Wald, article for the *Princetonian,* NYPL, Wald MSS; Wald, *House on Henry Street,* pp. 207–8.

28. "Proposed Constitution of the WTUL," 1907, attached to letter, Margaret Robins to Wald, 19 August 1907, CU, Wald MSS.

29. Nancy Schrom Dye, "Feminism or Unionism? The New York Women's Trade Union League and the Labor Movement," *Feminist Studies* 3: (Fall 1975): 111–25.

30. Robin Miller Jacoby, "Feminism and Class Consciousness in the British and American Women's Trade Union Leagues, 1890–1925," in *Liberating Women's History: Theoretical and Critical Essays,* ed. Berenice A. Carroll (Urbana: University of Illinois Press, 1976), pp. 137–60; Nancy Schrom Dye, "Creating a Feminist Alliance: Sisterhood and Class Conflict in the New York Women's Trade Union League, 1903–1914," *Feminist Studies* 2 (Fall 1975): 24–38.

31. Dock to Harriett W. Laidlow, n.d. SL, Laidlow MSS.

32. Mary E. Dreier, *Margaret Dreier Robins: Her Life, Letters, and Work* (New York: Island Press Cooperative, 1950), pp. 96–97.

33. Wald to Eleanor Roosevelt, 8 June 1929, NYPL, Wald MSS.

34. WTUL, "Annual Report," 1906–1917 gives clues to the contribution of Henry Streeters; for example, the largest contributors to the union in 1908, after the Dreier sisters, were the Lewisohns. Another source is the WTUL file in CU, Wald MSS.

35. Wald, *House on Henry Street,* p. 207.

36. Lorwin, *The Women's Garment Workers,* pp. 12–85, 144–67; Alice Henry, *The Trade Union Woman* (New York: D. Appleton, 1915), pp. 89–95; "The 1909 Strike," n.d., SL; Rose Schneiderman with Lucy Goldthwaite, *All for One* (New York: Paul S. Erikson, 1967), pp. 89–96.

37. Pearl Rose, "After the Victory," *Woman Voter,* September 1914, p. 9.

38. Wald, *House on Henry Street,* pp. 209–10; Schneiderman with Goldthwaite, *All for One,* p. 92.

39. Lorwin, *The Women's Garment Workers,* pp. 158–59.

40. Rose, "After the Victory," p. 10.

41. Roosevelt to Michael A. Schaap, 24 January 1913 in Elting E. Morison and John M. Blum, eds., *The Letters of Theodore Roosevelt*, 8 vols. (Cambridge: Harvard University Press, 1951), 7: 696–701.

42. Melvyn Dubofsky, *When Workers Organize: New York City in the Progressive Era* (Amherst: University of Massachusetts Press, 1968), p. 65; Lorwin, *The Women's Garment Workers*, pp. 168–95, 466–73, 218–32.

43. Henry Moskowitz, "The Power for Constructive Reform in the Trade Union Movement," *Life and Labor*, January 1912, p. 10–15; Wald, "Sanitary Control of an Industry by the Industry Itself," *Transactions of the Fifteenth International Congress on Hygiene and Demography* (Government Printing Office, Washington, D.C., 1913), 3: 881–90.

44. Elizabeth Hasanovitz, *One of Them: Chapters from a Passionate Autobiography* (Boston: Houghton Mifflin, 1918), p. 220.

45. Wald, "Sanitary Control," pp. 881–90.

46. Lorwin, *The Women's Garment Workers*, pp. 468–73; Hasanovitz, *One of Them*, pp. 147–54.

47. Wald, Speech to Cincinnati Woman's Club, October 1915, NYPL, Wald MSS.

48. Sidney Lens, *The Labor Wars: From the Molly Maguires to the Sitdowns* (Garden City, N.Y.: Anchor Press, 1974), pp. 195–216; Melvyn Dubofsky, *We Shall Be All: A History of the Industrial Workers of the World* (Chicago: Quadrangle Books, 1969), pp. 227–62.

49. Wald, *House on Henry Street*, pp. 278–79; Wald, *Windows*, pp. 18, 25–26.

50. Addams to Wald, 6 March 1912, CU, Wald MSS.

51. Wald to Dock, 22 December 1926, NYPL, Wald MSS.

52. Wald to Schneiderman, 17 February 1932; Sally Green to Wald, 24 August 1927, 12 October 1927; Wald's secretary to Green, 27 August 1927; Wald to Green, 13 October 1927, NYPL, Wald MSS.

53. Wald, "Organization among Working Women," pp. 638–645.

54. Josephine C. Goldmark, *Fatigue and Efficiency: A Study in Industry* (New York: Russell Sage Foundation, 1919); Goldmark, "The Study of Fatigue and Its Application to Industrial Workers," *Transactions of the Fifteenth International Congress on Hygiene and Demography* (Washington, D.C.: Government Printing Office, 1913), 3: 517–26.

55. Perkins in *Life and Labor*, April 1919, p. 77.

56. Wald, Speech, "Invasion of Women," 4 February 1909; Wald, Speech, "Health Laws, A Pressing Need," American Association for Labor Legislation, December 1920, NYPL, Wald MSS.

57. Eyewitness account related to Hasanovitz, *One of Them*, pp. 216–19.

58. Wald, *House on Henry Street*, pp. 208–9.

59. Matthew Josephson and Hannah Josephson, *Al Smith: Hero of the Cities, A Political Portrait Drawing on the Papers of Frances Perkins* (Boston: Houghton Mifflin, 1969), p. 128.

60. New York State Legislature, *Preliminary Report of the Factory Investigating Commission*. 3 vols. 1 March 1912. 3: pp. 1731–48. New York State Legislature, *Second Report of the Factory Investigating Commission*. 4 vols. 1913. 4: pp. 1563–71.

61. New York State Legislature, *Third Report of the Factory Investigating Commission.* 1914. pp. 2–21. New York State Legislature, *Fourth Report of the Factory Investigating Commission.* 5 vols. 1915. 1: pp. 10–13.

62. Wald to Abbot E. Kittredge, 29 October 1903, NYPL, Wald MSS.

63. Wald, *House on Henry Street,* pp. 171–76; Wald to Theodore Roosevelt, 9 April 1913, NYPL, Wald MSS; Wald to Maude E. Miner, 7 April 1913; Miner to Wald, 8 April 1913, CU, Wald MSS. Ruth Rosen, *The Lost Sisterhood: Prostitution in America, 1900–1918* (Baltimore: Johns Hopkins University Press, 1982) offers evidence that questions many of Wald's assumptions about the causes of prostitution.

64. Wald, Speech, "Immigrant Women in New York;" Wald, Speech, "Danger Surrounding the Young Immigrant Girl," Buffalo, New York, 16 June 1909, NYPL, Wald MSS. Egal Feldman, "Prostitution, the Alien Woman and the Progressive Imagination, 1910–1915," *American Quarterly* 19 (Summer 1967): 192–206 contends that the movement against prostitution was nativist in origin. It would explain why protectors of the immigrant like Wald sought to show that the alien woman was a helpless victim.

65. Beatrice Forbes-Robertson Hale, *What Women Want: An Interpretation of the Feminist Movement* (New York: Fred A. Stokes, 1914), pp. 88–89.

66. Roy Lubove, "The Progressive and the Prostitute," *Historian* 24 (May 1962): 308–30.

67. Catt, "The Traffic in Women," *Woman Voter,* March 1913, pp. 14–15.

68. Wald to Rockefeller, 21 October 1910, CU, Wald MSS.

69. Wald, "Testimony before the Legislative Committee on Prostitution," 27 February 1913, NYPL, Wald MSS.

70. Blackwell to Wald, 15 March 1913; Wald to Hamilton Holt, 16 November 1910; Wald to William Ivins, 6 September 1910, CU, Wald MSS; Blackwell, "The Legislature and the Social Evil," *Woman Citizen,* 18 January 1919, p. 687.

Chapter Eight

1. *Life and Labor,* January 1918, p. 5.

2. Harriot Stanton Blatch and Alma Lutz, *Challenging Years: The Memoirs of Harriot Stanton Blatch* (New York: G. P. Putnam's Sons, 1940), p. 210.

3. Anthony et al., *History of Woman Suffrage,* 6: 453, 486; Eleanor Flexner, *Century of Struggle: The Woman's Rights Movement in the United States* (Cambridge: 1923; reprint, Harvard University Press, Belknap Press, 1976), pp. 256–62; National WTUL, "Proceedings of the Third Biennial Convention," 12–17 June 1911, Boston, Massachusetts, pp. 42–46.

4. Perkins, COHC, pp. 192–93; Carrie Chapman Catt and Nettie Rogers Shuler, *Woman Suffrage and Politics: The Inner Story of the Suffrage Movement* (Seattle: University of Washington Press, 1970), pp. 280–99.

5. Catt to Wald, 11 September 1909, NYPL, Wald MSS.

6. Wald to Catt, 13 September 1909, NYPL, Wald MSS.

7. Catt to Wald, 29 September 1909, NYPL, Wald MSS.

8. "Minutes of the New York City Woman Suffrage Party," Carnegie Hall, New York, 29 October 1909; "Minutes of the New York City Woman Suffrage Party," 15 January 1910, CU, NYC WSP MSS; Ronald Schaffer, "The New York City Woman Suffrage Party, 1909–1919," *New York History* 43 (July 1962): 269–87.

9. Anthony et al., *History of Woman Suffrage,* 6: 451–63; Catt and Shuler, *Woman Suffrage and Politics,* pp. 280–92; Catt, "Plan of the Campaign of 1915," NYPL, Catt MSS.

10. Duffus, *Lillian Wald,* p. 170.

11. Wald to Helen Hall, 19 May 1936, NYPL, Wald MSS.

12. Ethel M. Adamson to Wald, 27 January 1915, NYPL, Wald MSS.

13. S. Adolphus Knopf, M.D., "Why I Believe in Woman Suffrage," *Woman Voter,* November 1911, p. 1–8.

14. Mrs. Barclay Hazard, Speech, "How Woman Can Best Serve the State," New York Federation of Women's Clubs, 30 October 1907, NYPL, Wald MSS.

15. Wald, Speech, "Women in the Campaign," reported in the *Evening Post,* 3 November 1913, NYPL, Wald MSS.

16. *Henry Street Settlement Journal,* December 1909, p. 8.

17. Wald to George Foster Peabody, 21 May 1912; Wald to Sylvia Pankhurst, 15 June 1912; Pankhurst to Wald, 30 April 1912; Peabody to Wald, 14 May 1912, 25 May 1912; Henry Moskowitz to Pankhurst, 17 May 1912, NYPL, Wald MSS.

18. Wald to Duffus, 2 November 1937, NYPL, Wald MSS; Wald, *Windows,* pp. 46–47.

19. Doris Stevens, *Jailed for Freedom* (New York: Boni and Liveright, 1920), pp. 143, 358.

20. Wald to Dock, 31 August 1917, 23 October 1917, 4 January 1916; Dock to Wald, 19 September 1917; W. Gwynn Gardiner to Wilson, 9 November 1917, NYPL, Wald MSS; Dock to Wald, 26 December [?], CU, Wald MSS.

21. Wald, [Speech?], no title, n.d.; Wald, "Why You Should Vote for Woman Suffrage," *New York World,* 26 October 1915, NYPL, Wald MSS.

22. Duffus, *Lillian Wald,* p. 113.

23. Alan P. Grimes, *The Puritan Ethic and Woman Suffrage* (New York: Oxford University Press, 1967), pp. 72–117; Schaffer, "NYC Woman Suffrage Party," pp. 269–74.

24. Edward Alsworth Ross, "American and Immigrant Blood," *Woman Voter,* January 1914, pp. 11–12.

25. Stanton and Shaw as quoted in Aileen S. Kraditor, *The Ideas of the Woman Suffrage Movement, 1890–1920* (New York: Columbia University Press, 1965), pp. 126–29.

26. Schaffer, "NYC Woman Suffrage Party," p. 274.

27. Catt to the editor of the *New York Times,* 23 November 1914, NYPL, Catt MSS.

28. Olivia Coolidge, *Women's Rights, the Suffrage Movement in America, 1848–1920* (New York: E. P. Dutton, 1967), p. 100.

29. Schaffer, "NYC Woman Suffrage Party," p. 275.

30. Josephine Goldmark, *Impatient Crusader* (Urbana: University of Illinois Press, 1953), p. 67.

31. Harry Roskolenko, *The Time That Was Then: The Lower East Side, 1900–1914, An Intimate Chronicle* (New York: Dial Press, 1971), p. 216.

32. Duffus, *Lillian Wald,* p. 134; Robert Archey Woods and Albert J. Kennedy, eds., *Handbook of Settlements* (New York: Arno Press, the *New York Times,* 1970), p. 206.

33. William O'Neill, *Everyone Was Brave: A History of Feminism in America* (Chicago: Quadrangle Books, 1969), pp. 94–95.

34. Goldmark, Boradcast Address, 10 April [?], NYPL, Wald MSS.

35. O'Reilly to Wald, 1 May 1913, NYPL, Wald MSS.

36. Wheeler, Notes for Debate against Mrs. Blatch, 1916; Wheeler to John S. Roberts, 25 February 1916; Wheeler to editor of the *Churchman,* 17 April 1917, NYPL, Wheeler MSS.

37. Wald to Wheeler, 17 February 1914, NYPL, Wald MSS.

38. Catt to the Speakers in the New York Campaign, 9 October 1915, NYPL, Catt MSS.

39. Wald, *House on Henry Street,* pp. 266–68; Wald, "Why You Should Vote for Woman Suffrage"; Wald, Speech, "The Foreign Vote," Equal Suffrage League of New York City, Hotel Astor, 5 December 1913; Wald, Speech, "Concerning the Ignorant Vote," Columbia University, 29 October 1915; Wald, Speech, "Mothering a Community," New York Woman's Suffrage Association, Rochester, 15 October 1914, NYPL, Wald MSS are representative of Wald's activities during the suffrage fight.

40. Elizabeth McCracken, "Woman Suffrage in the Tenements," *Atlantic Monthly* 96 (December 1905): 750–59.

41. Wald, Speech, "Mothering a Community"; Wald, Speech, "Concerning the Ignorant Vote," NYPL, Wald MSS; Wald, *House on Henry Street,* pp. 267–68.

42. Wald to the *Jewish Daily Mail,* 16 October 1917; Wald, Speech to the Educational Alliance, New York City, 21 March 1915, NYPL, Wald MSS.

43. *Woman Voter,* June 1914, p. 24; April 1915, p. 20; June 1915, p. 22; August 1915, p. 21; *New York Times,* 29 October 1915, p. 5.

44. Dock, "Suffrage on the East Side," *Woman Voter,* March 1911, p. 3; *Woman Voter,* July 1911, p. 12; April 1915, p. 20; February 1913, p. 33; March 1913, p. 33; May 1915, pp. 14–16. Dock did report that the Italians and Irish were the most difficult to convert to the cause.

45. Catt to Upstate Leaders, 1 April 1915, NYPL, Catt MSS.

46. *New York Times,* 28 October 1915, p. 5; 30 October 1915, p. 4.

47. Wald, *House on Henry Street,* p. 266.

48. Anthony et al., *History of Woman Suffrage,* 6: 474; *New York Times,* 4 November 1915, p. 2.

49. *New York Times,* 4 November 1915, p. 3.

50. Wald to the editor of the *New York Times,* 4 November 1915, NYPL, Wald MSS.

51. Abram Lipsky, "The Foreign Vote on Suffrage," *American Hebrew,* 26 November 1915, NYPL, Wald MSS.

52. Catt to All Chairmen, 4 November 1915, 5 November 1915, NYPL, Catt MSS; Catt and Shuler, *Woman Suffrage and Politics,* pp. 294–99.

53. "New Status of Suffrage," *Nation* 13 July 1916, pp. 28–29; *Woman Citizen,* 14 September 1918, p. 308; 3 November 1917, p. 432; 5 October

1918, pp. 366–67; Ida H. Harper in interview in the *Chicago Daily News,* 13 December 1915, SL, Harper MSS; Arthur S. Link, *Wilson: The New Freedom* (Princeton: University Press, 1956), pp. 257–59; John D. Buenker, "The Urban Political Machine and Woman Suffrage: A Study in Political Adaptability," *Historian* 33 (February 1971): 264–79.

54. Laidlow to Wald, 21 December 1916; Wald to Laidlow, 28 December 1916; Anne Watkins to Wald, 22 January 1917; Wald to Mary G. Hay, 20 January 1917, 24 January 1917, NYPL, Wald MSS. Wald was only one of many Vice-Chairmen for Manhattan and she later asked that Borg also be given the title as a reward for her work.

55. Wald to Borg, 27 February 1917, 10 March 1917; Wald to Vera Whitehouse, 6 March 1917; Wald to Hay, 30 November 1917; Wald to Watkins, 30 June 1917; Watkins to Wald, 11 June 1917, NYPL, Wald MSS.

56. "Report of the Eighth Congress of the International Woman Suffrage Alliance," 6–12 June 1920, pp. 212–13, NYPL, Catt MSS.

57. Wald to Vera Whitehouse, 26 February 1917, 6 March 1917, NYPL, Wald MSS.

58. Melvyn Dubofsky, "Organized Labor in New York City and the First World War, 1914–1918," *New York History* 42 (October 1961): 380–400.

59. *New York Times,* 8 November 1917, pp. 1–3; Anthony et al., *History of Woman Suffrage,* 6: 465–67; *Woman Citizen,* 10 November 1917, pp. 449–51.

60. Wald to Addams, 13 November 1917, NYPL, Wald MSS.

61. *Woman Citizen,* 10 November 1917, p. 451.

62. Wald to Addams, 13 November 1917; Wald to Hay, 30 November 1917, NYPL, Wald MSS.

63. Wald, "Memorandum in Regard to Civic Education for Woman Voters," November 1917; Wald, Notes to Henry Street Staff Meeting, 16 November 1917; Wald to Jean Norris, 26 November 1917; Wald to Borg, 14 November 1917, NYPL, Wald MSS.

64. Wald, Speech, "Women in Politics," 13 September 1920; Wald to Iva Clyde Clarke, 21 January 1920, NYPL, Wald MSS.

65. Carrie Chapman Catt, "Woman Suffrage, The First Ten Years," *New York Times Magazine,* 24 August 1930, pp. 3, 16; Florence Allen, "The First Ten Years," *Woman Journal,* August 1930, pp. 5–7, 30–32; Emily Newell Blair, "Are Women a Failure in Politics?" *Harper's Monthly Magazine* 150 (October 1925): 513–22.

66. Wald, "Why You Should Vote for Woman Suffrage," *New York World,* 26 October 1915; Wald to the *Jewish Daily Mail,* 16 October 1917, NYPL, Wald MSS.

67. Helen Hall, interview, 20 May 1975.

Chapter Nine

1. Marie Louise Degen, *The History of the Woman's Peace Party* (Baltimore: Johns Hopkins University Press, 1939), pp. 11–16; C. Roland March-

and, *The American Peace Movement and Social Reform, 1898–1918* (Princeton: University Press, 1972), pp. 186–87.

2. Jane Addams, *Peace and Bread in Time of War* (New York: Macmillan, 1922) pp. 3–22.

3. Wald, *Windows,* p. 337.

4. Sondra R. Herman, *Eleven against the War: Studies in American Internationalist Thought, 1898–1921* (Stanford: Hoover Institution Press, 1969), p. 138.

5. Emmeline Pethick-Lawrence, "Motherhood and War," *Harper's Weekly,* 5 December 1914, p. 542; Degen, *Woman's Peace Party,* pp. 24–37.

6. Dock to Wald, 19 May 1918, NYPL, Wald MSS.

7. *New York Herald,* 30 August 1914, p. 1.

8. Mercedes M. Randall, *Improper Bostonian: Emily Greene Balch* (New York: Twayne Publishing, 1964), p. 7.

9. Wald, *Windows,* pp. 285–99; Duffus, *Lillian Wald,* pp. 150–58: Minutes of the Executive Committee of AUAM, 29 November 1915–24 October 1916, SCPC, AUAM.

10. Wald, Speech, "Women and War," Cooper Union, New York, February 1915; Wald, Speech, "What Business Are Women About," 20 October 1915; Wald, Discussion of Emily Balch's paper "The Status of Women in War" delivered at the American Sociological Society Convention, Washington, D.C., 29 December 1915, NYPL, Wald MSS.

11. Addams, *Second Twenty Years,* p. 136.

12. Pethick-Lawrence, *My Part in a Changing World* (London: Victor Gollancz, 1938), pp. 308–11; Addams to Wald, 8 December 1914, NYPL, Wald MSS; Addams to Heads of Women's Organizations, 28 December 1914, SCPC, Addams MSS.

13. Degen, *Woman's Peace Party* pp. 28–63; "A Woman's Peace Party Full Pledged for Action," *Survey,* 23 January 1915, pp. 433–34; Pethick-Lawrence, "Motherhood and War," p. 542.

14. Bernice Nichols to Doris Daniels, 4 June 1976.

15. Degen, *Woman's Peace Party,* pp. 64–91.

16. Addams to Wald, 13 March 1915, CU, Wald MSS.

17. Wald to Addams, 25 March 1915, NYPL, Wald MSS.

18. Smith to Wald, 31 March 1915; Addams to Wald, 26 March 1915, 6 April 1915, NYPL, Wald MSS.

19. Addams, *Peace and Bread,* pp. 13–20; Degen, *Woman's Peace Party,* pp. 64–126; Randall, *Improper Bostonian,* pp. 142–92; "Memo on the Hague," 28 April 1915–1 May 1915; "Proposals for a Conference of Neutral Nations," 2 April 1915, SCPC, Addams MSS.

20. "Is the Women's Peace Movement 'Silly and Base'?," *Literary Digest,* 1 May 1915, pp. 1022–23.

21. Wald, Speech, "New Aspects"; Wald, Discussion of Balch paper, NYPL, Wald MSS.

22. Wald to Joseph Tumulty, 13 July, 1915, NYPL, Wald MSS.

23. "Memorandum of Henry Street Meeting," 27 September 1915, CU, Wald MSS.

24. Charles Seymour, ed., *The Intimate Papers of Colonel House: From Neutrality to War, 1915–1917*, 4 vols. (Boston: Houghton Mifflin, 1926), 2: 96.

25. Addams, *Peace and Bread,* pp. 26–71.

26. *New York Times,* 9 February 1916, p. 2; *New York Tribune,* 9 February 1916, p. 4.

27. *New York Times,* 7 April 1916, p. 3; *New York Tribune,* 7 April 1916, p. 2

28. Transcript of meeting with Wilson, 8 May 1916, NYPL, Wald MSS.

29. Wald, "Comments on Interview," 18 May 1916, NYPL, Wald MSS.

30. *New York Times,* 11 May 1916, p. 2; 16 May 1916, p. 5.

31. Wald to Wilson, 13 April 1917, NYPL, Wald MSS.

32. Wald to Waters, 14 August 1917, NYPL, Wald MSS.

33. Wald to Ella Phillips Crandall, 6 November 1914, NYPL, Wald MSS; Duffus, *Lillian Wald,* pp. 189–200.

34. Wald, *Windows,* pp. 308–12; Blanche Wiesen Cook, ed., *Crystal Eastman on War and Revolution* (New York: Oxford University Press, 1978), pp. 11–22, 254–62. Carroll Smith-Rosenberg, *Disorderly Conduct* (New York: Oxford University Press, 1985), p. 284, suggests that another reason for the "political alienation" from Eastman was her "sexual flamboyance." Wald was put off by the introduction of sexual liberation as a feminist goal.

35. Degen, *Woman's Peace Party,* p. 217; Addams, *Peace and Bread,* pp. 152–53.

36. Addams to Wald, 6 January 1917, 16 May 1917, SCPC, WPP MSS; Addams to Wald, November 1918, CU, Wald MSS.

37. Duffus, *Lillian Wald,* pp. 206–12; Alice Hamilton to Mary Smith, 1 May 1919; Addams to Smith, 1 May 1919, SCPC, Addams MSS.

38. Kelley to Smith, 22 May 1919, SCPC, Addams MSS.

39. Degen, *Woman's Peace Party,* p. 228–34.

40. Wald to McDonald, 22 December 1919, NYPL, Wald MSS.

41. Warburg to Wald, 25 May 1920, NYPL, Wald MSS.

42. Wald and others, Appeal to Fellow Women to Serve the Cause of Peace, 15 October 1920, NYPL, Wald MSS.

43. Wald, Speech, "Disarmament," Mecca Temple, New York, 11 November 1931, NYPL, Wald MSS.

44. Wald to Addams, 9 October 1931; Wald to Dorothy Detzer, 3 December 1931; Wald, Speech at Graduation exercises of Mt. Sinai School of Nursing, 3 February 1932, NYPL, Wald MSS.

45. Wald to MacDonald, 26 March 1930, 28 March 1930; Wald to Crowley, 27 July 1932, NYPL, Wald MSS.

46. Wald to John McDonald, 9 May 1933; Wald to Stephen Wise, 22 March 1933; Wald to Agnes Leach, 22 March 1933; Wald to Rebecca Eaton, 23 March 1933; Wald to FDR, 6 May 1933, NYPL, Wald MSS.

47. Wald to Rockefeller, 11 July 1934, NYPL, Wald MSS.

48. Wald to Kirchwey, 8 March 1938, NYPL, Wald MSS.

49. Helen Hall, interview, 20 May 1975.

50. Degen, *Woman's Peace Party,* p. 165.

51. Staughton Lynd, "Jane Addams and the Radical Impulse," *Commentary* 32 (July 1961): 57.

52. Addams, *Peace and Bread,* pp. 73–74.

53. *New York Times,* 27 February 1917, p. 2; 4 March 1917, p. 10.

54. Wald to Mrs. Henry Sharpe, 28 February 1923, NYPL, Wald MSS.

55. Wald to Draper, 16 March 1923, NYPL, Wald MSS.

56. Wald to Naomi Deutsch, 1 December 1924; Wald to Yssabella Waters, 3 September 1919, 14 November 1919; Wald to Anna Woerishofer, 28 November 1924, NYPL, Wald MSS.

57. Harding to Wald, 4 August 1917, NYPL, Wald MSS.

58. Wald to William J. Schieffelin, 10 September 1919, 24 September 1919, NYPL, Wald MSS.

59. Wald to Harding, 8 August 1917, NYPL, Wald MSS.

60. Wald to Dock, 16 August 1919, NYPL, Wald MSS.

61. Wheeler, an open letter, 27 December 1917; "How Suffrage was Imposed on New York State," n.d., NYPL, Wald MSS.

62. *New York Times,* 25 January 1919, pp. 1, 4; 26 January 1919, p. 1; Robert K. Murray, *Red Scare: A Study of National Hysteria, 1919–1920* (New York: McGraw-Hill, 1964), pp. 94–98.

63. Wald to Addams, 25 January 1919, SCPC, Addams MSS.

64. Wald to Dr. Schwarz, 12 March 1919, NYPL, Wald MSS.

65. Duffus, Notes on the Biography of Lillian Wald, n.d., in Wald Biographical Material, NYPL, Wald MSS.

66. Wald to Graham Taylor, 3 December 1919; Wald to Iva Clyde Clarke, 21 January 1920; Wald to Julius Rosenwald, 2 December 1919, NYPL, Wald MSS.

67. Murray, *Red Scare,* pp. 98–104; Norman Hapgood, ed., *Professional Patriots* (New York: Albert and Charles Boni, 1928), pp. 11, 107–12.

68. *Woman Citizen,* 10 April 1920, pp. 1107–9, 1114–17; Wald to Hughes, 16 January 1920, NYPL, Wald MSS.

69. Wald to Smith, 9 January 1920, 15 January 1920, 13 May 1920, 25 May 1920; Wald to Joseph Proskauer, 5 October 1920, 8 October 1920, NYPL, Wald MSS.

70. Murray, *Red Scare,* p. 239.

71. Wald to Alice and Irene Lewisohn, 19 January 1920, NYPL, Wald MSS.

72. Norman Hapgood, ed., *Professional Patriots* (New York: Albert and Charles Boni, 1928), pp. 10, 88–90.

73. Ibid., pp. 103–6; Stanley J. Lemons, *The Woman Citizen: Social Feminism in the 1920's* (Urbana: University of Illinois Press, 1973), pp. 213–25.

74. *Woman Patriot,* 1 June 1924, pp. 1–8; 1 January 1924, p. 2; 15 June 1924, pp. 1–8; 15 August 1925, pp. 121–23; 1 March 1927, pp. 25–39; 15 August 1927, pp. 57–61; 1 May 1927, pp. 65–67; 15 December 1928, p. 189; Pamphlet, no title, circulated to help defeat the Child Labor Amendment, SL, Dorothy Kirchwey Brown MSS.

75. The Shepperd-Towner legislation will be examined in Chapter 10. The *Woman Patriot* opposed it from its introduction into Congress and then fought the extension of the law in 1926. See *Woman Patriot,* 15 May 1926, pp. 73–80; 1 June 1926, pp. 81–88; 15 June 1926, pp. 89–96; 1 July 1926, pp. 97–104; 15 July 1926, pp. 105–12; 1 August 1926, pp. 113–20; 15 August 1926, pp. 121–28.

76. U.S., Congress, Senate, *Congressional Record,* 69th Congress, 1st session, 8 July 1926, pp. 12931–65.

77. Wald to MacDonald, 15 December 1927, 26 January 1932, NYPL, Wald MSS. As late as 1937, Wald was still defending the reputation of Kelley, who had died five years earlier.

78. Wald to Julia Cordley, 27 January 1932, NYPL, Wald MSS.

Chapter Ten

1. Shaw in Stanley J. Lemons, *The Woman Citizen: Social Feminism in the 1920's* (Urbana: University of Illinois Press, 1973), p. 228.

2. Wald, Speech[?] to the YWHA, n.d.; Wald, Speech, "The Volunteer in Social Work," 19 October 1922; Wald, Speech, "Social Possibilities of Club Work," n.d., NYPL, Wald MSS.

3. Henry Street Settlement residents, a tribute to Wald, 10 March 1923, NYPL, Wald MSS.

4. Sinclair Lewis, *Ann Vickers* (New York: Doubleday, Doran, 1933).

5. Wald to Vera Metcalf, 31 March 1933; Wald to Paul Kellogg, 4 January 1933, NYPL, Wald MSS.

6. Wald to Henry Street Family c/o Elsa Herrman, 8 March 1925, NYPL, Wald MSS.

7. Residents of the Nurses' Settlement to Wald, n.d., CU, Wald MSS.

8. Wald to each resident of the Henry Street Settlement, 6 February 1929, NYPL, Wald MSS.

9. Libbian Benedict, "Miss Wald of Henry Street," *American Hebrew,* 7 March 1926, pp. 876, 906, NYPL, Wald MSS; S. J. Woolf, "Miss Wald Has Seen an Ideal Blossom," *New York Times,* 1 December 1929, p. 11.

10. Wald to Dudley, 13 October 1931, NYPL, Wald MSS.

11. Wald, *Windows,* pp. 321–22.

12. Wald to Naomi Deutsch, 1 December 1924, NYPL, Wald MSS.

13. Wald's secretary Anne Geddis passed the information to J. C. Sutherland, 23 April 1925, NYPL, Wald MSS.

14. Genevieve Parkhurst, "Is Feminism Dead?" *Harper's* 160 (May 1935): 735–45.

15. *Equal Rights,* 6 July 1929, p. 171; 25 October 1930, pp. 300–301; 24 January 1931, pp. 405–6; Lois Scharf, *To Work and to Wed: Female Employment and the Great Depression* (Westport, Conn.: Greenwood Press, 1980), pp. 43–65.

16. Lemons, *Woman Citizen,* p. vii.

17. Charlotte Perkins Gilman, "Woman's Achievements Since the Franchise," *Current History* 27 (October 1927): 7–14.

18. Wald was one of the "Sponsors for the Rebecca Shelley Repatriation Committee" along with such other women as Alice Paul. The quote is from the letterhead of the group's stationery; Balch to Wald, [1920]; Wald to Crowley, [1932]; Wald to Rabbi I. L. Bril, 19 August 1931, NYPL, Wald MSS.

19. George Madden Martin, "American Women and Paternalism," *Atlantic Monthly* 133 (June 1924): 746; *Woman Citizen,* 14 February 1920, pp. 860–62; 28 February 1920, pp. 928–29; Dorothy Kirchwey Brown, "The Maternity Bill," *Survey,* 18 June 1921, pp. 399–400.

20. Dorothy Kirchwey Brown, "How Uncle Sam Is Legislating for the Children," *Woman Citizen,* 22 May 1920, pp. 1288–90, 1294–96; Dr. Anna Rude to Wald, 21 April 1920, 6 May 1920, 7 May 1920, NYPL, Wald MSS.

21. Lathrop to Wald, 25 March 1919, NYPL, Wald MSS.

22. Robert Bremmer, ed., *Children and Youth in America: A Documentary History,* 4 vols. (Cambridge: Harvard University Press, 1971), 2: 1019–20.

23. Wald, Notes for Speech to American Association for Labor Legislation, 8 January 1921; Wald, Speech for Dr. Felix Adler's Dinner, 3 February 1922; Wald, Speech, "Preventative Medicine" Democratic Union of Women, 4 June 1923; Wald, Speech, "Sheppard Towner Bill" YMCA, 6 June 1923; Wald to Mrs. Frank A. Vanderlip, 8 May 1923; Wald to Kelley, 22 May 1923; Wald to Bruce Bliven, editor of the *New York Globe,* 7 February 1921; Wald to Speaker of the House Frederick Gillette, 3 February 1921, NYPL, Wald MSS.

24. Kelley, "My Philadelphia," *Survey,* 1 October 1926, pp. 7–11, 50–57; Edith Abbott, "Grace Abbott: A Sister's Memories," *Social Service Review* 13 (September 1939); 392–94; Mary Anderson to Robins, 18 April 1930, SL, Anderson MSS; *Life and Labor Bulletin,* July 1930, pp. 1–2.

25. Wald, *Windows,* pp. 202–5.

26. Catt to editor of the *New York Times,* 5 October 1914, NYPL, Catt MSS.

27. Robert S. Gallagher, "The Fight for Women's Suffrage: An Interview with Alice Paul," in *Historical Viewpoints,* ed. John A. Garraty (New York: Harper & Row, 1975), p. 195.

28. Blatch to Wald, 23 September 1920, 11 November 1920, NYPL, Wald MSS.

29. Freda Kirchwey, "Alice Paul Pulls the Strings," *Nation,* 2 March 1921, pp. 332–33.

30. Josephine C. Goldmark, *Impatient Crusader,* (Urbana: University of Illinois Press, 1953), pp. 180–87.

31. The ERA is discussed in almost every issue of the WTUL's *Life and Labor* and the NWP's *Equal Rights* during the 1920s. In addition, magazines like *Good Housekeeping, Nation, Harper's* and *Atlantic Monthly* ran feature stories which offered their readers the arguments for and against the amendment.

32. *Equal Rights,* 26 April 1924, p. 84.

33. Eveline Brainerd to Wald, 20 April 1936, NYPL, Wald MSS. Goodrich's articles in favor of the ERA appeared in *Equal Rights,* 22 February 1924, p. 15; 3 November 1929, pp. 340–41; 15 March 1935, p. 3; 15 February 1938, pp. 211–13.

34. *Equal Rights,* 31 May 1924, pp. 125–26.

35. Dock to Wald, 23 October 1928, NYPL, Wald MSS.

36. Wald to Norris, 23 February 1938, NYPL, Wald MSS.

37. Wald to Faville, 23 February 1938, NYPL, Wald MSS.

38. Wald to Faville, 6 April 1938, NYPL, Wald MSS.

39. William O'Neill, *Everyone Was Brave: A History of Feminism in America* (Chicago: Quadrangle Books, 1969), pp. 275–94.

40. Clarke A. Chambers, *Seedtime of Reform: American Social Service and Social Action, 1918–1933* (Minneapolis: University of Minnesota Press, 1963), p. 78.

41. Wald to Dock, 18 October 1932, NYPL, Wald MSS.

42. Wald to Kelley, 9 July 1922, NYPL, Wald MSS.

43. Wald's secretary to Mrs. Henry Sharpe, 3 March 1923, NYPL, Wald MSS.

44. Kelley to Wald, 22 May 1925, NYPL, Wald MSS.

45. Wald's secretary, Anne Geddes, to Kelley, 26 September 1925; Geddes to Dock, 12 June 1925, NYPL, Wald MSS.

46. Wald to Mrs. Charles S. Brown, Jr., 28 April 1931, NYPL, Wald MSS.

47. Wald to Addams, 17 March 1927, NYPL, Wald MSS.

48. Wald to Ramsay MacDonald, 7 November 1928, 28 March 1930; Wald to Bondfield, 3 December 1930, NYPL, Wald MSS.

49. Wald, "What Keeps the Nurses Going?" *Survey*, 15 November 1932, pp. 590–91; Wald, *Windows*, pp. 227–50.

50. Wald to Perkins, 28 December 1931, 25 January 1932, 10 February 1932; Wald to Dock, 10 February 1932; Marguerite Wales to Mayor and Member of the NYC Board of Estimate and Apportionment, 8 June 1932, NYPL, Wald MSS.

51. Wald to Maud Nathan, 3 November 1931, NYPL, Wald MSS.

52. Wald to Rosa Fried Carton, 12 January 1932, NYPL, Wald MSS.

53. Wald to Bertha Franz, 14 December 1931; Wald to Mr. and Mrs. Sylvan Bier, 20 October 1931; Wald to Mrs. Arthur Holden, 20 October 1931; Wald to Mrs. John Palmer Gavit, 23 October 1931, NYPL, Wald MSS offer only a few examples of Wald's letters at this critical time.

54. Wald to Bondfield, 9 March 1932, Wald to Lina Rogers, 15 March 1932; Wald to Aaron Rabinowitz, 3 March 1932, NYPL, Wald MSS.

55. Wald to John Schiff, 8 January 1933, NYPL, Wald MSS. Wald's secretary, Eleanor Linton, informed her friends as to the nature of Wald's illness and her progress. For an example, see Linton to Jane Hitchcock, 13 April 1933, NYPL, Wald MSS.

56. Wald penciled this message over a letter to Mabel Vernon, 22 June 1932, NYPL, Wald MSS.

57. Wald to Elsa Herrmann, 5 April 1933, NYPL, Wald MSS.

58. Wald to Hamilton, 4 April 1933, NYPL, Wald MSS.

59. Wald to Mary Smith, 12 April 1933, NYPL, Wald MSS.

60. Wald to Perkins, 12 August 1935, NYPL, Wald MSS.

61. Wald to Milly Hamilton, 18 November 1932, NYPL, Wald MSS.

62. Wald to Mary Dreier, 5 April 1933, NYPL, Wald MSS.

63. Wald to Dock, 24 October 1932, NYPL, Wald MSS.

64. Wald to Ann Brenner, 27 September 1937, NYPL, Wald MSS.

65. Lehman, COHC, p. 151.

66. Wald to Josephine Bowen, 2 December 1935, NYPL, Wald MSS. Wald wrote to dozens of interested people to notify them of the changes at the

Settlement in 1933. In that year, she was named President of Henry Street and in 1937, President Emeritus.

67. Wald to Josephine Goldmark, 12 May 1936; Wald to Hall, 25 May 1936, NYPL, Wald MSS.

68. *New York Times,* 2 December 1940, p. 23.

69. Kellogg to Wald, 19 November 1937, NYPL, Wald MSS.

70. Wald to Board of Directors of the Foreign Policy Association, 9 January 1935, NYPL, Wald MSS.

71. *New York Call* quoted in Ann Gordon, Mari Jo Buhle, and Nancy Schrom, "Women in American Society: An Historical Contribution," reprinted from *Radical America* (July-August, 1971) Warner Modular Publications, 1973.

Bibliographical Essay

Personal Papers

The Wald papers are divided between the Rare Books and Manuscript Divisions of the New York Public Library and the Butler Library of Columbia University. There is also a small collection in the Archives of the Visiting Nurse Service of New York. Little remains of the papers from Wald's early life except for the letters to Jacob Schiff documenting her first years on the East Side. But shortly after moving to 265 Henry Street, Wald acquired the services of a secretary and typewriter and her papers for the period after about 1895 are a rich source of information, not only on her personal and public activities, but also on the movements and groups with which she was associated. The collections include her letters (both sent and received), speeches, many of the articles she authored, committee reports, position papers, and newspaper clippings.

The Manuscript Division of the NYPL also holds the papers of Everett Wheeler, the lawyer who chaired the Man Suffrage Association Opposed to Woman Suffrage and the American Constitutional League. The collection is invaluable in gaining an understanding of the opposition to Wald's work in both the suffrage and peace movements. Equally important are the papers of Carrie Chapman Catt that deal with the New York State suffrage campaign and show the methodical organization and planning necessary for this successful effort. Nicholas Kelley's papers contain a few of the personal letters of his mother, Florence Kelley, which give evidence of the long and loving relationship between Wald and Kelley.

In addition to the Wald papers, the Rare Book and Manuscript Library in Butler Library contains the remnants of the personal letters of Florence Kelley to her friends, her mother, and particularly to her young children, which reveal the private side of this remarkable woman. Columbia University is also the repository of the Nursing Archives in Special Collections, Milbank Memorial Library of Teachers College and it is a treasure trove of material for the early days of nursing. The M. Adelaide Nutting papers, in particular, include letters from Dock, Wald, and other nurse pioneers which detail their activities for the development of the profession.

The richest, most comprehensive source of manuscript material for women's history is the Woman's Archives of the Schlesinger Library, Radcliffe College. The diaries and papers of Leonora O'Reilly are critical to any study of Wald, life at Henry Street, the WTUL, and the attitudes of working women. Selective use of the papers of Clara Beyer, John Graham Brooks, Dorothy Kirchwey Brown, Elizabeth Glendower Evans, Mary Sewall Gardner, Harriett W. Laidlow, Mary Anderson, and Alma Lutz—all of which contain letters from or references to Wald—will yield substantial information on almost every cause with which Wald was associated.

The Jane Addams, the AUAM, and Woman's Peace Party papers in the Swarthmore College Peace Collection contain the letters of Addams, Balch, Wald, Hamilton, and others relating to the formation of the WPP, the American Union Against Militarism, and the WILPF, as well as the events that resulted in the Hague and Zurich conferences. There are, in addition, the records of the proposals for a Conference of Neutral Nations drawn up by Rosika Schwimmer and Julia Grace Wales. The Addams papers have interest, too, because they include a sampling of the hate mail she received from the part of the public critical of her peace activities. Some letters are so filled with venom and animosity that they make clear the hostility encountered by the women during the years of the Red Scare.

The Franklin D. Roosevelt Library in Hyde Park holds the papers of George B. Graves (an associate of Governor Alfred Smith) and Adolph A. Berle, who as a young man worked at the Henry Street Settlement and later was a member of the New Deal "Brain Trust." Both collections illustrate Wald's relationship with political leaders—as do a small sample of letters to FDR—and Berle's letters are testimony of the devotion shown to Wald by a former member of the Settlement family. Portions of the Eleanor Roosevelt papers have interest both as examples of Wald's political ties and of her friendship with a younger member of the women's network.

Lastly, the Manuscript Division of the Library of Congress contains the Blackwell Family papers. Elizabeth Stone Blackwell's letters to and from Wald are significant sources on suffrage, peace, women's health, and prostitution.

Organizational Material and Publications

The Henry Street Settlement published a *Settlement Journal* sporadically between 1904 and 1915, as well as three anniversary issues of "Report of the Henry Street Settlement" in 1913, 1918, and 1921, which detail the activities of the organization after 1893, when it was founded.

They also chronicle the growth of the Settlement and serve as evidence of the reasons for Wald's need to work so hard and long as a fundraiser.

The publications of the WTUL relate not only to the economic goals of working women, but also to their relationship to other women's organizations and movements like suffrage and the ERA. *Life and Labor* (renamed *Life and Labor Bulletin* after 1921) was published between 1911 and 1932 by the National WTUL and the New York League issued a *Bulletin* between 1911 and 1913. In addition, the national organization published such pamphlets as "Some Facts Regarding Working Women in the Sweated Industries" (New York: National Women's Trade Union League, 1914).

The suffrage movement is documented in the *Woman's Journal,* issued by the NAWSA until 1917, and the *Woman Citizen* (1914–1923), which was renamed the *Woman's Journal* in the 1920s. Together these publications describe the campaigns on the national level. Of greater value in a study of Wald's activities is the *Woman Voter,* published by the Woman Suffrage Party from 1910 to 1917, since it deals more extensively with the New York fight.

For the postsuffrage period, two other publications are essential. *Equal Rights* (1921–1940), the weekly organ of the National Women's Party provides the best single source of information on the arguments and attitudes of the proponents of the ERA. It also is rich in material on the Cable Act, Sheppard-Towner, the fight for female jurors and the attempt to end the dismissal of women workers during the depression. The second publication is the *Woman Patriot* for a view of the opposition to Wald and all feminists who supported women's equality, child welfare, maternity care, and any of the other reforms of the time.

Several other organizations issued material of use in this study. The Consumers' League (both New York and National) published such pamphlets as Florence Kelley and Dorothy Meyers, "Children's Compensation for Industrial Injuries," (New York: NCL, May 1927) and "The Forty Eight Hour Law: Do Working Women Want it?" (New York: Consumers' League of New York, n.d.), which shed light on the goals set for industrial workers. In another area, the publications of the Women's Temporary Committee on the State of New York Constitution (1915) offer evidence of the fight to have women represented at the convention that was convened to write a new state constitution. Information on Wald's student days can be derived from "School of Nursing of the New York Hospital, Fiftieth Anniversary, 1877–1927," published by the Society of the New York Hospital. And Lavinia Dock wrote "Some Urgent Social Claims," *Nurses Associated Alumnae of the United States,* a report of the Tenth Annual Convention of the Nurses' Association, 1906, which provides insight into Wald's attitudes toward her profession.

Oral Histories and Interviews

The best clues to Wald's personality and work methods are to be found in the "reminiscences" of George Alger, Bruno Lasker, Herbert Lehman,

Frances Perkins, and Isabel Maitland Stewart, all of which are located in the Columbia University Oral History Collection.

Additionally, a few people who knew Wald agreed to be interviewed for this book. Helen Hall, Benjamin Schoenfield (a retired banker who used the Settlement as a child and subsequently became a member of its board of directors), Betty Friedman (niece of Hyman Schroeder, who was probably the most loyal of Wald's "boys"), Clara Rabinowitz, and several people in Westport, Connecticut, whose memories of Wald are confined to her retirement years, had varying recollections. But most dealt primarily with Wald's charm and ability to get along with people of all sorts and while not equally valuable, collectively they provide material with which to reconstruct a portrait of Wald and life on Henry Street.

Government Publications

While Wald and/or her work figured in a large number of governmental actions and are included in many public records, only a few were of special interest for this study. The New York State Legislature's multivolumed *Reports of the Factory Investigating Commission,* published in four series between 1912 and 1915, includes Wald testimony and contributes to understanding of the fight for protective labor legislation after the Triangle Fire. Another labor source is the *Report on the Condition of Women and Child Wage-Earners in the United States* issued by the United States Congress in nineteen volumes from 1910 to 1913, publication of which was urged by Wald.

Students of the ERA have need of the *Congressional Record* for the committee hearings held on the amendment between 1925 and 1938. The arguments offered in testimony both for and against the measure clarify the nature of the division in the women's ranks.

One last federal publication of value is the *Transactions of the Fifteenth International Congress on Hygiene and Demography* (Washington, D.C.: Government Printing Office, 1913), which contains articles by Wald (the sanitary control of the garment industry) and Josephine Goldmark (fatigue among industrial workers).

Periodical Material

Even a partial listing of the articles useful in a study of Wald's life and work would exhaust the reader, since she and her associates were indefatigable writers for publications geared to both the lay public and to professional readers. It is worthwhile, however, to look through *Survey,* edited by Paul Kellogg, which was a periodical involved with every reform program of the Progressive years and which contains articles by Addams, Wald, Perkins, Brown, and Kelley, among others. Many of the same topics are covered and many of the same authors are included in *Commons* (the magazine of the Chicago Commons Settlement) and *Charities* (published by the New York Charity Organization Society). The two were merged in late 1905 into *Charity and Commons* and together with *Survey* are invaluable sources for social reform.

For more detailed articles on the issues that absorbed the women, the *Annals of the American Academy of Political and Social Science* is most helpful. Wald wrote articles in 1905, 1906, and 1909, and Kelley and Goldmark were frequent contributors to issues dealing with trade unionism, public health, women, and child labor. The issue entitled *Women in the Modern World* (May 1929) is particularly useful for work on the postsuffrage years.

The early days of nursing are documented in the *American Journal of Nursing* for which Dock wrote many articles and Wald wrote a few. In October 1950, the *Journal* published an anniversary issue with retrospective pieces by Dock, Goodrich, and Stewart, which is rewarding reading for students of the profession.

Popular magazines that carried frequent articles relevant to women's issues were *Forum, Atlantic Monthly, Nation, Harper's, Current History,* and the *New Republic,* and it is worth skimming these publications for the years through the early 1930s. Also recommended are *Ladies Home Journal* and *Good Housekeeping* (1919 to 1928), for articles on the ERA and other postsuffrage issues.

Autobiographical and Biographical Material

It was common practice for the women (and some of their male colleagues) to write of themselves and their activities. Frequently, too, they wrote biographies of each other in what was, perhaps, their own recognition of the fact that they lived during a golden age for women in public life. These are rarely analytical and are largely uncritical works whose chief value for this study is the information that can be gleaned on the various movements and causes with which the women were concerned. Also, these books and articles provide insight into the relationships among the various women. Their unqualified admiration of one another offers evidence of the women's network and testifies to their loving concern for each other.

Wald's *House on Henry Street* (New York: Henry Holt, 1915) and *Windows on Henry Street* (Boston: Little, Brown, 1934) reveal little of her early life and thought, but they are sources for her work at the Settlement. Several articles, presumably written with her assistance, provide bits and pieces of her personality. The best of them are Paul U. Kellogg, "A Pioneer Woman of the City Frontier," *New York Times Magazine,* 13 March 1927; S. J. Woolf, "Miss Wald Has Seen an Ideal Blossom," *New York Times,* 1 December 1929; Jerome Beatty, "She Never Gave Up," *Forum,* August 1936; and a profile for the *New Yorker,* 14 December 1929, written by Helena H. Smith and entitled "Lillian Wald: Rampant But Respectable."

Robert Duffus's biography, *Lillian Wald: Neighbor and Crusader* (New York: Macmillan, 1938), is the work of a friend and admirer and makes no attempt at evaluating Wald's work. But it has interest because it was written with her assistance and represents her view of her life and work. Two well-researched works are Allan Edward Reznick, "Lillian D. Wald: The Years at Henry Street," Ph.D. dissertation, Madison, Wisconsin, University Press, 1973, which examines Wald's early years—her most active and successful—at the Settlement, and *A Generation of Women: Education in the Lives of Progressive Reformers* (Cambridge: Harvard University Press, 1979) by Ellen Condliffe Lagemann, which covers the educational influences and experiences of five women, of whom Wald is one.

Of all the women, Jane Addams was the most prolific and articulate. More introspective than Wald, Addams's *Twenty Years at Hull House* (New York: Macmillan, 1910) and *The Second Twenty Years at Hull House, September 1909 to September 1929* (New York: Macmillan, 1930) give greater detail and thought to many of the same topics covered in the Wald books. Historians are drawn to Addams and she has been the subject of a number of published biographies such as Allen F. Davis, *American Heroine: The Life and Legend of Jane Addams* (New York: Oxford University Press, 1973), which is strongest on Addams's fall from popularity after World War I. Two differing, but most interesting interpretations of her life are to be found in Jill Conway, "Woman Reformers and American Culture, 1870–1930," *Journal of Social History* (Winter 1971–72) and Staughton Lynd, "Jane Addams and the Radical Impulse," *Commentary* (July 1961).

Addams wrote a loving biography, *My Friend, Julia Lathrop* (New York: Macmillan, 1935), which is also a study of the Children's Bureau. And Edith Abbott chronicled her sister's life in "Grace Abbott: A Sister's Memories," *Social Service Review* (September 1939). Not as well written, but equally laudatory is Mary Dreier's study of her sister, *Margaret Dreier Robins: Her Life, Letters, and Work* (New York: Island Press Cooperative, 1950). Both Frances Perkins, "My Recollections of Florence Kelley," *Social Science Review* (March 1954) and Josephine Goldmark, *Impatient Crusader* (Urbana: University of Illinois Press, 1953), wrote of their friend. Of the two, the Goldmark book has the greater value, particularly as an examination of Kelley's work with the NCL. Kelley never wrote a full autobiography, but she did author a four-part series of articles for *Survey* in 1926 and 1927, in which she explored her early life and education. Much the same period is covered by Dorothy Rose Blumberg in her admirable biography, *Florence Kelley: The Making of a Social Pioneer* (New York: Augustus M. Kelley, 1966).

Other women who fought for equal rights, peace, social reform, labor legislation, contraception, and improved health care wrote of their experiences. Some of the autobiographies are better than others, some refer to Wald directly, but all deserve at least a cursory reading for, taken together they provide a record of the way the women saw themselves and each other. They are: Elizabeth Hasanovitz, *One of Them: Chapters from a Passionate Autobiography* (Boston: Houghton Mifflin, 1918); Harriot Stanton Blatch and Alma Lutz, *Challenging Years: The Memoirs of Harriot Stanton Blatch* (New York: G. P. Putnam's Sons, 1940); Helen Hall, *Unfinished Business in*

Neighborhood and Nation (New York: Macmillan, 1971); Carrie Chapman Catt and Nettie Rogers Shuler, *Woman Suffrage and Politics: The Inner Story of the Suffrage Movement* (1923; reprint, Seattle: University of Washington Press, 1970); Margaret Sanger, *My Fight for Birth Control* (New York: Farrar Rinehart, 1931); Emmeline Pethick-Lawrence, *My Part in a Changing World* (London: Victor Gollancz, 1938); Vida Dutton Scudder, *On Journey* (New York: E. P. Dutton, 1937); Rose Schneiderman with Lucy Goldthwaite, *All for One* (New York: Paul S. Erikson, 1967); and Maud Nathan, *Once upon a Time and Today* (New York: G. P. Putnam's Sons, 1933) and *The Story of an Epoch Making Movement* (Garden City, N.Y.: Doubleday, Page, 1926); Alice Hamilton, *Exploring the Dangerous Trades* (Boston: Little, Brown, 1943); Barbara Sicherman, *Alice Hamilton: A Life in Letters* (Cambridge: Harvard University Press, 1984).

At least three of Wald's male associates wrote their memoirs. Stephen Wise, *Challenging Years: The Autobiography of Stephen Wise* (New York: G. P. Putnam's Sons, 1949), Graham Taylor, *Chicago Commons Through Forty Years* (Chicago: Chicago Commons Association, 1936), and Oswald Garrison Villard, *Fighting Years: Memoirs of a Liberal Editor* (New York: Harcourt, Brace, 1939) offer still another dimension to a study of her life.

Several biographies of Wald's colleagues are rich in material. Peace activities are covered in Mercedes Randall, *Improper Bostonian: Emily Greene Balch* (New York: Twayne Publishing, 1964) and Blanche Wiesen Cook, *Crystal Eastman on Women and Revolution* (New York: Oxford University Press, 1978). Social reform movements are detailed in Clarke A. Chambers, *Paul Kellogg and the Survey: Voices for Social Welfare and Social Justice* (Minneapolis: University of Minnesota Press, 1971). And Wald's closest political allies are the subjects of Arthur Mann, *Laguardia: A Fighter against His Times, 1882–1933* (Philadelphia: J. B. Lippincott, 1959); Robert F. Wesser, *Charles Evans Hughes: Politics and Reform in New York, 1905–1910* (Ithaca: Cornell University Press, 1967); Allan Nevins, *Herbert H. Lehman and His Era* (New York: Scribner's, 1963), which is important since Lehman paid tribute to Wald and his Henry Street experiences in shaping his social philosophy; Matthew Josephson and Hannah Josephson, *Al Smith: Hero of the Cities, A Political Portrait Drawing on the Papers of Frances Perkins* (Boston: Houghton Mifflin, 1969); and Oscar Handlin, *Al Smith and His America* (Boston: Little, Brown, 1958).

Lastly, there are a number of works that deal specifically with some aspect of Wald's life. She contributed to Cyrus Adler's *Jacob H. Schiff: His Life and Letters* (Garden City, N.Y.: Doubleday, Doran, 1928), a family-authorized biography that reads like a eulogy. But, given the relationship between the banker and the social worker, it is valuable. While the latter book describes Wald's friendship with an "uptown" Jew, Rose Cohen's *Out of the Shadow* (New York: George Doran, 1918) is the best source for Wald's influence on the life of an immigrant working girl. Less directly relevant to Wald, is Emma Goldman, *Living My Life* (New York: Knopf, 1931), which offers a contrasting view to Wald's of life in Rochester at the turn of the century. Two other books detail an aspect of Wald's work. Alice Lewisohn Crowley, *The Neighborhood Playhouse* (New York: Theater Arts Books, 1959) is the autobiography of a woman who remained Wald's friend and disciple for life, and Carole Klein, *Aline* (New York: Harper & Row, 1979) tells of the influence of the playhouse on a woman who went on to become one of the theater's outstanding scenic and dress designers.

The nursing sisters were apt to act as biographers for each other and information on these women is most often found in brief articles in professional journals. Wald wrote "Comrade Annie W. G.," *Henry Street Nurse* 4 (May-June 1923) and "Adelaide Nutting," *American Journal of Nursing* (June 1925). Goodrich was also the subject of Mary Roberts in the *AJN* of February 1955. Only Lavinia Dock wrote of her own experiences in a "Self Portrait," *Nursing Outlook* (January 1977), a "little biographical sketch" written in 1932, in which she attempted to explore the ingredients of her own personality and social philosophy. Dock figures in three other biographical pieces; two were written in 1956, the year of her death, for the *AJN* and *Nursing Outlook* and the third is part of a series by Teresa Christy on the early nurse leaders—Wald, Dock, et al.—printed in *Nursing Outlook* in 1969 and 1970.

Other Printed Material—Primary and Secondary

There are a number of works that throw light on Wald's childhood environment and clarify the influences on her development. Information on Rochester and Judaism (both Conservative and Reform) is to be found in a reading of Blake McKelvey, "The Jews of Rochester: A Contribution to Their History During the Nineteenth Century," *Publications of the American Jewish Historical Society* 40 (September 1950) and "Women's Rights in Rochester—A Century of Progress," *Rochester History* 10 (July 1948). Nathan Glazer's *American Judaism* (Chicago: University of Chicago Press, 1957) details the development of Reform Judaism and Zosa Szajkowski, "The Attitude of American Jews to East European Immigration (1881–1893)," *Publications of the American Jewish Historical Society* 40 (March 1951) tells of the antagonisms that evolved between the new and the old immigrants. The most relevant work for a life of Wald is Stuart Rosenberg, *The Jews of Rochester, 1843–1928* (New York: Columbia University Press, 1954), since it deals in detail with the people of her home town.

While dozens of nursing histories have been written since its publication, M. Adelaide Nutting and Lavinia L. Dock, *A History of Nursing: The Evolution of Nursing Systems from Earliest Times to the Present* (New York: G. P. Putnam's Sons, 1907) remains the most valuable because of its detail on the nurse registration fights and Wald's role in the development of the profession. Dock also authored "The History of Public Health Nursing," for *The Public Health Nurse* 14 (October 1922). Wald's articles on public health nursing for *The Trained Nurse and Hospital Review* (June 1928), the *Bulletin of the American Academy of Medicine* (August 1910), *University Studies* (October 1905–January 1906), and the *Women's City Club Bulletin* (11 February 1919) and Henry Street nurse Yssabella G. Waters, *Visiting Nurses in the United States* (New York: Charities Publication Committee, 1909) are worth looking at for factual information as well as for examples of Wald's propagandizing methods.

The thesis in the chapter on nursing is close to that of Jo Ann Ashley, *Hospitals, Paternalism, and the Role of the Nurse* (New York: Teachers College Press, 1976), although there is not complete agreement on the extent to which nurse leaders acquiesced to domination by physicians. Louise M. Fitzpatrick's *The National Organization for Public Health Nursing, 1912–1952: Development of a Practice Field* (New York: National League for Nursing, 1975) is another valuable secondary source.

The attempt to link the development of professionalized nursing with women's revolt against their traditional role has created speculation about the motivations of the founder of modern nursing. Elaine Showalter's "Florence Nightingale's Feminist Complaint: Women, Religion, and Suggestions for Thought," *Signs* 6 (Spring 1981) is a provocative example.

For background on immigrant life on the East Side, the following are worth reading: Hutchins Hapgood, *The Spirit of the Ghetto: Studies of the Jewish Quarter of New York* (New York: Schocken Books, 1966); Harry Roskolenko, *The Time That Was Then: The Lower East Side, 1900–1914, an Intimate Chronicle* (New York: Dial Press, 1971); Jacob A. Riis, *How the Other Half Lives: Studies among the Tenements of New York* (New York: Hill and Wang, 1957); Edward Steiner, "Russian and Polish Jews in New York," *Outlook* 72 (1902); Charles D. Kellogg, "The Situation in New York City, the Winter of 1893–94," *Journal of Social Science* 32 (1894); Lillian Wald, "Russian Jewish Immigrant," *American Hebrew,* (14 April 1911); and two excellent secondary sources, Moses Rischin, *The Promised City: New York's Jews, 1870–1914* (Cambridge: Harvard University Press, 1967) and Irving Howe, *World of Our Fathers* (New York: Harcourt Brace Jovanovich, 1976).

The settlement movement is described in many of the biographies already mentioned and in Robert Archey Woods and Albert J. Kennedy, *The Settlement Horizon* and the *Handbook of Settlements,* which the two men edited. Both works were republished in 1970 by the Arno Press and the New York Times. A more critical view of the accomplishments of the settlement workers may be found in some of the articles in Michael Freund and Robert Morris, eds., *Trends and Issues in Jewish Social Welfare in the United States, 1899–1952* (Philadelphia: Jewish Publication Society of America, 1966).

The best secondary sources on the settlements are Allen F. Davis, *Spearheads for Reform: The Social Settlements and the Progressive Movement, 1890–1914* (New York: Oxford University Press, 1967) and Clark A. Chambers, *Seedtime of Reform: American Social Service and Social Action, 1918–1933* (Minneapolis: University of Minnesota Press, 1963). Also valuable and most relevant for Wald is John P. Rousmaniere, "Cultural Hybrid in the Slums: The College Woman and the Settlement House, 1889–1894," *American Quarterly* 22 (Spring 1970).

It is worth skimming some of the works that concentrate on the individual campaigns of the women in order to study the methods of lobbying and propagandizing. They also show the importance of the network in the public sector. Some of the best are: Susan Tiffin, *In Whose Best Interest? Child*

Welfare Reform in the Progressive Era (Westport, Conn.: Greenwood Press, 1982); Walter Trattner, *Crusader for the Children: A History of the National Child Labor Committee and Child Labor Reform in America* (Chicago: Quadrangle Books, 1970); Jeremy P. Felt, *Hostages of Fortune: Child Labor Reform in New York State* (Syracuse: Syracuse University Press, 1965); Frederick Smith Hall, *Forty Years, 1902–1942: The Work of the New York Child Labor Committee* (Brattleboro, Vt.: E. L. Hildreth, 1943); James A. Tobey, *The Children's Bureau: Its History, Activities and Organization* (Baltimore: Johns Hopkins University Press, 1925); and James H. Timberlake, *Prohibition and the Progressive Movement, 1900–1920* (Cambridge: Harvard University Press, 1963).

Any evaluation of Wald's place in the women's movement requires an understanding of the motivations, ideas, and goals of the feminists of her time. For this purpose, Sophonisba P. Breckinridge, *Women in the Twentieth Century: A Study of Their Political, Social and Economic Activities* (New York: McGraw-Hill, 1933); Floyd Dell, *Women as World Builders: Studies in Modern Feminism* (Chicago: Forbes, 1913); Charlotte Perkins Gilman, *Women and Economics,* ed. Carl Degler (1898, reprint, New York: Harper & Row, 1966); Rheta Child Dorr, *What Eight Million Women Want* (Boston: Small, Maynard, 1910); and especially Beatrice Forbes-Robertson Hale, *What Women Want: An Interpretation of the Feminist Movement* (New York: Fred A. Stokes, 1914) are helpful.

Since suffrage was the goal around which all feminist reforms revolved, it is not surprising that this aspect of the women's movement is rich in literature. The best single primary source of information remains the six-volume Susan B. Anthony, Elizabeth Cady Stanton, and Ida Husted Harper, eds., *History of Woman Suffrage* (1881–1922; reprint, New York: Source Book Press, 1970). The militant tactics of the National Woman's Party are detailed by Doris Stevens, *Jailed for Freedom* (New York: Boni and Liveright, 1920) and is useful because of its mention of Lavinia Dock. The NWP's general biographer is Inez Haynes Irwin, *The Story of the Woman's Party* (New York: Harcourt, Brace, 1921).

Most secondary sources for suffrage starting with Eleanor Flexner, *Century of Struggle: The Woman's Rights Movement in the United States* (Cambridge: Harvard University Press, Belknap Press, 1975) emphasize the work of the traditional middle-class Anglo-Saxon women. The anti-immigrant sentiment of this group is discussed in Alan P. Grimes, *The Puritan Ethic and Woman Suffrage* (New York: Oxford University Press, 1967) and it provided ideas that conflicted with Wald's experiences in New York. The chapter on suffrage also gained from John D. Buenker, "The Urban Machine and Woman Suffrage: A Study in Political Adaptability," *Historian* 33 (February 1971) and Ronald Schaffer, "The New York City Woman Suffrage Party, 1909–1919," *New York History* 43 (July 1962).

Some of the suffrage studies attempt to explain the decades after 1920 in light of the great campaign. The best example is William O'Neill, *Everyone Was Brave: A History of Feminism in America* (Chicago: Quadrangle Books, 1969) in which social feminists, for whom the vote was a means of furthering social reform are separated from hard-core feminists, who wanted the vote for its own sake. William H. Chafe, *The American Woman:*

Her Changing Social, Economic and Political Roles, 1920–1970 (New York: Oxford University Press, 1972) and Stanley J. Lemons, *The Woman Citizen: Social Feminism in the 1920's* (Urbana: University of Illinois Press, 1973) rely on the O'Neill model to explain why feminism died after suffrage was won. All claim that the social feminists promised too many things to get the vote and then could not deliver and this added to the split among women over the ERA that killed the women's movement after 1920.

The evidence of Wald's life would indicate that she continued to work on women's issues after 1920 and that her failure resulted from political and economic changes in the nation rather than from the actions of the feminists. Several works deal with these same ideas. They are Estelle B. Freedman, "The New Women: Changing Views of Women in the 1920's," *Journal of American History* 61 (Spring 1974); Susan Ware, *Beyond Suffrage: Women in the New Deal* (Cambridge: Harvard University Press, 1981); Susan D. Becker, *The Origins of the Equal Rights Amendment: American Feminism between the Wars* (Westport, Conn.: Greenwood Press, 1981); and Nancy F. Cott, "Feminist Politics in the 1920's: The National Woman's Party," *Journal of American History* 71 (June 1984).

Substantial material on working women came from Alice Henry, *The Trade Union Woman* (New York: D. Appleton, 1915) and *Women and the Labor Movement* (New York: George Doran, 1923). The goals of the women were ably expressed by Florence Kelley, *Modern Industry in Relation to the Family, Health, Education, Morality* (New York: Longmans, Green, 1914) and *Some Ethical Gains through Legislation* (New York: Macmillan, 1905). Since Wald worked primarily with the women in the clothing trades, two valuable sources are Lewis Levitzki Lorwin [Lewis Levine], *The Women Garment Workers: A History of the International Ladies' Garment Workers Union* (New York: B. W. Heubsch, 1924) and Mabel Hurd Willett, *The Employment of Women in the Clothing Trade* (New York: Columbia University Press, 1902). And the Schlesinger Library has a short pamphlet written by a woman worker on "The 1909 Strike" which also yielded information.

General labor histories traditionally are weak on women workers, but it is worth looking at three works by Melvyn Dubofsky: "Organized Labor in New York City and the First World War, 1914–1918," *New York History* 42 (October 1961); *We Shall Be All: A History of the Industrial Workers of the World* (Chicago: Quadrangle Books, 1969); and *When Workers Organize: New York City in the Progressive Era* (Amherst: University of Massachusetts Press, 1968). Sidney Lens, *The Labor Wars: From Molly Maguires to the Sitdowns* (Garden City, N.Y.: Anchor Press, 1974) and Irwin Yellowitz, *Labor and the Progressive Movement in New York State, 1897–1916* (Ithaca: Cornell University Press, 1965) are also helpful.

Surveys on the history of working women include: Barbara Mayer Wertheimer, *We Were There: The Story of Working Women in America* (New York: Pantheon Books, 1977); Philip S. Foner, *Women and the American Labor Movement: From the First Trade Unions to the Present* (New York: Free Press, 1979); and Alice Kessler-Harris, *Out to Work: A History of Wage-Earning Women in the United States* (New York: Oxford University Press, 1982).

The history of the WTUL may be found in Gladys Boone, *The Women's Trade Union League in Great Britain and the United States* (New York: AMS Press, 1942) and Allen F. Davis, "The Women's Trade Union League: Origins and Organization," *Labor History* 5 (Winter, 1964). *Feminist Studies* is always helpful to writers of women's history, but volume three (Fall 1975) of the publication is particularly worthwhile for work in labor history and the WTUL because of articles by Robin Miller Jacoby and Nancy Schrom Dye.

George Kneeland, *Commercialized Prostitution in New York City* (New York: The Century Co., 1917) remains a valuable primary source on prostitution. But two secondary works, Egal Feldman, "Prostitution: the Alien Woman and the Progressive Imagination, 1910–1915," *American Quarterly* 29 (Summer 1967) and Roy Lubove, "The Progressive and the Prostitute," *Historian* 24 (May 1962), hold greater interest because of their concern with the middle-class reaction to prostitution. Ruth Rosen, *The Lost Sisterhood: Prostitution in America, 1900–1918* (Baltimore: Johns Hopkins University Press, 1982) offers thoughtful new interpretations about the "oldest profession." The same author edited *The Maimie Papers* with Sue Davidson (Old Westbury, N.Y.: The Feminist Press, 1977), which makes references to Wald.

The loving relationship between the women and the benefits they received from living in a women's world are the subject of Estelle Freedman, "Separatism As Strategy: Female Institution Building and American Feminism, 1870–1930," *Feminist Studies* 5 (Fall 1979); Kathryn Kish Sklar, "Hull House in the 1890s: A Community of Women Reformers," *Signs* 10 (Summer 1985); and Carroll Smith-Rosenberg, *Disorderly Conduct: Visions of Gender in Victorian America* (New York: Oxford University Press, 1985). Useful, also, are two articles that allude to lesbian relationships between women in the network. James R. McGovern, "Anna Howard Shaw: New Approaches to Feminism," *Journal of Social History* 3 (Winter 1969–70) and Blanche Wiesen Cook, "Female Support Networks and Political Activism: Lillian Wald, Crystal Eastman, Emma Goldman," *Chrysalis* 3 (Autumn 1977) argue that the female friendships had an erotic element.

The peace movement is the subject of two very good books by its participants, Jane Addams, *Peace and Bread in Time of War* (New York: Macmillan, 1922) and Emily Greene Balch, *Approaches to the Great Settlement* (New York: B. W. Huebsch for the American Union Against Militarism, 1918). *The Intimate Papers of Colonel House: From Neutrality to War, 1915–1917*, 4 vols. (Boston: Houghton Mifflin, 1926), edited by Charles Seymour, is of interest because it shows the reactions of a presidential insider to the efforts of the women.

The chapter on Wald's pacifist activities and the repercussions of the Red Scare period drew heavily on Marie Louise Degen, *The History of the Woman's Peace Party* (Baltimore: John Hopkins University Press, 1939); Gertrude Carmen Bussey and Margaret Tims, *Women's International League for Peace and Freedom, 1915–1965* (London: George Allen and Unwin, 1965); Allen F. Davis, "Welfare, Reform and World War I," *American Quarterly* 19 (Fall 1967); Sondra R. Herman, *Eleven against War: Studies in American Internationalist Thought, 1898–1921* (Stanford: Hoover

Institution Press, 1969); Roland C. Marchand, *The American Peace Movement and Social Reform, 1898–1918* (Princeton: Princeton University Press, 1972); David S. Patterson, "Woodrow Wilson and the Mediation Movement," *Historian* 33 (August 1971); Norman Hapgood, ed., *Professional Patriots* (New York: Albert and Charles Boni, 1928); and Robert K. Murray, *Red Scare: A Study of National Hysteria, 1919–1920* (New York: McGraw-Hill, 1964).

Name Index

Subject Index

The Feminist Press at The City University of New York offers alternatives in education and in literature. Founded in 1970, this nonprofit, tax-exempt educational and publishing organization works to eliminate sexual stereotypes in books and schools and to provide literature with a broad vision of human potential. The publishing program includes reprints of important works by women, feminist biographies of women, and nonsexist children's books. Curricular materials, bibliographies, directories, and a quarterly journal provide information and support for students and teachers of women's studies. In-service projects help to transform teaching methods and curricula. Through publications and projects, The Feminist Press contributes to the rediscovery of the history of women and the emergence of a more humane society.

New and Forthcoming Books

Black Foremothers: Three Lives, 2nd ed., by Dorothy Sterling. Foreword by
    Margaret Walker. Introduction by Barbara Christian. $9.95 paper.
Families in Flux (formerly *Household and Kin),* by Amy Swerdlow, Renate
    Bridenthal, Joan Kellly, and Phyllis Vine. $9.95 paper.
Get Smart: A Woman's Guide to Equality on Campus, by Montana Katz and
    Veronica Vieland. $29.95 cloth, $9.95 paper.
"How I Wrote Jubilee" and Other Essays on Life and Literature, by Margaret
    Walker. Edited by Maryemma Graham. $29.95 cloth, $9.95 paper.
Islanders, a novel by Helen R. Hull. Afterword by Patricia McClelland Miller. $10.95
    paper.
*Library and Information Sources on Women: A Guide to Collections in the Greater
    New York Area,* compiled by the Women's Resources Group of the Greater New
    York Metropolitan Area Chapter of the Association of College and Research
    Libraries and the Center for the Study of Women and Society of the Graduate
    School and University Center of The City University of New York. $12.95 paper.
Lillian D. Wald: Progressive Activist, edited by Clare Coss. Including the play,
    Lillian Wald: At Home on Henry Street, by Clare Coss, and selected writings by
    Lillian D. Wald. $6.95 paper.
Lone Voyagers: Academic Women in Coeducational Universities, 1869–1937, edited
    by Geraldine J. Clifford, $29.95 cloth, $12.95 paper.
My Mother Gets Married, a novel by Moa Martinson. Translated and introduced by
    Margaret S. Lacy. $8.95 paper.
Not So Quiet: Stepdaughters of War, a novel by Helen Zenna Smith. Afterword by
    Jane Marcus. $9.95 paper.
Ruth Weisburg: Paintings, Drawings, Prints, 1968–1988, edited and curated by
    Marion E. Jackson. With an essay by Thalia Gouma-Peterson. $15.00 paper.
Seeds: Supporting Women's Work in the Third World, edited by Ann Leonard.
    Introduction by Adrienne Germain. Aferwords by Marguerite Berger, Vina
    Mazumdar, Kathleen Staudt, and Aminita Traore. $29.95 cloth, $12.95 paper.
Sultana's Dream and Selections from The Secluded Ones, by Rokeya Sakhawat
    Hossain. Edited and translated by Roushan Jahan. Afterword by Hanna
    Papanek. $16.95 cloth, $6.95 paper.
These Modern Women, edited and with a revised introduction by Elaine Showalter.
    $8.95 paper.
We That Were Young, a novel by Irene Rathbone. Introduction by Lynn Knight.
    Afterword by Jane Marcus. $10.95 paper.
What Did Miss Darrington See? An Anthology of Feminist Supernatural Fiction,
    edited by Jessica Amanda Salmonson. Introduction by Rosemary Jackson. $29.95
    cloth, $10.95 paper.
Women Activists: Challenging the Abuse of Power, by Anne Witte Garland. Foreword
    by Ralph Nader. Introduction by Frances T. Farenthold. $29.95 cloth, $9.95 paper.
Women Composers: The Lost Tradition Found, by Diane Peacock Jezic. Foreword by
    Elizabeth Wood. $29.95 cloth, $12.95 paper.

For a free catalog, write to The Feminist Press at The City University of New York, 311 East 94 Street, New York, NY 10128. Send individual book orders to The Talman Company, Inc., 150 Fifth Avenue, New York, NY 10011. Please include $1.75 for postage and handling for one book, $.75 for each additional.